BLUE HELMETS AND BLACK MARKETS

BLUE HELMETS AND BLACK MARKETS

THE BUSINESS OF SURVIVAL

IN THE SIEGE OF SARAJEVO

Peter Andreas

CORNELL UNIVERSITY PRESS
ITHACA AND LONDON

First published 2008 by Cornell University Press

Printed in the United States of America

            Library of Congress Cataloging-in-Publication Data
Andreas, Peter.
   Blue helmets and black markets : the business of survival in the siege of Sarajevo / Peter Andreas.
      p.cm.
   Includes bibliographical references and index.
   ISBN 978-0-8014-4355-8 (cloth : alk. paper)
   1. Sarajevo (Bosnia and Hercegovina)—History—Siege, 1992–1996.
2. Smuggling—Bosnia and Hercegovina—Sarajevo.   3. Black market—Bosnia and Hercegovina—Sarajevo.   4. United Nations—Bosnia and Hercegovina—Sarajevo.   5. Humanitarian assistance—Boania and Hercegovina—Sarajevo.
I. Title.
   DR1313.32.S27A57   2008
   949.703—dc22   2008013721

   Cornell University Press strives to use environmentally responsible suppliers and materials to the fullest extent possible in the publishing of its books. Such materials include vegetable-based, low-VOC inks and acid-free papers that are recycled, totally chlorine-free, or partly composed of nonwood fibers. For further information, visit our website at www.cornellpress.cornell.edu.

Cloth printing 10 9 8 7 6 5 4 3 2 1

CONTENTS

PREFACE

Inside the UN-run airport in besieged Sarajevo hung a makeshift sign: *Maybe Airlines*. Along the edges of the sign, aid workers, journalists, and diplomats had posted stickers—*CNN, ITN, CBS, RTL, MSF, VOX, UNICEF,* the French flag, the Canadian flag, the Swedish flag, and so on. Above the sign was a piece of plywood with the word *destinations* handwritten at the top, with a changeable placard below (the placard choices included *New York, Geneva, Rome, Berlin, Zagreb, Paris,* and *Heaven*). "Maybe Airlines" was the nickname given to the unreliable UN flights in and out of wartime Sarajevo—the longest-lasting airlift ever attempted and the centerpiece of the international humanitarian response to the war in Bosnia-Herzegovina.[1] Meanwhile, underneath the airport tarmac ran a narrow and damp 800-meter tunnel that bypassed both UN controls and the siege lines. Protected from Serb shelling and sniper fire, thousands of people and tons of food, arms, and other supplies moved through the underground passageway every day (which the UN pretended did not exist), providing both a vital lifeline for the city and an enormous opportunity for black market profiteering. While the UN airlift was part of the highly visible front stage of the siege, the tunnel was part of the much less visible but equally important backstage action. Together, they helped Sarajevo survive for over three and a half years, setting a siege longevity record.[2]

The 1992–95 battle for Sarajevo was not only the longest siege in modern history but also the most internationalized—an urban

A United Nations sign at the Sarajevo airport, 1994. Photo reproduced with permission of Ron Haviv/VII.

The tunnel under the Sarajevo airport. Photo reproduced with permission of the Historical Museum of Bosnia-Herzegovina.

magnet for aid workers, diplomats, UN "Blue Helmet" soldiers, journalists, artists, celebrities, peace activists, adventure seekers, embargo
busters, and black market traders. Sarajevo under siege became the
most visible and recognizable face of post–Cold War "ethnic conflict"
and humanitarian intervention. At the same time, the less visible and
less recognized face of the siege included aid diversion, clandestine
commerce, and peacekeeper corruption. As the Sarajevo experience
powerfully illustrates, just as changes in fortifications and weapons
technologies transformed siege warfare through the ages, so too has
the arrival of CNN, NGOs, satellite phones, UN peacekeepers, aid
convoys, and diaspora remittances. The internationalization of the
siege changed the repertoires of siege-craft and siege defenses. It
changed the strategic calculus and opportunities and constraints of
both the besiegers and the besieged.

Given the overwhelming military advantage of the Serb besiegers,
many at first expected the poorly defended city and its government to
fall quickly and easily. At the same time, because of the intensity of international political and media attention, many expected that the Serb
leadership would back down and the siege would be short-lived. It
did not turn out that way. Why not? What sustained the siege for such
an unexpectedly long period of time? These questions are particularly
puzzling because siege warfare in Europe was supposed to be
obsolete—and in Sarajevo it not only returned with a vengeance, but
contrary to all expectations stubbornly persisted. Moreover, it was
being broadcast live across the globe. As one Western journalist described it: "A European city was being reduced to nothing; Carthage
in slow motion, but this time with an audience and videotaped
record."[3]

This book is about the imposition, maintenance, lifting, and aftermath of the siege of Sarajevo. I focus on the Sarajevo case not simply because it is a particularly fascinating and important historical story. The
siege offers a powerful lens through which to scrutinize the relationship between the material and performative aspects of conflict, international intervention, and postwar reconstruction. In a highly confined
and intensely contested geographic space, the siege provides a striking
illustration of the interdependence between the upper-world and underworld, formal and informal, front stage and backstage in armed
confrontations and external involvement. At the broadest level, this is a

book about the dynamics of war economies, humanitarian and media access to conflict zones, and the political repercussions of relief aid told through the story of Sarajevo. More specifically, issues of aid diversion, embargo busting, trading with the enemy, war profiteering, and irregular combatants all come together and crystallize in the Sarajevo case. In concentrated form, the siege illuminates important elements of the political economy of contemporary conflict and the dilemmas, contradictions, and unintended consequences of humanitarian action.

I examine the bottom-up, micro-dynamics of the siege in the context of top-down international conditions and developments. I show how and why the internationalization of the siege, which aimed to end the conflict, paradoxically helped to perpetuate it by becoming incorporated into the war economy. A peculiar and in many ways unintended symbiosis developed on the ground between key actors among the besiegers, besieged, and external interveners. I explain the logic and trace the causal mechanisms of this siege symbiosis and show how it was finally broken. For comparative leverage, I briefly extend the analysis to other siege cases both within Bosnia (Srebrenica) and outside the region (Leningrad, Grozny, Falluja), helping to illuminate what is and is not distinctive about the Sarajevo experience.

Pointing to the symbiotic aspects of the Sarajevo siege is not meant to suggest that the besieged and the international interveners did not want the siege lifted, that the besiegers would not have preferred a quick and decisive military victory, or that all sides benefited equally from the siege and were equally responsible for its continuation. However, it does draw attention to the ways in which moves on all sides often ended up being reinforcing, even if not necessarily intentionally. No elaborate conspiracy was required, making the siege symbiosis all the more durable.

For many local and international actors, the partial and continuously negotiated permeability of the city made the siege politically tolerable, militarily acceptable, and economically profitable. Siege dynamics were often more about controlling humanitarian supplies and smuggling routes in and out of the city than making the siege militarily succeed or fail. While the vast majority of the city's inhabitants struggled for survival and lived in a state of terror, a semi-porous siege kept the city formally and informally supplied and served various local and international interests.

Dissecting the anatomy of the siege shows how and why it proved to be not only sustainable but rewarding for some key players on all sides. For the nationalist Serb besiegers, the siege kept the city bottled up and useful as a political lever while helping to distract attention away from far more severe atrocities elsewhere; for the inner circle of Sarajevo's political leadership, the siege helped keep them in power, consolidate their party's political position, marginalize opponents, and generate and sustain international sympathy and support; for the UN and its Western sponsors, the siege provided a remarkably viable working environment to showcase aid provision in the Bosnian war, avoid more direct military entanglement, and contain a further flood of refugees; for foreign journalists, the siege offered a front-row seat in a high-drama spectacle and the most accessible war zone in Bosnia; and for well-placed black market entrepreneurs on all sides the siege conditions assured a captive market with highly inflated profits. As described by Hasib Salkić, the secretary general of the Liberal Party of Bosnia, the siege was "the best course in market economy one can get. I learnt it and I use it today. Naturally some used it as education, some for getting rich, for wheeling and dealing, for stealing."[4]

I should say a few words about what this book is not. It is certainly not meant to provide an exhaustive account of the battle for Sarajevo— that challenging task is best left to military historians. It also does not offer a detailed examination of the historical roots of the conflict, but instead focuses on the political economy of its conduct, longevity, outcome, and aftermath. This book is also not meant to be a polemic against crime, corruption, and black market profiteering. Although I examine these activities with a critical eye, the primary purpose is to explain and understand rather than to expose and condemn. All too often, denouncements of corruption and criminality substitute for critical evaluation and fuel politically motivated speculation. Rather than simply joining the chorus of voices loudly condemning such behavior, I often stress its double-edged character: the criminalized side of the conflict involved both looting and saving Sarajevo, it contributed to both the persistence and ending of the war, and it fostered both state formation and deformation. Equally important, an analytical focus on the criminalized dimensions of the siege is not meant to discredit the remarkable defense of Sarajevo and survival skills of its inhabitants. My goal is not to diminish the heroics and sacrifices of Sarajevo's citizens but to shed light on a dimension of conflict that is too often either neglected or distorted. Crucially, this includes acknowledging and critically evaluating the role of international actors and their interaction with local players in shaping and enabling the criminalization of the siege and wider war. Indeed, as I stress, the particular mode of external intervention was critical in turning the conflict into such an enormous black market business opportunity.

Much of what has been written about the siege of Sarajevo involves eyewitness reports by journalists, diplomats, military officials, and local residents. This book draws extensively on these memoirs, diaries, and other on-the-ground accounts to develop a more focused and systematic argument about the role of formal and informal mechanisms and practices in sustaining the siege. Those who typically pay the most attention to on-the-ground micro-processes of conflict, such as journalists, have usefully documented these dynamics but have tended not to systematically analyze or theorize about them. Although my account of the siege is not a full-blown ethnography, I do take seriously the anthropological emphasis on bottom-up analysis of micro-dynamics,[5] while also taking into account top-down international forces and contexts.[6]

A heavy dose of caution is called for regarding the subject matter of this book. Focusing on the role of black market operators, criminals turned combatants, and smuggling networks runs the risk of exaggerating their importance, providing an overly criminalized narrative of the siege. In its crudest form, this can generate a knee-jerk cynical dismissal of all actors as simply greedy and corrupt. It is not my intention to reduce the dynamics of the siege merely to crime and profiteering. This is only one (albeit important) dimension of a complex conflict. Rather than invalidating or supplanting other accounts, I aim to incorporate and thus illuminate a commonly overlooked or misunderstood aspect of the siege and wider war. Moreover, the criminalized component of the conflict has left a powerful legacy—including the emergence of new elites who profited from the war and the persistence of politically protected wartime smuggling networks—that needs to be taken more fully into account in order to understand the challenges for postwar reconstruction.

There are inherent obstacles to doing research on this topic. Not surprisingly, information on smuggling and criminal actors tends to be incomplete and imprecise, and is often unreliable and hard to obtain. The available documentation is usually fragmentary and represents rough estimates at best. This requires extra caution and care regarding the credibility and political biases of sources, the accuracy of the data, and an appreciation for the built-in constraints of this type of research. Much remains untold—indeed, I suspect I have only begun to scratch the surface. Readers should keep these limitations in mind in the chapters that follow. Yet, however uneven and imperfect the empirical evidence, my hope is that this book provides some insight into an often obscured and poorly understood dimension of conflict and its aftermath. This is by its nature a rather messy and difficult realm of inquiry—and no doubt it is partly for this reason that many scholars have tended to shy away from it. In this regard, there are practical advantages to focusing on the Sarajevo story: there is more on-the-ground reporting and eyewitness accounts from Sarajevo than most conflicts, given the city's high wartime profile.

The research for this book included in-depth interviews and extensive review of local and international media reporting, official testimonies and reports, internal documents, court transcripts, war diaries and memoirs, and secondary literature. Much of the research was conducted during trips to Sarajevo and elsewhere in the region during the summers of 2001, 2002, 2003, and 2006, as well as a brief final trip in the fall of 2007. This involved nearly 100 interviews (ranging from one to three hours each) with a wide assortment of local and international informants, including current and former diplomats, government officials, UN personnel, army officers, aid workers, representatives of non-governmental organizations, journalists, soldiers, and policemen. Most of the interviews took place in Sarajevo, but some were in Belgrade, Zagreb, New York, Washington, and elsewhere. I thank all those who generously agreed to be interviewed (in some cases multiple times). Sarajevans are understandably fatigued from years of intense scrutiny under a global microscope, and thus I am doubly appreciative of those who took the time to talk with me.

Many thanks as well to those who provided research assistance or translation work: Edward Ahn, Sanja Bajin, Rebecca Braswell, Cornelius Friesendorf, Nedim Duraković, Selma Duraković, Erica Haskell, Brett Heeger, Craig Kennedy, and especially Jasmina Burdžović

Andreas. A huge debt is owed to John Fawcett, who provided unpublished materials (much of it drawing from his years of experience as an aid worker in wartime Sarajevo). In Sarajevo, valuable research materials were obtained through the University of Sarajevo library, the Soros Media Center, and FAMA International. The Historical Museum in Sarajevo generously gave permission to reproduce photographs from their siege exhibit. Saša Skoko created the map of Sarajevo for the book. Additional useful information on wartime humanitarian aid distribution was obtained from the library of the Geneva headquarters of the United Nations High Commission for Refugees.

Many friends and colleagues provided critical feedback on the conference papers and chapter drafts that culminated in this book. This includes Joel Andreas, Deborah Avant, Keith Brown, Chuck Call, Alex Cooley, John Fawcett, Pauline Jones-Luong, Cathy Lutz, John Mueller, Will Reno, Cathy Schneider, Rich Snyder, Herman Schwartz, and especially Aida Hozić and James Ron. Roger Haydon at Cornell University Press had confidence in this project at a very early stage. I am grateful not only for his encouragement and guidance, but also for his patience, since there were some unexpected delays and detours along the way. The three external reviewer reports for the press provided enormously helpful comments.

Some material in this book was presented at the annual meeting of the American Political Science Association, the annual meeting of the International Studies Association, Brown University, Carleton University, Columbia University, Cornell University, the Central European University, Marquette University, Ohio State University, Reed College, Yale University, the International Peace Academy, the Woodrow Wilson International Center for Scholars, and the Bosniak Institute in Sarajevo. Small portions of the book draw from articles I originally published in *International Studies Quarterly* (Spring 2004), and *Problems of Post-Communism* (May/June 2004). Used by permission.

Just as I stress the material basis for the longest siege in modern history, so, too, must I acknowledge the material basis for a book project that took longer than expected. The research would not have been possible without the financial support provided by the Smith Richardson Foundation and the United States Institute of Peace. Additional funding was provided by Brown University (the Watson Institute for International Studies and the Department of Political Science) and Reed College. The book was completed while on a teaching leave fellowship at Brown's Cogut Center for the Humanities.

Last but not least, a personal confession: I am a war profiteer. I would not have met my wife, Jasmina, had it not been for the siege of Sarajevo—and certainly would not have written a book about it had it not been for her companionship and support (often including as a translator and local "fixer"). Forcibly displaced from their home in the Serb-held neighborhood of Grbavica when the siege began in the spring of 1992, Jasmina and her family fled Sarajevo, joining the hundreds of thousands of Bosnian refugees scattered across the globe. Jasmina eventually ended up in Ithaca, New York—hosted by the same family from whom I rented an attic apartment while I was in graduate school. During our first years together, we watched, along with the rest of the world, the drama of the Sarajevo siege unfold on the nightly news and on the front page. Years later we traveled to Sarajevo as the city was slowly rebuilt under uneasy international supervision. I dedicate this book to Jasmina (no one has ever been more deserving of a book dedication), but also to her father, Jusuf, who suffered far too much and died far too young.

PETER ANDREAS

Providence, Rhode Island

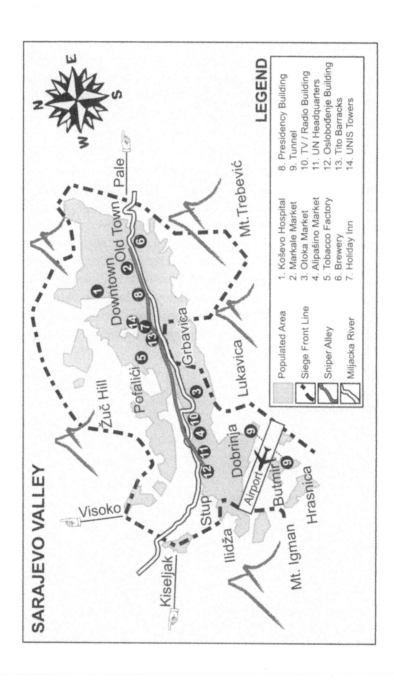

SARAJEVO VALLEY

LEGEND

Populated Area

Siege Front Line

Sniper Alley

Miljacka River

1. Koševo Hospital
2. Markale Market
3. Otoka Market
4. Alipašino Market
5. Tobacco Factory
6. Brewery
7. Holiday Inn

8. Presidency Building
9. Tunnel
10. TV / Radio Building
11. UN Headquarters
12. Oslobodenje Building
13. Tito Barracks
14. UNIS Towers

Žuč Hill
Pofalići
Downtown
Old Town
Pale
Grbavica
Mt. Trebević
Lukavica
Visoko
Stup
Dobrinja
Airport
Butmir
Hrasnica
Ilidža
Kiseljak
Mt. Igman

CHAPTER 1

THE LONGEST SIEGE

Bosnia has a special place in the post-Cold War landscape of armed conflict and international intervention. The 1992–95 war in the former Yugoslav republic became the poster child for "ethnic conflict"—indeed, the term "ethnic cleansing" was popularized during the Bosnia experience (although the practice is certainly not new). Bosnia and the other conflicts related to the bloody break-up of Yugoslavia represented the first outbreak of war in Europe since the end of World War II and erased the widespread assumption that war on the continent was unthinkable.[1] Bosnia was also the first drawn out humanitarian crisis of the decade, prompting a far more expansive and ambitious interventionist role for the United Nations—and the humbling experience significantly undermined the early enthusiasm for its conflict prevention and resolution capacity. No other war is as closely associated with humanitarian assistance as is the Bosnia conflict. More than 100,000 foreigners, at least a dozen UN agencies, and over 200 non-governmental organizations (NGOs) were estimated to be part of the humanitarian relief operation in Bosnia.[2] By the middle of 1995, two-thirds of all UN blue-helmeted peacekeepers in the world were deployed in the region, with the number of troops in Bosnia peaking at about 22,500.[3]

The Bosnian war and the other conflicts in the western Balkans that were part of the breakup of Yugoslavia were largely carried out through a series of large and small sieges by nationalist Serb forces. This included the destruction of Vukovar and the shelling of Dubrovnik during the war in neighboring Croatia, the early sacking of towns in eastern Bosnia such as Zvornik, and the fall of Srebrenica and execution of thousands of Muslim men and boys late in the war. Given the siege-style warfare that defined much of the conflict, frontlines tended to run around urban centers and the road networks that linked them.

Sarajevo, the capital and largest city in Bosnia (with a prewar population of some 350,000), was the site of the biggest and most prominent siege of the war. The fate of Sarajevo was critical: if the city had fallen or been cut in half, the duration and outcome of the conflict would have been radically altered. On April 6, 1992, Serb forces began shelling the city from hillside positions and quickly occupied neighborhoods such as Grbavica and Ilidža. With the city surrounded and poorly defended, few could have imagined that the siege would last for some three and a half years.

This book is about the long siege of Sarajevo and the international response. I combine detailed tracing of the micro-mechanisms and processes on the ground with attention to international contexts and conditions. The story of the siege sheds light on much larger issues related to the political economy of contemporary conflict, humanitarian intervention, and its aftermath. The siege provides a laboratory of sorts to study the interaction between local and international actors, playing both formal and informal roles, in creating and sustaining the material conditions for conflict.

In-depth case studies are particularly illuminating when they have puzzling characteristics and defy conventional expectations.[4] In the case of Sarajevo, the siege was not supposed to happen: siege warfare in Europe was assumed to be a relic of the past, yet a modern European city that had hosted the 1984 Winter Olympics was being shelled less than a decade later. It was not supposed to last: given the extreme military power imbalance, many (including the besiegers) thought it would be over quickly and that the Sarajevo government would be forced to capitulate. Alternatively, many expected (and hoped) that international pressure would force a quick lifting of the siege. Yet the Sarajevo siege not only persisted but set a siege longevity record. A siege formally characterized by intense ethnic-based animosities is not expected to involve cross-ethnic collaboration, yet in the Sarajevo case there was substantial informal economic exchange across the frontlines.[5] A siege is defined as a military encirclement, but while Sarajevo

was surrounded by vastly superior forces and its population terrorized, the siege was also semi-porous and globally connected. Indeed,
paradoxically, Sarajevo became a peculiar type of "global city" precisely because it was under siege.[6] A city under military siege by its
nature should be a particularly inaccessible and dangerous place for
international actors such as UN monitors and negotiators, aid workers, and journalists. Sarajevo was certainly violent and dangerous, as
one would expect of a besieged city, but it was also the most accessible
war zone and viable working environment for international actors in
Bosnia—which also helped turn Sarajevo into a global media spectacle. In this book I interrogate these puzzling features of the siege.

Sarajevo on Center Stage

During the course of the siege, Sarajevo became the centerpiece
and most important test case of an expanded UN commitment to humanitarian intervention, reflected in an ambitious UN-led relief aid
effort for the city that included the longest-lasting airlift ever attempted. The siege took place under international supervision and
was televised to a global audience, with the UN taking on the role of
referee and mediator. The global political and media spotlight was so
intense that journalist David Rieff called the besieged city "the most
famous place in the world."[7] The siege was formally internationalized
through UN monitoring and aid provision, diplomatic initiatives,
sanctions and embargoes, an influx of humanitarian workers, and
continuous global media coverage. And it was informally internationalized through smuggling networks and mechanisms used to clandestinely supply and finance the opposing sides and evade UN sanctions
and embargoes. These formal and informal dimensions were very
much interdependent, representing the front-stage and backstage action in the long siege drama.

The use of theatrical metaphors to characterize the siege dynamics
is not meant to belittle the conflict or understate its seriousness. The
death toll and physical damage make clear that it was brutally serious.[8] Inspired by the work of the sociologist Erving Goffman, the
point here is not to belittle or dismiss the siege as "mere theater," but
rather to draw attention to discrepancies between the formal scripts

and the more informal behavior behind the scenes, the multiple roles that actors can simultaneously play, and the relationship between the visible, audience-directed official "face work" on the front stage and the less visible, unofficial action backstage.[9]

There were many reasons why Sarajevo was on center stage: it was in Europe, it was a capital city, it was relatively accessible, and it had the basic infrastructure needed for international media coverage.[10] This included access to the city via the UN-controlled airport and airlift, availability of food and lodging for the foreign press corps in the dilapidated but functional Holiday Inn hotel, and a bunker-like television and radio building with modern broadcast equipment and facilities.

Sarajevo's high visibility and accessibility contrasted sharply, for example, to Mostar, some 130 kilometers from the capital, where the intense close-in fighting and devastation was far less noticed by the outside world. Mostar was simply too dangerous and inaccessible to sustain much of a humanitarian or media presence. As Nik Gowing, an editor for Britain's *Channel Four News,* comments, "Because of the logistics nightmare, coverage of Mostar was minimal and the city's predicament never grabbed world attention like Sarajevo. Conditions were too dangerous for TV crews to work. Broadcasters could not risk deploying their satellite dishes." As a result, "there was never the same drip feed of emotive real-time siege stories to catch international sympathy, as happened with Sarajevo."[11] On a rare visit to the besieged town, one reporter observed: "Conditions here may make those in Sarajevo look like easy living. . . . The Croat siege of Eastern Mostar has made the Serb siege of Sarajevo seem positively porous. Here, there is no street market to buy even a loaf of bread or cigarettes. Nor is there the kind of Serb-fed black market that flourishes in Sarajevo and helps keep people alive there, albeit at high prices in German marks."[12]

Sarajevo was besieged yet accessible, and as such it profoundly shaped international engagement with (and perceptions of) the war. As the historian Robert Donia observes in his biography of Sarajevo:

> The daily violence was conducted under the scrutiny of international civil servants, aid workers, 'peacekeepers,' journalists, and scholars (including this author) who could travel with relative ease on conveyances not available to the local population. Sarajevo was the lens through which most outsiders viewed the

conflict; the agony of Sarajevo became the embodiment of the Bosnian war's savagery and senselessness. At most times, the army of privileged observers could get into and out of the city, stay in relative comfort at the Holiday Inn (the sole hostelry that functioned throughout the war), ride in armored vehicles along the city's most dangerous routes, and send dispatches to the outside world using the latest communications technology.[13]

The Sarajevo story is thus a particularly extreme illustration of what the political scientist Stathis Kalyvas labels "urban bias" in the study of internal wars. He argues that internal wars "tend to be viewed through a heavily urban lens by both scholars and practitioners" and that "most observers cluster in cities." The war in Bosnia, he notes, was "mostly covered from Sarajevo."[14] The former U.S. military strategist Ralph Peters bluntly acknowledges the strategic prioritization of urban areas in the post-Cold War era: "But who cares about Upper Egypt if Cairo is calm? We do not deal with Indonesia—we deal with Jakarta. In our recent evacuation of foreigners from Sierra Leone, Freetown was all that mattered."[15]

Kalyvas warns scholars of the pitfalls of such urban bias, which he equates with a top-down, macro-level approach.[16] Yet as I stress in the case of Sarajevo, urban bias can also be an integral part of the microdynamics of war rather than only a problem that limits and distorts the analysis of war. Far from simply reflecting a top-down approach, urban bias in the case of Sarajevo has important bottom-up consequences—profoundly influencing the strategies and interactions of key actors on the ground. Here, urban bias not only shaped the interpretation of the conflict by outside observers but also the conduct of key participants in the conflict. Thus, rather than simply avoiding urban bias in research and looking elsewhere to understand the logic of organized violence, as Kalyvas advises, the Sarajevo case instead points to the explanatory utility of embracing it, unpacking it, and making it a core part of the study of war dynamics and international responses. While Kalyvas largely brackets and takes for granted international actors and contexts in his own recent work on civil wars,[17] bringing outside influences and players more centrally into the story necessarily requires a more urban lens—after all, urban areas are typically the hubs and nodes that link internal conflicts to the external world. Urban landscapes are key sites of interaction between "locals" and "internationals." And nowhere is this more powerfully illustrated than in the case of Bosnia's besieged capital city of Sarajevo.

The Cast of Characters

The siege of Sarajevo involved a diverse cast of characters playing multiple roles among the besiegers, besieged, and international interveners. The key actors among the besieging Serb forces included the nationalist political leadership of the Serbian Democratic Party (SDS), led by Radovan Karadžić and headquartered in the nearby mountain town of Pale; the Army of the Bosnian Serb Republic (VRS) and its Sarajevo-Romanija Corps; and an assortment of paramilitary units and other irregulars (including "weekend warriors" from Belgrade and elsewhere). The besiegers enjoyed geographic advantage and overwhelmingly superior firepower (especially in heavy weapons, such as tanks, mortars, artillery, and rocket launchers, inherited from the well-stocked Yugoslav army). Backed by neighboring Serbia, their political objective was ethnic partition of the ethnically mixed, newly independent state. The siege of Sarajevo was a central component of achieving this objective. The initial military goal was to bisect the city and force the Sarajevo government to capitulate, but when this failed the goal shifted to simply bottling the city up and using it as a hostage and political negotiating card.

Key actors within besieged Sarajevo included the head of the presidency, Alija Izetbegović, and his inner political circle of Party of Democratic Action (SDA) loyalists; the newly formed Army of Bosnia-Herzegovina (ARBiH) and its Sarajevo Corps, with responsibility for defending the siege lines divided among various rag-tag brigades and their unit commanders (some of whom were leaders from the Sarajevo underworld); and a variety of police units. A small part of the siege line was initially manned by Croatian Defense Council (HVO) militia forces until relations with the Sarajevo government deteriorated and eventually collapsed, as Bosnian Croats (backed by Zagreb) pushed their own nationalist ethnic partition agenda in the central and western part of the country. The main political objective of the Sarajevo government was territorial integrity, since Bosnia was internationally recognized as an independent sovereign state (which was threatened by Serb and Croat partition plans). The city's defenders had a man-power advantage over the besieging Serbs, but lacked weapons or even an organized army when the war broke out (and were further handicapped by an international arms embargo, which made it partic-ularly difficult to access heavy weapons). The Sarajevo government therefore repeatedly called for international military intervention and a lifting of the UN arms embargo.

However, the international interveners—the so-called "international community"[18]—primarily provided humanitarian aid and diplomatic initiatives rather than military support. Their basic objective was to contain the crisis, feed the civilian population, and achieve a negoti-ated settlement. Backed by major Western powers, the United Nations played the lead role on the ground: the UN High Commission for Refugees (UNHCR) was designated the lead agency coordinating humanitarian relief operations, including the Sarajevo airlift. The massive aid effort provided the beleaguered agency an opportunity to substantially expand its mandate, increase funding, and enhance its global prestige and profile—turning it into the world's largest relief agency.[19] The United Nations Protection Force (UNPROFOR), com-posed of "Blue Helmet" soldiers from various nations, was charged with protecting and facilitating the delivery of humanitarian aid.[20] The UN force in the Sarajevo area reached nearly 5,000 personnel by early 1995. About two-thirds were French, and the rest were Ukrainian, Egyptian, and Russian (with the Russians based in Serb-held terri-tory).[21] An assortment of other UN officials and agency representatives were sent to monitor, mediate, and negotiate. Whether visiting the city for a few days or only a few hours, some international actors made high-visibility cameo appearances (such as French president François Mitterrand and UN Secretary General Boutros Boutros-Ghali). In the air, NATO enforced a no-fly zone (and in moments of crisis was called on to threaten—and on a few occasions carry out—air strikes against the besiegers). Contributing to the relief effort were hundreds of international non-governmental aid agencies, religious charities, and other organizations (though only a handful had substantial staffing), all loosely working under the umbrella of the UNHCR. The foreign press corps, which both reported on and shaped the siege and the international response, ranged from major print and broadcast media outlets with a regular staff to dozens of stringers and freelance journalists.

The critical supporting cast for this large and diverse international presence was the small army of Sarajevans hired as translators, assistants, drivers, cooks, photographers, secretaries, guides, and so on. This local support staff (typically English speaking) not only played a key mediating role between the international interveners and the local environment,[22] but many of them also enjoyed some of the privileges of the internationals, such as access to hard currency, imported food and other basic supplies, and transportation across the frontlines (including foreign travel). These privileges, in turn, helped to support local extended families.

Front Stage and Backstage: Formal and Informal Roles

International and local actors played both formal and informal roles during the course of the siege. While their front-stage behavior was often carefully staged and choreographed for various audiences, sticking closely to the official script and engaging in what Goffman calls the "art of impression management," backstage there was greater room for improvisation and deviation. Thus, for example, while the Bosnian Serb leadership played the front-stage role of orchestrating the siege of the city under the official banner of ethnic grievance and animosity, backstage they profited from the siege through clandestine business dealings that included cross-ethnic economic exchange across the frontlines. Similarly, some of the city's key defenders played the formal role of repelling Serb military incursions while also engaging in illicit trading with their counterparts. While on the front stage they protected Sarajevo, backstage they engaged in theft and looting (a "siege within the siege"). This was particularly true of Sarajevo's combatants with criminal backgrounds and their charismatic leaders who became overnight heroes during the city's initial defense. Some of them sought the limelight, basking in their new celebrity status, while others hid from the light. Many of these local actors on both sides of the frontlines can be characterized as "violent entrepreneurs," fighting for turf and turning the siege into a profitable protection racket.[23]

The international interveners also played multiple roles. For instance, in their formal roles, UNPROFOR soldiers secured the Sarajevo airport for the delivery of humanitarian aid and became siege gatekeepers by not allowing Sarajevans to enter or leave the city across the airport grounds. But some UN soldiers also informally helped turn the airport into a conduit for smuggling—at times simply taking bribes to look the other way and at other times becoming more active participants by moving black market goods into the city and smuggling people out. UNHCR personnel ran the Sarajevo airlift, but in order to officially move the goods into the city they also unofficially bribed Serb checkpoint guards (preferring to think of such bribes as "gifts"). And the favored items used for bribes—such as whiskey and cigarettes—had to be quietly smuggled in via the airlift (never appearing on cargo manifests, which were checked by Serb authorities).

Members of the press corps also performed both front-stage and backstage roles. They formally covered the siege, keeping the global media spotlight on the city and participating in the public ritual of the daily UN press briefings. But informally they were also important contributors to the siege economy—ranging from buying black market fuel discretely supplied by the Ukrainian contingent of UNPROFOR (siphoned off from their Armored Personnel Carriers) to smuggling in money-filled letters for local residents (sent from friends and relatives abroad), who in turn would use the desperately needed cash to purchase food and other items on the black market.

Finally, the locals working for the internationals were actively engaged on both the front stage and the backstage: formally, they provided a major part of the support structure for both the UN-directed humanitarian relief effort and global media reporting. At the same time many of them informally took advantage of their privileged position and access to smuggle goods and money into the city, and their wages in hard currency also helped their extended families to purchase essential black market supplies. Understandably, some eventually used their position to permanently exit the city—joining the growing Bosnian diaspora abroad, which itself became a source of external support for the city's population and defense effort.[24]

Some might object to this characterization of the roles of the various siege actors, arguing that their informal backstage behavior was a sideshow compared to the formal front-stage action. However, focusing on the front stage—which is the standard, conventional approach—overlooks too much and explains too little. On its own, the front-stage action cannot fully account for how the city survived and defended itself for such a remarkably long period of time. For instance, humanitarian aid supplied through formal channels was essential but was also woefully inadequate. Black market supplies—albeit at highly inflated prices—provided a crucial supplement. It was not only the humanitarian effort that sustained the city, but also the opportunities that the UN aid and presence created for black marketeering and maintenance of a criminalized war economy. Officially, humanitarian aid helped feed Sarajevo's civilian population; unofficially, it also fed soldiers on both sides of the line through skimming and diversion. While UNHCR officials publicly denounced or denied the use of aid to feed combatants, privately they awkwardly acknowledged that this was unavoidable—part of the price paid to access the city.

Moreover, in the context of an international arms embargo and anemic local military production, only by taking into account informal backstage behavior can we explain how the Sarajevo government managed to generate and sustain a covert trickle of weapons and ammunition into the city—sometimes with the behind-the-scenes complicity of international actors formally committed to upholding the UN weapons ban.

Meanwhile, even as the front-stage activities of the foreign press corps kept the media spotlight on Sarajevo, backstage activities were essential in keeping the show going—ranging from feeding the foreign journalists with smuggled food and drinks at the Holiday Inn (Sarajevo's only functional hotel) to powering their satellite dishes and laptops with generators running on black market fuel. So while the siege of Sarajevo played out on center stage in the glare of the global media spotlight, some of the most important action took place backstage, away from the cameras. And much of this backstage activity sustained the action on the front stage.

Conflict Narratives

The story line of the siege of Sarajevo and the broader conflict in Bosnia can take various forms, directing attention to some actors and activities and not to others. The dominant conflict narratives draw attention to the front-stage action. Paying closer attention to backstage dynamics, as I emphasize throughout this book, provides a necessary corrective. These dominant narratives—evident in distinct scripts favored by different local and international actors—defined much of the play on the front stage. For example, the narrative of ethnic animosity was strategically promoted by the besieging Serbs, and was perpetuated in media accounts and resonated in many Western policy circles. It provided a seductively simple narrative of the conflict and conveniently offered a ready-made script for those who argued against more forceful external intervention to stop the carnage. In the most extreme variant, the conflict was depicted as a reflection of irrational Balkan barbarism and "ancient ethnic hatreds" beyond external control.[25] Bosnia was even characterized as a fault-line war in a planetary cultural "clash of civilizations."[26]

Although ethnicity certainly mattered, the popularity of the ethnic hatreds storyline masked far more complex and ambiguous realities on the ground. The focus on ethnic grievances explained too little and obscured too much, particularly the material conditions that enabled and sustained the conflict. It also conveniently overlooked the fact that, while interethnic relations were historically often uneasy and far from harmonious, they were largely peaceful and involved increasing levels of intermarriage (especially in urban areas such as Sarajevo). A singular focus on primordial ethnic animosities also ignored and could not explain the substantial amount of wartime interethnic economic cooperation in the form of clandestine trading. Indeed, dense interethnic social ties in prewar Sarajevo provided the social capital to facilitate wartime black marketeering and smuggling across ethnically divided frontlines.[27] And in the postwar period, the ability to transcend ethnic divisions was nowhere more advanced than in the expansive smuggling economy. A narrow focus on ethnic-based hatreds misses and cannot account for such high levels of clandestine cross-ethnic collusion.

For the Sarajevo government and many sympathetic international observers, the favored public script was a narrative of victimization, which contained some important truths. The Bosnian Serb leadership and their Belgrade sponsors *were* the main aggressors, bearing disproportionate responsibility for the war, and Sarajevans *were* indisputably victims—given that they were on the receiving end of regular shelling and sniper fire. Indeed, the high visibility of this victimization was a crucial weapon for the Sarajevo government in cultivating international support—and was an unstated reason for why it imposed tough restrictions on Sarajevo citizens wishing to leave the city.[28] The main limitation of the victim narrative, however, is that it is more about outrage and condemnation than explanation and understanding.[29] The victim narrative is particularly prevalent in media reporting, which "encourages the production of short, unambiguous, neatly scripted stories, replete with villains and heroes."[30] Nowhere was this more evident than in Sarajevo, where foreign camera crews were concentrated and could count on capturing graphic, close-in images of the victims of sniper fire and shelling.[31] Yet as Kalyvas argues, "Repetitive descriptions of violence stressing its most grotesque aspects substitute emotion for coherent political analysis."[32] The common tendency to simply denounce such violence as "senseless," whether in Sarajevo or elsewhere, inhibits efforts to actually make sense of it.

Moreover, the murkier reality on the ground in Sarajevo included a less visible internal siege (made possible by the external siege conditions)—ranging from theft and looting by criminals-turned-combatants within the city, to profiteering by unit commanders on the frontline, to the political power grab by the SDA leadership in sacking competent officials and replacing them with party loyalists. The victim narrative, however accurate, discouraged critical scrutiny of the siege within. As one American journalist candidly acknowledges:

> Those of us [among the foreign press corps in Sarajevo] who were convinced of the rightness of the Bosnian cause tended to underplay the corruption of Bosnian political elites, who, throughout the war, even in Sarajevo, were making fortunes off the conflict, doing private deals with the Serbs, and placing family members, friends, and mistresses in cushy jobs abroad. We also wrote less than we should have about the relation between war and crime on the front line, where the black market flourished even in the worst moments of the fighting.[33]

The UN interveners and their Western government backers, meanwhile, read from the official humanitarian script—drawing attention to the flurry of formal diplomatic initiatives and an unprecedented relief effort as an indicator of international concern and determination. This narrative highlighted the delivery of food and other supplies to besieged populations, projected an apolitical image of humanitarianism and a commitment to impartiality,[34] and pushed for a negotiated peace between the "warring factions" through diplomatic pressure and engagement.[35]

The massive UN-directed aid operation in Bosnia was indeed impressive—with the Sarajevo airlift the much-celebrated centerpiece—signaling that the West was "doing something." But the insistence on sticking to the humanitarian script, as critics have rightly pointed out, conveniently substituted for more direct and forceful action by the Western governments underwriting the relief operation. As one senior UNHCR official commented, "Every time the question of settling the conflict came up, the donors responded by saying that they were going to give more money to the humanitarian effort."[36] The particular form of humanitarianism in Bosnia served the strategic objective of avoiding more direct and risky military engagement, with profound political repercussions on the ground.[37] In Sarajevo, it made the siege manageable and thus internationally tolerable—even as it was ritualistically condemned.

The official humanitarian script also obscured the ways in which the relief effort itself was unofficially helping to sustain the war economy, both feeding soldiers and enriching black marketeers. Most important, it overlooked the fact that, on its own, humanitarian aid was far from sufficient to sustain the city's population. According to one estimate, the UN-directed relief operation supplied an average of only 159 grams (about 0.35 lbs.) of food per person per day in Sarajevo during the siege.[38] In early 1993, the weekly humanitarian ration was reportedly merely 870 grams per person, which is sufficient for only a day and a half of basic sustenance.[39] During the twenty-month period between November 1993 and the end of August 1995, the UNHCR calculated that it was able to fully meet its monthly food aid target/need for Sarajevo only six times.[40] Clandestine commercial flows into the city thus played an essential role in keeping the population supplied,[41] indicating that we should pay much greater attention to the siege's backstage dynamics, including its criminalized component.

Criminalized Conflict Narratives

In this book, I develop a narrative of the siege that draws greater attention to the backstage action (and its relation to the front-stage play), including the local and international mechanisms that created and sustained a criminalized war economy. Smuggling networks and quasi-private criminal actors are essential in helping to explain key aspects of the siege. This includes the unexpected ability of the city to defend and supply itself with the help of criminals-turned-combatants and underground trading networks; the role of black market food and fuel in enabling journalists to cover the siege (and thus keeping Sarajevo in the global media spotlight); and the eventual shift in the military balance on the ground in the wider Bosnian war facilitated by clandestine evasion of the arms embargo, which helped to establish the conditions for a diplomatic settlement.

Although there is a massive literature on the war in Bosnia, much of which contains valuable information on clandestine trading, criminal combatants, and manipulation and diversion of humanitarian aid, these topics tend not to be the central analytical focus and are not generally highlighted as part of a causal argument. Many observers have commented that the UN-led humanitarian approach contributed to the prolongation of the siege and wider war, yet the on-the-ground micro-mechanisms that made this particular international response both viable and sustainable over such an extended period of time have not been sufficiently explained and traced in detail. Equally important, most accounts focus largely on the formal, front-stage side of the conflict and its internationalization, paying far too little attention to the informal, backstage side and the interaction between the two.

Rather than providing a comprehensive examination of the siege and the wider war, the more focused and limited purpose here is to show the analytical mileage that can be gained by a detailed tracing of the interaction between the formal and informal dimensions of the siege, particularly between humanitarian assistance and a criminalized war economy. In developing this narrative, I build on and bring together emerging interdisciplinary literatures on war economies[42] and the political repercussions of humanitarian action.[43] Although scholars have increasingly focused on the role of international intervention in shaping internal wars, less attention has been devoted to examining how such intervention can (often unintentionally) become part of the war economy with long-lasting consequences. In concentrated form, the Sarajevo siege provides a stark illustration of this dynamic.

All types of wars—large and small, past and present—have some sort of criminalized dimension. But it is particularly evident in internal conflicts that take place in a context of anemic state capacity, limited production, and reliance on external funding and supplies. Such conflicts are partly made possible by "taxing" and diverting humanitarian aid, informal diaspora funding,[44] illicit trading across frontlines and other forms of smuggling, and the black-market selling of looted goods. They may use irregular combatants who operate in the absence of, alongside, and sometimes within formal military units, and are especially prevalent when at least one side does not have a regular army and is not a full-fledged state.

The importance of the criminalized war economy becomes especially apparent in the context of evading international economic sanctions and arms embargoes. In this respect, external intervention contributes to the criminalization of conflict, creating an economic opportunity structure for clandestine commerce and making the competing sides more reliant on smuggling channels. Under these conditions, war can be a continuation of business by clandestine means: military success on the battlefield can hinge on entrepreneurial success in the murky underworld of smuggling. Moreover, the black market networks and embargo-busting infrastructure built up during wartime can persist into the postwar reconstruction period.[45]

The criminalized dimensions of conflict are too often either neglected or treated too narrowly and one-dimensionally. For example, while security scholars have increasingly taken into account the external aspects of internal wars,[46] the emphasis tends to be on how these conflicts are formally internationalized (through UN interventions, diplomatic mediation efforts, provision of aid, peacekeeping, human rights monitoring and media reporting, and so on), paying far less attention to how they are also informally internationalized (through sanctions evasions, clandestine arms shipments, and other smuggling practices). This reflects a more general tendency for international relations scholars to shy away from scrutinizing the "covert world" and the illicit dimensions of the global economy.[47] Smugglers, arms traffickers, and criminals-turned-combatants are typically not treated as central players—strikingly apparent by the virtual absence of these actors from the pages of the leading journals in the field.[48] As evident in wartime Sarajevo, these actors do not merely profit from and feed off of military conflict but can be decisive in its conduct, longevity, and outcome. They are not simply the by-products of war but can be integral to the very practice of war. Moreover, as the Sarajevo case illustrates, many of these actors emerge from the devastation of war as part of a new elite with close ties to political leaders and the security apparatus, often impeding reforms and complicating post-conflict reconstruction efforts.

The potential danger of focusing on these type of actors and activities is to present an over-criminalized narrative of the conflict. John Mueller, for instance, suggests that the violence in Bosnia was largely provoked and perpetuated by relatively small groups of marauding thugs and common criminals, leading him to conclude that such organized violence resembles crime more than warfare. Mueller's provocative argument is a valuable antidote to popular accounts of ethnicity-driven mass violence. But it goes too far in reducing conflict narrowly to the actions of apolitical bands of opportunistic loot-seekers. What is needed is a more nuanced and complex understanding of the criminalized dimensions of conflict. For example, contrary to Mueller's assertion that "criminal armies simply do not have the ability, or more accurately the will, to stand and fight, and they will fade away," not all criminal combatants are necessarily cowardly—and indeed, as evident early on in the siege of Sarajevo, can sometimes show impressive resolve, stand their ground, and even be heroic in dire circumstances.[49]

A broader analysis also needs to go beyond the role of criminal combatants to include the much more diverse set of local and international actors, including arms dealers, embargo busters, and local black market entrepreneurs that make up the criminalized side of warfare. Equally important, this should not mean taking politics out and simply reducing all behavior to criminality and personal material gain. Differentiations between what is political and what is criminal are too easily overstated and indeed present a false dichotomy. Some economic approaches to conflict, for example, have framed the analysis around a separation between greed and grievance motives, when in fact the distinction can substantially blur in practice.[50] As evident in the story of the siege of Sarajevo and the wider war in Bosnia, criminality and private predation do not simply trump politics in wartime but rather interact with it in complex ways. Some aspects of the criminalized side of conflict are state-sponsored and directly serve political interests, such as when political leaders subcontract out key tasks to criminals and smugglers, because they either cannot or prefer not to perform these tasks themselves. This has long been recognized by American military strategists. For instance, a U.S. Army field manual on urban operations observes:

> Criminal elements or organizations may not always work against Army commanders. They can be co-opted or influenced to serve friendly objectives. For example, during World War II the US Navy worked covertly with the Mafia in New York City to secure the New York harbor from German U-boats believed to be torpedoing ships there. The Mafia controlled most dock activities [in] New York harbor and was perfectly positioned to monitor other subversive waterfront activity. This capability provided needed information to the Navy for its counterintelligence and security tasks. New York civil authorities therefore agreed to permit a Navy-Mafia alliance to operate at the port for the greater good of the country.[51]

Political sponsorship of criminal actors and smuggling practices can provide a license for robbery and war profiteering—while at the same time contributing to strategic war objectives and state-building projects. There can also be much variation in political motives for collusion with the criminal underworld beyond self-enrichment. In the Bosnian war, for example, the early Serb use of criminal combatants in irregular paramilitary units (mostly away from the Sarajevo area) helped to obscure the complicity of the Belgrade government[52] and compensate for desertions and recruitment difficulties in the regular army.[53] For the Sarajevo government, in contrast, the initial military dependence on criminals-turned-combatants was more of a survival strategy, providing a desperately needed substitute for a regular military force before a formal army with an operational command structure was fully in place. In some respects, this is reminiscent of the old practice of using mercenaries and privateers in early European state-building.[54]

Thus, while the Bosnian conflict is characterized as the archetypal example of a so-called "new" type of warfare,[55] it also partly reflects a throwback to a much older form of organized violence—but in a radically different global setting.

The Sarajevo experience also indicates that all aspects of criminalized conflict are not uniformly negative and in fact can be essential for daily survival. Indeed, Bosnia as a state would probably not exist (or certainly not in its present form) without the assistance of criminal combatants, black market traders, and arms embargo busters. In this regard, the Sarajevo story represents a case of criminally enabled state-making—a modern-day variant of Charles Tilly's famous characterization of "war making and state making as organized crime."[56]

The criminalized side of conflict can have a double-edged and contradictory character. As the defense of Sarajevo illustrates, criminal gangs can perform important military functions while also robbing and abusing those they are supposed to be defending. The criminalized dimensions of conflict can contribute to the stubborn persistence of war, but also to its ending, for example by tilting the military balance through clandestine weapons procurement. Smuggling is certainly about profits and greed, but at the same time can be essential for daily sustenance. Smuggling is thus not just about illicit enrichment but about coping and surviving under desperate circumstances. In the case of wartime Sarajevo, black marketeers were often depicted as opportunistic vultures, feeding on the city's misery. Many certainly fit this description. Yet the sheer diversity of actors and activities involved in the smuggling economy suggests there were many shades of gray, blurring distinctions between patriots and profiteers.

Preview

The story that follows traces the creation, maintenance, lifting, and aftermath of the siege of Sarajevo. The next two chapters focus on the buildup to the siege, its imposition, and its persistence. First, major players in Sarajevo's criminal underground spearheaded the defense of the city during the first critical weeks and months of the siege before a substantial international presence was established. While also robbing local residents, many of these criminals-turned-soldiers were embraced as war heroes for their leadership role before a regular army was fully formed and operational. Second, a thriving black market trade soon emerged that crossed the siege lines, providing an essential supplement to official relief aid. Third, vital military equipment and supplies gradually filtered into the city through various smuggling channels—sometimes with the complicity of the international interveners and even the besiegers. As documented in chapter 3, the UN-directed international relief effort not only conditioned and structured the political economy of the siege, but international actors on the ground also became deeply enmeshed as facilitators and even direct participants in the war economy. Chapter 4 shows how the siege conditions also provided a convenient cover and opportunity to redistribute wealth, privilege, and power within Sarajevo—a "siege within the siege" that largely took place backstage.

Chapter 5 turns to the lifting of the siege. Although minimal access to arms and ammunition placed the Sarajevo government on the defensive throughout most of the conflict, evading the UN arms embargo through smuggling channels proved essential not only in sustaining their war effort but in eventually shifting the military balance on the ground. On the front stage, the siege was lifted with the help of NATO air strikes, but backstage the war was brought to an end with an influx of smuggled arms to Bosnian government forces (covertly aided by friendly countries such as Iran and quietly encouraged by the United States). Thus, smuggling helped to sustain the conflict—but also helped to bring it to an end.

Chapter 6 examines the legacy of the criminalized side of the siege and wider war, evident in the emergence of a new elite enriched by war profiteering, and an expansive postwar smuggling economy partly based on political protections and informal trading networks built up during wartime. For comparative insights, chapter 7 briefly extends the analysis to other sieges within Bosnia (Srebrenica) and outside the region (Leningrad, Grozny, Falluja), revealing variations across place and time that illuminate what is and is not distinctive about the Sarajevo case. I conclude the book with an evaluation of broader implications and lessons for scholars and practitioners.

CHAPTER 2

IMPOSING THE SIEGE

S arajevo, crowded into a narrow valley between steep foothills and mountains, could not be more perfectly situated for siege planners. Straddling the narrow Miljacka River, the city is thirteen kilometers long on an east-west axis and only three to four kilometers wide. It is in an exceptionally poor defensive position. By the start of the siege in early April 1992, hundreds of artillery pieces, mortars, and tanks encircled the city, dug into positions prepared months in advance. The Serb-held hillside suburb of Grbavica was close to the downtown area and overlooked what became known as "sniper alley," and the more distant mountains provided perfect terrain for artillery positions.

This story begins with the buildup to the siege, its imposition, and the city's surprisingly effective and criminally enabled resistance. Rather than bringing a quick end to the siege, the international reaction instead helped establish the rules of the game and further criminalize the conflict, with long-lasting repercussions. The point here is not to provide a general explanation of the origins of the war or a detailed, blow-by-blow account of its beginning, but rather to show how the covert preparations for conflict, the formative moments during its outbreak, and the nature of the international reaction all set the stage for a highly criminalized and unexpectedly long siege and wider war.

The Road to Siege Warfare

In the spring of 1992, Bosnia, one of six republics of the Socialist Federal Republic of Yugoslavia, declared independence following the earlier international recognition of Slovenia and Croatia as independent states. Bosnia's ethnic Serbs, following the leadership of the Serbian Democratic Party (SDS), feared minority status in the new Bosnian state and thus opposed independence. The Bosnian Croats and Muslims, following the respective leaderships of the Croatian Democratic Union (HDZ) and the Party of Democratic Action (SDA), strongly favored independence as a way of avoiding the dominance of neighboring Serbia.[1] As the European Community announced recognition of Bosnia as an independent state in early April 1992, one of the most brutal conflicts in recent times began between the Belgrade-aided Bosnian Serbs on one side and Bosnian Croats and Muslims (in an on-and-off alliance of convenience) on the other. The war, which marked the return of siege-style warfare in Europe, lasted from April 6, 1992, to October 12, 1995.

Just a few years earlier, the SDS, HDZ, and SDA, had formed a coalition of convenience that brought these nationalist political parties to power. As Mirko Pejanović notes, "They decided to cooperate for the sake of one basic goal: to keep the democratic, liberal, and leftist parties out of power."[2] But beyond the immediate goal of winning the November 1990 elections they could not agree on core issues regarding Bosnia's future. Once in power, Robert Donia observes, the "leaders of the three nationalist parties engaged in a systematic division of personnel appointments in every government entity, institution, and enterprise in the city. The kingpins of nationalist party patronage networks spent much of 1991 securing their fair share of jobs at all levels, in some cases running roughshod over professional qualifications and frequently overriding established succession practices."[3]

By mid-1991, the short-lived uneasy alliance between the three nationalist parties had come undone. SDS officials moved to set up parallel institutions in many Sarajevo municipalities. SDS leaders such as Radovan Karadžić harbored plans to besiege the city as early as September.[4] In November, the Sarajevo newsweekly *Slobodna Bosna* published a document revealing that the SDS had established a war staff with plans to besiege the city if war were to break out.[5] Most Saraje-vans, nevertheless, continued to optimistically believe that war would be avoided, and were thus caught largely unprepared for both its out-break and longevity. Even as war engulfed neighboring Croatia in 1991, including the Serb sieges of Dubrovnik and Vukovar, and the bloodshed began to spill over into Bosnia in early 1992, most Saraje-vans stubbornly held onto the belief that the conflict would not reach their city.

In hindsight, the lack of a strong international response to these earlier Serb military sieges in Croatia may have helped pave the way for the siege of Sarajevo. Robert Toscano, a senior official in the Italian Foreign Ministry's Directorate of Political Affairs, comments, "It is widely believed that if the international community had 'drawn the line' in Dubrovnik, it might have avoided the tragedy of Sarajevo."[6] Warren Zimmerman, the former U.S. ambassador to Belgrade, argues similarly:

> Vukovar and Dubrovnik led directly to the merciless attacks on Sarajevo and other Bosnian cities. Yet no Western government at the time called on NATO's military force to get the JNA [Yugo-slav National Army] to stop shelling Dubrovnik, although NATO's supreme commander, General John Galvin, had pre-pared contingency plans for doing so. The use of force was sim-ply too big a step to consider in late 1991. I did not recommend it myself—a major mistake. The JNA's artillery on the hills sur-rounding Dubrovnik and its small craft on the water would have been easy targets. Not only would damage to the city have been averted, but the Serbs would have been taught a lesson about Western resolve that might have deterred at least some of their aggression against Bosnia.[7]

Much ink has been spilled trying to explain the outbreak of the war in Bosnia. Some arguments stress external economic and political con-ditions as primary explanations,[8] others place greater causal weight on domestic factors, such as opportunistic political elites or economic competition over the redistribution of productive assets in the transi-tion to a market-based economy,[9] and still others view the conflict as the product of historically rooted ethnic animosities.[10] These various perspectives, operating at different levels of analysis, share a tendency to take for granted or understate how the competing sides actually obtained and sustained their physical capacity to wage war in the first place.[11] Antagonistic group history, manipulative politicians, and economic crisis and transition certainly helped create a fertile environment for conflict. But armed conflict by definition requires arms, and there is nothing automatic about the ability to acquire them. While some security scholars argue that "weapons are so readily available through so many channels that any group, including governments, bent on the use of force have no difficulty finding them,"[12] the Bosnia experience shows that there can be enormous unevenness in access to weapons, and that this can powerfully shape the strategic calculus to go to war.

The Bosnian Serbs had the overwhelming advantage of being backed by the Yugoslav People's Army (JNA), whose Bosnia-based forces had quietly become Bosnian Serb-dominated by early 1992. In January 1992, Serbian president Slobodan Milošević secretly ordered that all Bosnia-born Serb JNA officers be transferred to Bosnia.[13] By April 1992, the vast majority of the 90,000 JNA troops in the republic were Bosnian Serbs.[14] When the JNA officially withdrew from Bosnia on May 19, 1992 (some six weeks after the outbreak of the war), most of the army stayed behind—along with their heavy weapons, ammunition, and supplies—and simply became part of the newly formed Bosnian Serb army (VRS). In the Sarajevo area, the JNA Fourth Corps was formally disbanded and became the Sarajevo-Romanija Corps of the VRS.

The nationalist Bosnian Serb forces were also heavily advantaged by being covertly armed through trafficking networks from Belgrade. An international arms embargo (UN Security Council Resolution 713) was imposed on the region in September 1991 with the intention of limiting the circulation of weapons and inhibiting war, but in practice the embargo simply cemented the military advantage of the Bosnian Serbs, who were well positioned geographically to access arms and other supplies through smuggling channels to neighboring Serbia.[15] Indeed, it was for this reason that Milošević supported the embargo.[16] The embargo was particularly important in reinforcing the enormous imbalance in heavy weapons in favor of the Bosnian Serb forces. Thus, while publicly endorsing the arms embargo on the front stage,

Milošević quietly supported and supplied Bosnian Serb forces backstage.

The prewar covert arming of the Bosnian Serbs was substantially orchestrated by Yugoslav State Security and the Ministry of the Interior, and facilitated by the SDS. Two State Security officials, Franko Simatović ("Frenki") and Radovan Stojičić ("Badža"), were key architects of the arming efforts.[17] JNA military generals were also selectively recruited as part of the development of a clandestine network.[18] The strategic objective was to use SDS local chapters for deployment of arms and ammunition. Simatović and Stojičić traveled regularly to Bosnia to organize the SDS and deploy weapons and ammunition. Mihalj Kertes, a leading member of the Milošević's ruling Socialist Party, also played a central logistical role, organizing clandestine convoys of weapons and munitions to the Serb regions in Bosnia in 1990 and 1991.[19]

While arms were supplied to local Bosnian Serb militias through conduits working for the Serbian Ministry of the Interior, Belgrade-supported paramilitary groups mobilized for action across the border in Bosnia. The covert arming of Bosnian Serbs and subcontracting of irregular paramilitaries helped to obscure the complicity of the Belgrade government, providing the convenient political cover of plausible deniability.[20] In other words, Belgrade could keep up the appearance of non-involvement on the front stage, while engaging in covert facilitation backstage. Many of these irregular fighters from Serbia were wooed to Bosnia by the prospect of looting and selling stolen goods on the black market.[21] Indeed, many of the irregulars were common criminals.[22] In the 1980s and early 1990s, many Yugoslav criminals operating in Western Europe had returned home in the face of intensifying police pressure and tighter immigration restrictions. Conveniently, "the Bosnian war had just started," wrote a journalist for the Belgrade independent weekly *Vreme*, "creating the opportunity for low-risk robbery in patriotic costume."[23]

Some well-known paramilitary leaders were gangsters with close ties to the Yugoslav State Security and Secret Police. The most infamous was Željko Ražnatović ("Arkan"), whose paramilitary units ("Tigers") took a lead role in the early ethnic cleansing campaigns in eastern Bosnia.[24] Arkan spent much of his youth robbing banks in Western Europe. Having escaped from prison, he returned to Belgrade in the 1980s. At the end of 1990 he became the head of Delije, the official fan club of the local Red Star soccer team, from which he selectively found recruits for his Serbian Volunteer Guard. He reportedly made a fortune on the Belgrade black market by selling looted goods from his military exploits in Bosnia.[25] Access to clandestine arms flows and irregular Serb paramilitary units would provide the means to quickly capture and ethnically cleanse some 70 percent of Bosnian territory at the start of the war while much of international attention was fixated on developments in Sarajevo. By the first summer of the war, most of eastern Bosnia was in the hands of Bosnian Serb forces.

JNA backing, paramilitary support, and a successful clandestine arming effort bolstered Bosnian Serb confidence that they could win quickly and decisively, enhancing their willingness and incentives to go to war. They expected a short conflict with limited resistance due to their enormous military power advantage. The Bosnian Serb leadership, Tim Judah observes, possessed so many weapons that "it was convinced it would win a crushing victory within weeks."[26] International observers had similar expectations. John Fawcett and Victor Tanner note that "there was a widespread assumption on both sides of the Atlantic that Serb forces would rapidly prevail."[27] Bosnian Serb leader Nikola Koljević was reported to have claimed in April 1992 that the war would end within ten days.[28] Momčilo Krajišnik similarly commented in March that "everything is ready. In ten days, it will all be over."[29] Radovan Karadžić was even more confident and optimistic, apparently expecting a victory in six days.[30] At a heated meeting of the Bosnian parliament on the night of October 14–15, 1991, Karadžić warned Muslim politicians: "Do not think that you will not lead Bosnia-Herzegovina to hell . . . because the Muslim people cannot defend themselves if there is war. . . . How will you prevent everyone from being killed in Bosnia-Herzegovina?"[31]

The Sarajevo government was woefully under-prepared for war,[32] naively counted on international military support if war broke out, was the most vulnerable to an arms embargo, and was in an extremely weak geographic and financial position to access arms supplies on the international black market. Not only did the Sarajevo government lack an organized military, but President Alija Izetbegović deliberately avoided stockpiling weapons and supplies for the possibility of war. Indeed, an important source of arms for the government was confiscated weapons from Serbs in the city who had been covertly supplied by the SDS (thus, in a roundabout way, the SDS ironically helped to supply the defense of the city).[33] The International Peace Research Institute in Stockholm calculated that Bosnian government forces were outgunned nine-to-one by Serb forces.[34]

Backstage war preparations by Bosnian Muslims were largely limited to two paramilitary formations, the Patriotic League and the Green Berets. The Patriotic League was established in May 1991 under SDA control, soon followed by the creation of the Green Berets. The SDA-paramilitary was informally headquartered in Sarajevo's Café Herceg-Bosna.[35] According to Izetbegović, the first military experts (mostly former JNA) joined the Patriotic League in July 1991, the first truckload of weapons delivered in August, military training commenced in September, and the first units were established in October. Nevertheless, the Patriotic League's organizational capacity and access to arms remained extremely limited, and was especially anemic in comparison to the Bosnian Serb military arsenal and preparations.[36] Local police forces of the Ministry of the Interior, particularly the elite special unit commanded by Dragan Vikić, were also a crucial source of manpower, light weapons, and organization for the city's defense.

Izetbegović apparently believed that more extensive and overt front-stage military preparations would be too risky and provocative, and would undermine international sympathy and willingness to intervene.[37] One can interpret this as either dangerously naïve or as a cynical strategic calculation. Regardless, the stakes were extraordinarily high, with Izetbegović gambling that war would either not come, or if it did that it would spark a strong Western military response on the side of the Sarajevo government. His repeated calls for an international peacekeeping force in the months leading up to the war fell on deaf ears.

The Start of the Siege and the Criminally Aided Defense

Sarajevo held a special place in Bosnian Serb war plans. The initial objective was not to destroy or sack the entire city, but rather to partition it and force the government to surrender. Karadžić stressed that "here [Sarajevo], we are near the viper, and one holds a viper by the throat and not the tail. It is here that the state must be built—Sarajevo is our city."[38] "The Bosnian Serb nationalists," Donia notes, "aimed to achieve the division of Sarajevo, the capital city, as a microcosm of Bosnia-Herzegovina."[39] In April 1992, SDS vice president Nikola Koljević urged that the partition of Bosnia should begin in Sarajevo.[40] Karadžić publicly advocated accomplishing this objective by building a wall through the middle of the city: "Our vision of Sarajevo is like Berlin when the Wall was still standing."[41]

In early March 1992 armed SDS supporters set up barricades at major intersections throughout Sarajevo shortly after the republic's independence referendum (which was boycotted by most Bosnian Serbs). SDA supporters responded with their own set of barricades and checkpoints, sometimes directly across from the SDS positions. The barricades froze traffic in the city and prompted the mobilization of thousands of street demonstrators demanding their removal. The barricades were dismantled, but this would prove to be merely a short-lived pause in an escalating crisis. On April 5, barricades again appeared at key intersections, and once again thousands of peace demonstrators marched through the city. As the crowd approached a roadblock, Serb forces opened fire, killing a young medical student. The crowd swarmed into the General Assembly building, and throughout the next twenty-four hours speakers made impassioned calls for nationalist government leaders, including President Izetbegović, to resign in the hope of keeping the peace. On April 6 (the day the European Community recognized Bosnia as an independent state), Serb snipers on the top floor of the Holiday Inn near the Assembly Building targeted the swelling crowds, killing six and wounding more than a dozen more. That same day, Bosnian Serb forces began shelling Sarajevo from hillside positions, officially marking the start of what would become a three and a half year war.

If Sarajevo were to fall or be bisected, the most likely time would have been when the siege was first imposed, before the city was fully mobilized militarily and a substantial international presence had been established. Thus, Sarajevo was most vulnerable during the first critical weeks and months of the siege when the frontlines were most fluid and contested. On May 2, two Serb armored columns came within 50 meters of the presidency building, with the apparent aim of cutting the city in half.[42] As the first Serb tanks crossed the Miljacka river over the narrow Skenderija bridge, they were repelled by scarce anti-armor weapons. The destroyed armored vehicles blocked further military advancement into the city.[43] According to Bosnian military officials, the availability of even a few shoulder-fired rocket launchers changed the military calculus of the Bosnian Serbs, who were wary of exposing their tanks and other armored vehicles in the narrow streets of Sarajevo.[44] Also decisive were the military clashes of May 14–16, when local military units pushed Serb forces out of the neighborhood of Pofalići, creating a secure corridor between central Sarajevo and the government-controlled western parts of the city.[45] Judah describes the fighting on May 14 as having "changed the course of the war" and "the single greatest Serbian defeat of the war."[46] If Serb forces had succeeded in bisecting the city, he suggests, the Sarajevo government would likely have collapsed and surrendered.

The Sarajevo government announced the formation of the Bosnian army on April 15, but it would take months for it to grow into a force that actually resembled any kind of formal, organized military structure. Sarajevo's defenders initially numbered perhaps 10,000 to 15,000 armed personnel.[47] In the absence of an established military defense system, Sarajevo's criminal underground is widely credited for playing a critical role in saving the city. What Sarajevo lacked was not manpower but rather arms, organization, coordination, and initiative in setting up the basic elements of a perimeter defense. The city's criminal gangs—teamed up, ironically, with police forces[48] and local residents defending their homes—were relatively well armed and well organized, providing some semblance of cohesion that initially substituted for a formal military structure. Their leadership role at the start of the siege also had a huge psychological effect, providing Sarajevans with a much-needed boost of optimism and sense of defiance in the face of military encirclement. Indeed, some of Sarajevo's criminal defenders became instant heroes—embraced and celebrated as a kind of "patriotic mafia."

One of Sarajevo's leading criminal defenders was Jusuf "Juka" Prazina. Juka was a thief and debt collector before the war, reportedly commanding a network of some 300 armed "collectors" who would later be the core of his army.[49] He had been in prison five times and was one of the city's best-known underworld figures. Juka's early leadership role in the defense of the city, however, transformed him into a local hero overnight. "At that time every armed man was important, and Juka's men were well equipped, well trained, and well armed," notes a senior Interior Ministry special unit commander. "No one can deny the fact that Juka with his men arrived to defend the city when it was most needed."[50] Juka's "wolves," as his men were called, grew to as many as 3,000 and were armed with sawed-off shotguns and Kalashnikovs. They reportedly "wore crew-cuts, black jump-suits, sunglasses, basketball shoes, and sometimes masks."[51] Juka rode around town in a stolen red Audi, with his name on the license plate instead of numbers.

Posters of Juka appeared throughout the city, and the local media turned him into a celebrity figure. The singer Senad Ramić appeared on a local television program singing a song praising Juka's heroics, and an upbeat television commercial featured Juka getting into a car with his bodyguards and a Doberman.[52] The commercial included a song with the lyrics:

They're destroying our town.
Shame on them!
But they didn't know
About Juka.[53]

The government rewarded Juka's heroics by giving him multiple official titles, including commander of the Special Forces of the Reserve Brigade of the Ministry of the Interior, and the commander of the Special Units of the Army.[54] These were actually fictional titles meant to appease and impress Juka, who craved recognition and respect and aspired to be the city's top military leader. As Juka allegedly proclaimed, "They all say I'm a great criminal, why shouldn't I be a great general too?"[55]

Other key criminal defenders included Ramiz Delalić and Ismet Bajramović, both of whom were nicknamed "Ćelo"—which meant "baldy," though both men had plenty of hair. The journalist Gojko Berić writes that "Ćelo" was the "most famous nickname in war-time Sarajevo," which was "common among petty criminals who returned from prison with shaven heads; there were apparently thirteen with the right to that nickname, though only two of them were powerful during the war."[56] In striking contrast to Juka, Ćelo Delalić, the commander of the 9th Motorized Brigade, shunned public attention and the media spotlight—so much so that he prohibited journalists from filming him or taking his picture. The other Ćelo, Ismet Bajramović, had been imprisoned for rape, assault, and armed robbery before the war broke out. But as a result of his leadership in the early days of the siege he was, ironically, put in charge of the central prison, and also served as a senior member in the Bosnian military police until the beginning of 1993. He played a key leadership role in capturing scarce anti-tank weapons and ammunition from the Marshal Tito JNA barracks in early June, and was also instrumental in the defense of Dobrinja, a strategically critical Sarajevo suburb near the airport. He led several major military police actions (including one against renegade soldiers who were abusing and robbing citizens) while at the same time engaging in smuggling, racketeering, and cross-frontline trading.[57] "I put Ismet in jail during peacetime, and during the trial the court found he was a psychopath," noted Jusuf Pušina, the Bosnian interior minister at the start of the war. "Then," during wartime, "suddenly I found he had more authority than me. It was a surreal moment."[58]

Some of those who rose to leadership positions in the initial phase of the city's defense did not have criminal backgrounds but ran their military units as their own private gangs and refused to conform to a formal military command structure. The most famous and feared was Mušan "Caco" Topalović, a nightclub musician and martial arts expert who oversaw frontline defenses in the area from Skenderija on the left side of the Miljacka River eastward. Operating in the frontline neighborhood next to Caco's was the local crime boss Mujo Zulić, who was able to exploit his underworld acumen to mobilize the defense of the Trebevic line and rise to become the commander of the 1st Mountain Brigade. Zulić used a local coffee shop as his headquarters, barking out orders on his walkie-talkie to his men on the front lines.[59] Criminal turf became military turf.

Many of Sarajevo's small-time criminals rushed to pick up arms at the start of the siege simply thinking it would be fun, short-lived, and offer a mechanism for quick advancement. For example, a commander of a small, forty-seven-person unit in Dobrinja at the start of the war recalls that most of his men had some kind of criminal background, and that 30–50 percent of them were killed early on "trying to be Rambos." As he explains it, they grew up watching Rambo-type movies, and genuinely believed that these films depicted what war was actually like, that it would be an adventure. Many assumed they could easily take out tanks with Molotov cocktails, thinking that this would work just as it did in the movies. While most Sarajevans were reluctant at the start of the war to pick up a gun, these men and others like them across the city were eager to do so. "They didn't need to be very smart," he says, "just more dangerous and daring than the average person."[60] Juka, for example, had a custom-made "bulletproof vest"—oblivious to the fact that it was not actually bulletproof.[61] Zulić had allegedly been turned down from military service before the war due to mental incompetence (which was extremely difficult to achieve), but the initial defense of the city required bravado more than brainpower.[62] A penchant for risk-taking and adventurism helped to make up for a lack of military training.

Placing key sections of the city's perimeter security in the hands of people like Juka, Zulić, Caco, and the two Ćelos came at a high price, however. A substantial portion of the perimeter defense was privatized and criminalized, with the government in effect subcontracting out military tasks that it could not perform on its own. The full repercussions were recognized only slowly, with some of the city's key defense lines claimed as personal turf and divided up into individual fiefdoms and protection rackets. In practice, the military command structure was more personal than professional—for example, Sarajevo's army brigades were commonly referred to not by their formal titles (such as the "1st Mountain Brigade") but rather by their leader (such as "Zulić's unit"); and similarly, rather than identifying a soldier as a member of a particular brigade they were more commonly identified simply as one of "Ćelo's boys" or "Juka's boys." Some of these defense lines became profit centers that controlled key access routes into and out of the city. They formally served as sites of military confrontation, but informally regulated and facilitated cross-frontline commercial collaboration and exchange. The city was never entirely sealed off, with those on both sides who controlled the access points essentially functioning as gatekeepers and toll collectors. And, as discussed in detail in the next chapter, the substantial international presence in the city became an integral part of this dynamic.

As the city's hodge-podge assortment of loosely organized and co-ordinated defense forces swelled during the early months of the siege, it became increasingly difficult for the besiegers to overcome their manpower deficit. Former Bosnian army general Jovan Divjak claims that the Serb army had fewer than 29,000 people along a sixty-four-kilometer-long siege line.[63] While the nationalist Serbs enjoyed over-whelmingly superior firepower and had enough men to surround the city, their numbers were insufficient to take the city block-by-block and were extremely reluctant to risk heavy casualties. Their military hardware could keep Sarajevo bottled up and its residents in a state of terror, but had limited use in close-in street fighting once inside the city. This provided the initial conditions for a siege stalemate, which would be powerfully reinforced and institutionalized by the particu-lar international response to the conflict.

The International Response

As shells fell on Sarajevo and Serb forces made large territorial gains elsewhere in Bosnia, Western governments scrambled to "do something" to contain if not resolve the escalating conflict. Beyond fre-quent front-stage condemnations of the violence and calls for peace negotiations, the main international response was a combination of economic sanctions on the Milošević regime for its support of the rebel Serbs in Bosnia (which turned much of the Serbian economy into a sanctions-busting black market economy), reaffirmation of the re-gional arms embargo (which placed the Sarajevo government at a sub-stantial disadvantage and made it dependent on black market arms), and large-scale delivery of humanitarian aid to the victims of the con-flict, coordinated by the UNHCR and supported by a limited contin-gent of UN troops. These UN-led efforts offered Western leaders a highly visible and symbolically appealing alternative to risky military intervention and a political shield against charges of inaction.[64] The UN provided a convenient vehicle to both condemn and contain the conflict without having to intervene more directly. And some UN agencies, such as the UNHCR, were eager to demonstrate their rele-vance to Western governments, viewing the conflict as an opportunity to take a center-stage role and enhance funding, status, and visibility.

The most important component of the international response to the Bosnian war was an ambitious UN-led humanitarian aid operation, with Sarajevo and its airport as the centerpiece. UN Security Council Resolution 757, in addition to imposing sanctions on the Belgrade government, reaffirmed that supplying besieged Sarajevo with humanitarian aid should be the UN's priority. It called for creating the "necessary conditions for unimpeded delivery of humanitarian supplies to Sarajevo and other destinations in Bosnia and Herzegovina, including the establishing of a security zone encompassing Sarajevo and its airport." In practice, however, the UN separated out protecting the city and protecting the airport, viewing the latter as its primary task—essentially signaling that the siege of the city could continue as long as aid deliveries were let in.

The idea of a humanitarian airlift gained political support and momentum after a successful two-day U.S. military airlift to Sarajevo in mid-April 1992. The gesture was largely symbolic (the 92,000 ready-to-eat military rations were perhaps enough to feed less than half of the city's inhabitants for a day), but it had a powerful demonstration effect. Importantly, Serb military officials in control of the airport cooperated with the entire operation—even as they continued to shell the city. Fawcett and Tanner, who were in Sarajevo during the siege working for humanitarian assistance organizations and the United Nations, argue that "the April airlift was a critical forerunner of the UNHCR airlift that began at the end of June 1992. In terms of operations, it set important precedents and operational criteria for the later airlift." Most important, "it showed that humanitarian access to Sarajevo could be negotiated with the Serb leadership. . . . From the Serb leadership's perspective, they doubtless drew the lesson that consent on the humanitarian front—the fact that they had been asked to grant permission for the relief effort—allowed them to get away with otherwise unacceptable behavior, such as shelling the city during the visit of U.S. officials."[65]

A humanitarian response to the Sarajevo siege was not only politically appealing in Washington policy circles but in European capitals as well. The French were particularly eager to find alternatives to military intervention. Adding a key endorsement to the humanitarian approach that was gaining popularity, French president François Mitterrand took center stage during his dramatic visit to Sarajevo in late

June and singled out the opening of the airport as the number one priority: "The city is shut off, closed and isolated from the rest of the world, and all the while, it is being subjected to practically constant gunfire that is destroying its vital centers and killing many of its people. This is not acceptable." He concluded: "Therefore, it is necessary to open the airport by one means or another."[66]

The UN brokered an airport agreement on June 5, 1992, and the UN-directed airlift was up and running by the end of the month, bringing in more than 150 tons of food and medical supplies a day.[67] The UNHCR embraced its new task of running the airlift. As Lowell Martin, chief of the UNHCR's evaluation section, comments, "Although several western governments were willing to assume responsibility for the airlift, UNHCR was eager to demonstrate its effectiveness, and worked hard to secure responsibility for this aspect of the relief effort. Once the airlift began, the operation gained a much higher political profile and the need for UNHCR's presence in former Yugoslavia ceased to be debated internally."[68]

Bosnian Serb leaders had multiple motives and incentives for agreeing to the airlift and turning over the airport to UN forces. Doing so helped to inhibit more forceful Western action, which was far more likely if the city was cut off. As Laura Silber and Alan Little note, "Karadžić was as concerned as anybody to avoid the starvation of Sarajevo: it would have further increased calls by senior western politicians—including Margaret Thatcher and Bob Dole—for military intervention. Would the world really stand by and watch a European capital starve to death? Karadžić planned happily to vacate the airport, making it look like a major concession and throwing the burden of 'responsible behavior' back on the Bosnian government."[69] Karadžić told a senior UN official that he did not want the city sealed off entirely because the Muslims in Sarajevo "needed to breathe" (even as he oversaw an ethnic cleansing campaign elsewhere in Bosnia).[70]

Importantly, the terms of the airport agreement specified assuring safe access to the airport and the corridors into the city only for aid delivery—which Serb leaders interpreted to mean they could continue to besiege the rest of Sarajevo unimpeded. The airport agreement, and its implicit acceptance of the siege conditions, was therefore a major Serb victory that would powerfully constrain the UN's role in Sarajevo throughout the war. In this regard, the initial mission of the UN

Protection Force (UNPROFOR) deployed to Sarajevo was narrowly conceived as providing protection for the airport and support for humanitarian aid deliveries, not protection for the city's besieged population. Indeed, as part of the terms of the airport agreement, the UNPROFOR became siege enforcers by not allowing people to exit or enter the city across the airport grounds. While the UNPROFOR's mandate would expand during the course of the war (to include, for example, monitoring cease-fires and the NATO enforced no-fly zone in Bosnian airspace), securing the airport and providing support for the humanitarian operation would remain its core task. .

These highly restrictive rules of engagement, along with a formal commitment to consent and impartiality, generated intense local bitterness and resentment toward the UNPROFOR. The presence of the UNPROFOR also inhibited external military action for fear of placing the troops in jeopardy (and indeed, some UN soldiers would later be taken as hostages by Serb forces). Equally important, the UNPROFOR leadership had an interest in avoiding confrontations and antagonistic relations with the besieging Serbs, since their mobility and access to the city required Serb consent.

The UNPROFOR was initially formed as a small peacekeeping force in Croatia in early 1992, but it would be substantially expanded through the aid mission in Sarajevo and then elsewhere in Bosnia— becoming the largest and most costly peacekeeping effort ever undertaken by the United Nations.[71] What began as a force with fewer than 2,000 personnel in the summer of 1992 grew to over 9,000 troops by the middle of 1993 (though never reaching anywhere near what was considered the necessary size). UN Security Council Resolution 761 on June 29, 1992, authorized additional UNPROFOR troops "to ensure the security and functioning of Sarajevo airport and the delivery of humanitarian assistance." In early July, 1,000 Canadian troops arrived to manage the airport and make the airlift operationally viable.

Not coincidentally, once the airlift was operational, Western powers immediately stopped insisting on a cease-fire and withdrawal of heavy weapons around the city. The airlift made the siege locally manageable and therefore internationally palatable. Shortly after the airlift was underway, General Lewis MacKenzie, the Canadian UNPROFOR commander, commented, "We're getting used to working around the shooting."[72] Some UN officials later tried to even avoid calling the situation a siege, preferring to describe it as a "militarily advantageous encirclement" for the Serbs and a "tactical disadvantage" for the city's defenders.[73]

Making the siege manageable also meant that it would be economically rewarding for those who controlled access to the city. As Fawcett and Tanner note, the Bosnian Serb leadership may "have begun to realize that a prolonged siege offered promising commercial opportunities."[74] They not only had to approve all aid coming into the airport, but also profited by taking a sizeable cut. As stipulated in the airport agreement, almost one-quarter of all aid allocated for the city would be handed over to the besiegers. The UN was, in this sense, literally buying access to the city. The Bosnian Serb leadership also imposed the terms of the airport agreement on land convoys, which also had to enter the city via the airport grounds.[75]

Some critics warned that this policy of supplying and relying on the consent of the besiegers in order to feed the besieged was counterproductive and a form of appeasement.[76] In his memoir, the former U.S. diplomat Richard Holbrooke describes the UN's policy of consent in harsh terms: "By allowing the Bosnian Serbs to determine what got in, the U.N. had, in effect, become an unintentional accomplice to Serb policy. In its press releases, the UNHCR boasted about the amount of food it had brought in, not the inadequacy of the system or the rising death toll."[77] Indeed, from the very start, the airlift was played up as an international success story, with UNPROFOR commander MacKenzie lobbying and manipulating his superiors to give him the high-profile job of running the airport.[78]

Setting up the UN airlift had immediate political consequences. Most important, it dramatically reduced the prospects of Western military intervention.[79] Local actors were keenly aware of the political ramifications of the airlift, which is why Karadžić pushed for it despite opposition from some of his own military leaders.[80] On the Sarajevo government side, President Izetbegović welcomed the airlift even as Vice President Ejup Ganić made a sober assessment of the implications: "By getting out of the airport, just in time, [Serbian leaders] have given the Western powers just enough to allow them to avoid the hard decision of intervening here with military force."[81]

In retrospect, the airport agreement and handover of the airport to the UN was the defining moment of international engagement in the war in Bosnia. It provided the key mechanism for major powers to make Bosnia first and foremost a humanitarian problem. Based on their experience as senior aid workers in Sarajevo, Fawcett and Tanner argue that "the airport agreement was the turning point in the transformation of the perception of the Bosnian conflict from a war of aggression into a complex humanitarian emergency. It defined the crisis as a humanitarian tragedy that called for humanitarian solutions, rather than as a political crisis in need of political measures. It institutionalized the siege of Sarajevo. It made it politically acceptable."[82] The airlift became "the most visible manifestation of Western policy in Bosnia."[83]

Similarly, Mark Cutts, a senior UNHCR official, acknowledges that "the airlift developed into a high-profile, donor-led operation which served the political interests of powerful nations who wanted to demonstrate to the world that they were 'doing something' in Bosnia. As a tangible and highly visible symbol of the international community's efforts to intervene constructively in Bosnia, it became something of an obsession."[84] Pragmatism and expediency trumped: "UNHCR, UNPROFOR and the international community had decided that it was better to have the airlift operating on terms laid down by the Bosnian Serb authorities, than not at all," Cutts explains. "The problem was that this further empowered the Bosnian Serbs, who turned the tap on and off as they pleased. It gave them enormous leverage over the international community. Throughout the war, much time was wasted by international negotiators returning almost religiously to Karadžić's headquarters in Pale, beseeching the Bosnian Serbs to cooperate and pleading with them to turn on the tap to Sarajevo again."[85]

The Sarajevo airlift and the entire humanitarian approach to the Bosnian conflict quickly took on a life of its own, becoming an end in itself. Keeping the airlift going became the driving international policy objective, with day-to-day successes measured by how much aid was or was not getting in. UNHCR officials and Washington policymakers became preoccupied with the quantitative indicators—tonnage of food delivered, the number and size of cargo planes and flights per day, and so on. Recalling daily calls from the White House, one administration official put it bluntly: "When the President of the United States wants to know how many tons of lentils have been delivered that day, you *know* you have no [expletive] policy."[86] Another State Department official lamented: "They needed guns, we sent them flour."[87]

The limitations and compromises involved in the airport agreement are strikingly illustrated by comparing the Sarajevo and Berlin airlifts:

> The allies would certainly not have succeeded in delivering such large quantities to Berlin, and in eventually forcing Stalin to back down and lift the blockade, if they had started off with an agreement which allowed the East Germans to dictate the terms of the airlift, to inspect all arriving cargo, to receive a pay-off of one quarter of all arriving supplies, and to have the remainder pass through an East German road checkpoint before being allowed into the city.[88]

The airlift also provided a politically useful front-stage distraction for the besieging Serbs: it focused international attention and concern narrowly on Sarajevo, keeping the rest of the war-torn country off-stage and out of the media spotlight (where some of the worst atrocities were taking place, including the mass execution and expulsion of Muslims from towns and villages and the setting up of concentration camps). With Sarajevo occupying center stage, much of the rest of Bosnia was treated as a sideshow. As Donia observes, "Developments in Sarajevo, and access to the city through its airport, became the dominant factors in UN decision making, so that policy toward Sarajevo heavily influenced UN policy toward Bosnia-Herzegovina."[89]

Importantly, UN control of the airport not only drew media attention to the airlift but also greatly facilitated the influx of foreign journalists into the city, who could conveniently fly in and out to nearby Germany, Croatia, and Italy via the airlift. The opening of the airport turned a city under siege into the most accessible war zone in Bosnia. This partly explains why Sarajevo was transformed into a global media spectacle, becoming the most familiar face of the war.[90] The so-called "CNN effect" was real, but provided a narrow and distorted picture: as preparations were being made to get the airlift going, CNN optimistically reported that "some [UN] officials here say the lull in the fighting has given them new hope, that they can return to the job of clearing the airport and making it safe—a first step toward bringing saneness [sic] back to the region."[91] Meanwhile, away from the front-stage cameras in Sarajevo, the killings and mass expulsions continued elsewhere in Bosnia. Bosnian Serb leader Nikola Koljević later acknowledged that the international attention on Sarajevo in the summer of 1992 "had allowed us to get on with what we had to do in northern Bosnia."[92] Koljević told a foreign journalist that he and other Western observers had essentially been conned: "It amazes me that you all took so long to get the point. Poor Sarajevo! That was all you could think about."[93]

Opening the airport and starting up the airlift brought desperately needed (though never sufficient) aid to the city: from the summer of 1992 until January of 1996 (longer than the Berlin airlift) there were 12,951 UN aid flights into the city using planes from twenty countries, bringing in 160,677 tons of humanitarian supplies (144,827 tons of food and the rest non-food items such as medical supplies). During some months, the airlift brought in more than 85 percent of the aid arriving in the city.[94] The fleet of aircraft that composed the airlift represented Sarajevo's most important link to the rest of the world.

But as the airlift helped to keep the city from starving, it also made the siege tolerable and therefore internationally acceptable—reducing the likelihood of it being lifted. Humanitarian action became, in effect, a new form of containment. It provided a mode of managing the situation without having to resort to direct military force. It also avoided the specter of hundreds of thousands of refugees exiting the city: delivering aid would help to deter a further mass exodus of Bosnian refugees.[95] The result of this process, as Michael Ignatieff puts it, is that "the U.N. allowed itself to become the administrator of the Serbian siege of Sarajevo."[96] At the end of a visit to the city, George Soros put it in even stronger terms: "Sarajevo is a concentration camp and the UN is part of the system that maintains it."[97]

The airlift not only served the political interests of major powers but also provided a useful mechanism for UN agencies, most notably the UNHCR, to showcase their activities on the front stage and raise their global profile. The Bosnian war and the siege of Sarajevo in particular were key ingredients in the UNHCR's effort to reinvent itself and become a much bigger player. As Gil Loescher notes, "From being a much-maligned agency in 1989, the UNHCR suddenly became one of the most valued and esteemed of all UN agencies."[98] The UNHCR came to be viewed as an "indispensable actor" in keeping the aid operation going in Bosnia: "The prestige of the High Commissioner

soared as she [Sadako Ogata] had access to the world's political leaders and regularly briefed the UN Security Council on developments in
Bosnia."[99] Indeed, "Bosnia transformed the UNHCR into the world's
largest relief agency"—an especially impressive achievement given
that it had previously been "an obscure humanitarian agency with no
emergency relief profile."[100] Although the UNHCR had some earlier
operational experience as a relief agency, this was the first time the
UNHCR played this role in an ongoing conflict and on such a massive
scale. And remarkably, this transformation all took place in a matter of
months.[101] Designated as the lead UN agency in the conflict, the
UNHCR's influence and status also grew by supervising and coordinating all other international relief organizations, which were rushing
in to play a humanitarian role. The UNHCR thus became a quasi-
government, overseeing a growing number of agencies (more than 250
by the end of 1995).[102]

Far from prompting a quick lifting of the siege of Sarajevo, the international response instead institutionalized it, making the city sufficiently accessible to be manageable and sustainable. The Serb besiegers, the besieged Sarajevo government, and the international
interveners (major powers working through the UN) all preferred a
different outcome than the creation of a high-profile siege stalemate.
Nevertheless, the situation offered certain advantages to key actors
on all sides, who found it preferable to some of the possible alternatives.

For the besieging Serb forces, their first preference, of course,
would have been for the Sarajevo government to simply capitulate
early on, quickly partition the city and the rest of the country, and
avoid any kind of external intervention that would complicate and
challenge their plans. This would have preempted turning Sarajevo
into a center-stage conflict under intense international scrutiny. In the
absence of this immediate outcome, however, Bosnian Serb leaders
and their supporters in Belgrade could cope with (and profit from)
economic sanctions, were militarily advantaged by the UN arms
embargo, and could gain significant political leverage and economic
rewards from the mass influx of humanitarian aid. Moreover, this outcome substituted for and inhibited their least preferred outcome: a
strong international military response.

For the Sarajevo government, its clear preference would have been an early and decisive external military intervention to deter Bosnian Serb aggression and Belgrade sponsorship. Its least preferred option, however, was no international response at all—to simply be ignored (not unlike a number of other conflicts around the world) and be left purely at the mercy of the besieging Serb forces. The humanitarian compromise that emerged assured that Sarajevo would remain in the global spotlight, even if this neglected much of the rest of the country and did not necessarily translate into immediate military intervention and a quick end to the conflict. For key players within the city, the situation would prove economically and politically rewarding.

For the major powers, their first preference would have been for the conflict to simply blow over and stay off center stage. But with the Sarajevo government stubbornly digging in its heels and the plight of the city capturing global media attention, this was no longer an option. Highly visible UN delivery of humanitarian aid signaled that Western leaders were helping the victims of the war, imposing economic sanctions signaled that they were punishing the main neighboring sponsor of the war, and sustaining the arms embargo signaled that they were against the weapons of war. These measures were politically useful and symbolically attractive for the major powers, and served the larger goal of avoiding their least preferred option: direct military engagement. But as discussed in the next chapter, the practical effect of these front-stage actions on the ground was to further criminalize and perpetuate the conflict—turning the siege into the longest and most internationalized siege in modern history.

SUSTAINING THE SIEGE

The siege of Sarajevo began as a Serb military operation with the immediate instrumental goal of defeating the enemy, but it eventually became an end in itself. Similarly, international humanitarian intervention began with the immediate instrumental goal of curbing the conflict and facilitating a negotiated peace, but it also became an end in itself. Thus, the siege and the international response each took on a life of their own. In the pages that follow, I trace the front-stage and backstage mechanisms through which the siege was maintained and sustained for such an unexpectedly long period of time.

During the course of the long siege, various explicit and implicit "rules of the game" emerged that were regularly tested and renegotiated. For instance, it was considered against the rules for Serb forces to block all humanitarian food supplies and starve the city (depriving the besiegers of a classic siege strategy), but it was within the rules to manipulate and skim off such supplies. It was against the rules to openly divert humanitarian aid to feed combatants, but doing so discretely was tolerated as long as this was kept largely backstage. It was against the rules for the besiegers to shell public spaces where large groups of people gathered (such as breadlines and marketplaces), but it was within the rules to shell the rest of the city and terrorize civilians with sniper fire (the former had a greater media shock effect, and thus could provoke NATO air strikes, while the latter prompted only routine international condemnation). It was against the rules for the opposing forces to openly trade across the siege lines, but it was within the rules to do so quietly and covertly backstage. The rules dictated that the UN be formally impartial in the conflict, yet the terms of the UN's access to the city meant not only de facto acceptance of the siege but also complicity in enforcing it.[1]

Diverting and Manipulating Humanitarian Aid

Formally, the UN-directed humanitarian aid operation fed Sarajevo's civilian population, becoming the centerpiece of the international response to the siege and wider war. Informally, the relief effort fed the opposing armies and enriched black marketeers on all sides. This happened through a variety of mechanisms. In order to gain access to the city, the UN agreed to hand over almost one-quarter of all aid to the Serb besiegers regardless of need (and the actual amount could be much greater through theft and plunder).[1] Much of this aid, in turn, would trickle into Sarajevo backstage via smuggling channels. As one foreigner who was part of a Sarajevo-bound aid convoy puts it, "To get food to the starving Sarajevans the UN had to make a deal, but the irony was that by making the deal the UN became involved in providing goods that would later sell on the black market."[2] Former SDS party leader Biljana Plavšić claims that some war profiteers became millionaires in a matter of months by smuggling humanitarian aid, and that Radovan Karadžić "was fascinated by such people. He admired them, he consorted with them, and then he followed in their footsteps."[3]

Beyond the automatic cut taken by the Bosnian Serb forces surrounding the city, the aid community typically expected to "lose" about 30 percent en route.[4] This was especially the case for aid shipped by land rather than via the airlift, since more checkpoints had to be crossed (moving goods by air, on the other hand, was much more expensive). Widely recognized but rarely publicly discussed was the fact that the UNHCR and other aid agencies pragmatically tolerated and accepted a certain amount of theft and diversion as the price of admission. Portions of this aid would, in turn, end up being sold as commercial goods. This was evident by the appearance of UNHCR-marked items in Sarajevo's public markets that locals rarely, if ever, saw in their official aid packages.[5]

There were three layers of aid "disappearances."[6] The first layer involved the hijacking of aid convoys. While this sometimes included the loss of entire shipments, more common was the selective skimming of goods at checkpoints en route to or entering the city. A warehouse at a Serb checkpoint near Sarajevo, for instance, was reportedly lined wall-to-wall with UNHCR-marked containers.[7] Similarly, Croat forces often collected "tolls" from aid convoys that reached Sarajevo via Croat-held territory. Some entrepreneurial Croat soldiers freelanced by establishing spurious checkpoints and ambushing trucks.[8]

The second layer of "disappearances" allegedly involved the complicity of local UNHCR drivers and warehouse workers. This often amounted to little more than diverting small amounts of the highest quality aid for personal use (including for friends and family members), but there were also reports of larger-scale abuses. For instance, according to one UN official, a UN police raid on the UNHCR warehouse at the Sarajevo airport in the summer of 1993 uncovered a number of serious abuses, with some local workers losing their jobs and others arrested.[9] Fuel also reportedly disappeared: according to a former Bosnian government official, local drivers hired by the UN were bribed to stage accidents, driving their trucks off the road where the fuel would then be siphoned off and sold on the black market.[10] The truck driver would be paid "a few thousand marks to do it," claims the former official. "Then the local mafia would sell [the fuel], sometimes for 30 marks a liter."[11]

Problems of theft and diversion were compounded by the fact that the UNHCR delivered all humanitarian aid to a few central warehouses, leaving the final distribution to local authorities. While this division of labor was understandable given the circumstances, it invited manipulation and abuse. As the journalist Chuck Sudetic reports, "Inevitably, the local authorities diverted some of the aid to their respective armed forces and sold some of it on the open market. The sale of aid and authority over its distribution created local mafias and gave them the power and the authority to press for local interests and act, in many cases, independently of the central government."[12]

The third layer of "disappearances" involved manipulating the counting system in aid lists, including creating fictional recipient names or keeping active the names of the deceased or of those who had left the city. Using fictional recipient lists and oversupplying legitimate institutions (such as hospitals) was an important mechanism for feeding the army. A former UNHCR aid monitor estimates that more than 20 percent of humanitarian aid was diverted to the Bosnian army.[13] Official UN policy prohibited the feeding of combatants, but this was difficult to enforce in practice. This was particularly true on the Bosnian Serb side, where the UNHCR had little monitoring capacity and no leverage anyway over how and where aid was distributed. Thus, the UNHCR went through the motions of making sure that all the paperwork at least appeared to be in order—even while privately admitting that the recipient lists were inflated and partly fictional.[14] According to a local interpreter for a major European news agency, the UNHCR spokesperson acknowledged to foreign journalists that aid was being diverted to the army, but would not say so in front of the cameras.[15] One reporter visiting a local distribution center witnessed boxes of UN aid being handed over to soldiers.[16] Sarajevans typically did not complain about this particular form of aid diversion since it contributed to the defense effort. One local "fixer" and translator for foreign journalists, for example, claims that diverting aid to the army was the one story she discouraged her employers from covering and was careful not to feed them any information about it.[17]

Aid convoys were at times deliberately stalled in order to inflate prices in the city. One Bosnian government official even claims that in late 1993 he witnessed members of the Bosnian army "shoot it up for fifteen days, have the convoys stop, let the city run out of stuff, drive up the prices, and then have the aid sent in." This was allegedly done in collaboration with black marketeers.[18] Tim Ripley claims that a similar dynamic afflicted the airlift: "One low-level Serb commander in Ilidža was dubbed 'King of Sarajevo' because of his ability to control the price of black-market goods in the city. At the behest of Bosnian gangsters, he would fire on aircraft flying into the city's airport to force the humanitarian airlift to shut down, driving up the price of food."[19]

Exploiting the Privileges of Mobility and Access

The UN-led humanitarian assistance effort not only created opportunities for plundering and diverting aid but also infrastructure and cover for a wide range of smuggling activities. Particularly important in this regard was possession of the highly coveted UN "blue card" ID given to international aid workers and many of their local staff, which provided privileged mobility and access across the siege lines. While facilitating smuggling was certainly not the UN's intention, it ultimately contributed to the objective of increasing the overall amount of goods entering Sarajevo (even if at exorbitant prices). Supplying the city via smuggling was especially important given that the UN relief effort provided, according to one estimate, an average of only 159 grams of food per person per day (about 0.35 pounds).[20] Simply put, the city could not have survived on official aid alone.

Among those who enjoyed the greatest mobility and access across the siege lines were, of course, members of the UNPROFOR. For some UNPROFOR troops, their informal role as black market suppliers was arguably as important as their formal role as protectors and facilitators of the UN humanitarian aid effort. As the BBC correspondent Martin Bell concludes, "The principal contribution of the Egyptian and Ukrainian [UNPROFOR] battalions was to ease the hardship of those citizens [of Sarajevo] with German marks by selling their food and fuel on the black market."[21] Locals served as brokers and intermediaries. For example, a Bosnian State Security Service internal memo in early 1993 noted that a local shop owner regularly procured alcohol and other goods at night from the UNPROFOR.[22] Maggie O'Kane reported, "The UN soldiers here are making themselves and the Sarajevo mafia rich. The soldiers are the importers and the locals are the middlemen for a trade in cigarettes, alcohol, food, prostitution and heroin, worth millions of dollars."[23] As Ćelo Bajramović, one of Sarajevo's better-known criminal defenders, candidly explained it, "You know what a good business it is, dealing with the UNPROFOR? You take one ton of petrol at night and sell it by next morning, so you're ahead 2,000 or 3,000 Deutschmarks, even more."[24]

Members of the Ukrainian contingent of the UNPROFOR were particularly notorious for making business deals on the side, specializing in selling fuel siphoned off from their Armored Personnel Carriers.[25] A former UNPROFOR soldier recalls that the Ukrainian troops were "a problem from day one," and that "one had to be blind not to notice that they were involved in a lot of funny business." Their official role in UNPROFOR activities, he says, such as being paired with the French in anti-sniping teams, had little to do with their effectiveness and everything to do with "keeping up the appearance of a multinational team effort."[26] Ukrainian UNPROFOR soldiers were also suspected of importing heroin into the city in UN vehicles and shipping cars (especially Volkswagen Golfs) out of the city in UN container trucks—first transported to Belgrade to obtain false documents, and then on to the Ukraine.[27] Some of the Ukrainian soldiers reportedly even returned to Bosnia after the war to continue their smuggling activities, including bringing in stolen German luxury cars to sell on the black market.[28]

Some UNPROFOR soldiers reportedly also took advantage of their position to engage in smuggling people out of the city, motivated by profit, sympathy, or a mixture of both. This allegedly included selling seats on humanitarian aid flights for 1,000–2,000 German marks per head (while this provided the quickest exit out of the country, the downside was that the passenger did not always know at which foreign airport the plane would land).[29] French troops in their Armored Personnel Carriers would allegedly pick people up at their homes like a taxi service, charging 500–2,000 German marks for a ride out of town.[30] Similarly, it was an open secret in Sarajevo that Ukrainian soldiers would smuggle Serbs out of Sarajevo to nearby Pale for 1,000 German marks per person.[31] One former UNPROFOR soldier writes in his memoir that he and some of his colleagues ran a free clandestine shuttle service out of the city. In one case this involved dressing the smuggled passengers up in UNHCR hats and blue flak jackets to impersonate aid workers.[32]

The UNPROFOR insisted that there were only isolated incidents of abuse and black marketeering within its ranks, and occasionally sent members home. The commander of the Ukrainian corps, for example, was relieved of his duties in the fall of 1992 for collusion with local smugglers in selling oil, cigarettes, and alcohol.[33] By late August 1993, twenty-two soldiers (nineteen Ukrainians and three French) had been dismissed for war profiteering.[34] Austrian major general Gunther Greindl was dispatched to Sarajevo in 1993 to look into the mounting allegations of UNPROFOR crime, corruption, and profiteering. Yet, as one journalist notes, Greindl hardly spoke to any locals during his investigation and "ignored the prostitution that was visible around most of the UN barracks in the city."[35] Most sensitive and controversial were local accusations that members of the UNPROFOR had frequented a Serb brothel at a women's concentration camp outside the city during the summer of 1992.[36] Greindl's final report in March 1994 (the full contents of which were not made public) concluded that there were some problems with particular individuals but that these were merely isolated cases and did not reflect systemic corruption.[37] The UN denied that their employees were involved in smuggling people out of the city, calling such charges "baseless," and could not substantiate claims of prostitution.[38]

Many locals employed by the UNPROFOR, UNHCR, and the 100–150 other international humanitarian agencies in Sarajevo (according to one estimate, international organizations employed approximately 5 percent of the city's population in 1994)[39] also had privileged access and mobility across the siege lines that came with possession of a blue card. For some locals, these jobs not only provided desperately needed hard currency to purchase black market goods for household survival,[40] but also cover and travel opportunities to engage in part-time smuggling. Munir Alibabić, the chief of the state security service in Sarajevo during part of the siege, recalls that "only a small privileged group had the opportunity to leave the city often and without special procedure. This category of Sarajevo residents included individuals who served in certain UNPROFOR departments—that is, as translators, drivers, and other auxiliary personnel. And unfortunately, some of these individuals abused this privileged status by smuggling and other illegal activities."[41] This meant, for instance, that a job as a driver for an international organization could informally double as a smuggling job. As a senior UNHCR official with extensive experience in wartime Bosnia observes, "Many of the citizens of Sarajevo saw them [local drivers hired by the UNHCR] as opportunists and capitalists, and believe they were part of the black market. One or two of them were. We did dismiss some."[42] In one smuggling scheme, five UNHCR trucks loaded with aid would make regular deliveries to the Serb-held neighborhood of Grbavica, always using the same drivers. These trucks would make the scheduled deliveries and then return from Grbavica filled with smuggled goods (such as coffee, cigarettes, and meat), which were relatively inexpensive in Grbavica but extremely expensive in the rest of the city.[43]

Blue card holders could also exit and enter the city on the UNHCR airlift. On the return flight, the amount of personal luggage was restricted by weight but often not subjected to rigorous inspections. This made it possible to engage in low-volume yet profitable smuggling: a kilo of instant coffee, for example, could sell for 450 German marks on the black market, a substantial sum for the average city resident.[44] While the amount of goods entering the city this way was presumably modest on an individual level, the cumulative amounts were potentially quite substantial. Lax airport inspections also reportedly enabled Bosnian government delegations to smuggle in goods on return flights from diplomatic negotiations abroad. For instance, the head of the Bosnian army writes in his memoir that five members of the official delegation he was traveling with from Zagreb to Sarajevo in February 1994 brought back forty suitcases. While one person argued with the UNPROFOR about the large number of suitcases, others in the delegation used the distraction to discretely label the bags as inspected and approved.[45]

Blue card-holders could also purchase goods at non-inflated prices at the UN's PX-style store located at the airport and at UNPROFOR headquarters in town. These items could then be resold at a substantial markup on the black market. For instance, a carton of Marlboros selling for 20 German marks at the UN store could be resold for 250 marks (or equivalent in bartered goods),[46] and chocolate chip cookies purchased for $2 could be resold for $11.[47] At first there was little monitoring or regulation of UN store sales, but the UN imposed limits as it became evident that this was supplying the black market.

Thus, not surprisingly, blue cards were in high demand since they could be used for all kinds of purposes beyond their official intent. For instance, Muhamed Kulašević, described as a local "liquor magnate" in one press account, somehow managed to secure a blue card even though he served no clear humanitarian purpose.[48] Even the U.S. diplomat Richard Holbrooke used a doctored blue card to pass through Serb checkpoints on an unofficial visit to Sarajevo.[49] The UN allocated blue cards to individuals who either had a copy of a contract from a registered aid organization or a letter of appointment with a designated job title from the organization's director.

One former international aid worker for a religious-based relief agency explains that his most important task was acquiring UN blue cards for the local staff (numbering about 40 people), given that he was the only person in the office who spoke English and had developed a good relationship with the UNHCR officer in charge of authorizing and allocating the IDs. Everyone in the agency's office wanted a blue card regardless of need. To help qualify for a blue card, staff members were given important-sounding job titles that had little practical meaning. For example, the aid worker himself had various fancy titles, such as "Program Director" and "Project Manager"—even though he was not actually directing or managing anything and did not even have a formal job description. Indeed, he had no previous experience in relief work, but his knowledge of English made him a useful liaison between his office and the UN and other organizations.[50] He also recalls that he sometimes brought in large amounts of hard currency on return trips to Sarajevo. This was not uncommon. According to one press report, "UN officials say it has long been common for airport security officials to find hundreds of thousands of German marks in small denominations inside the suitcases of Islamic aid workers bound for Sarajevo."[51]

Finally, some of the smallest local aid outfits were humanitarian organizations in name only, simply providing a convenient front for black marketeering.[52] As Vesna Bojičić and Mary Kaldor point out, part of the reason there were so many humanitarian organizations registered in Sarajevo during the siege is that this provided many small store owners a cover for engaging in black market trading and made it possible for them to obtain permits to exit and enter the city.[53]

The UN-Controlled Airport as Smuggling Hub

The UN-controlled airport was the most valuable piece of real estate in besieged Sarajevo. On the front stage, it was the entry point for the vast majority of international humanitarian assistance, with the airlift bringing in an average of 350–500 metric tons of aid per day.[54] But backstage it was a gateway for both land and air-based smuggling. The airport thus played both formal and informal roles in accessing the besieged city. It was the weakest link in the Serb siege lines due to both UN management of the airport and the particular geography of the siege. Sarajevo was surrounded on three sides by Serb forces, with the UN-controlled airport the only point where one could enter or exit the city without directly crossing Serb lines. Bosnian government forces controlled the areas at each side of the airport (Dobrinja and Butmir), while the Serbs controlled areas at each end (Lukavica and Ilidža).

Dashing across the airport grounds, taxiway, and runway required avoiding both Serb sniper fire and UNPROFOR patrols. As part of the airport agreement with the Bosnian Serbs, the UN agreed to police the tarmac and apprehend individuals trying to cross it. Pyers Tucker, military assistant to UNPROFOR General Philippe Morillon, recalls:

> About 200 French soldiers, every night, spent all night driving up and down the airport in their vehicles, trying to catch these civilians and taking them back to where they came from. . . . Another aspect of these civilians trying to run across the airport was that the Bosnian Serbs had set up snipers with nightsights and machine-guns with nightsights and they fired at the civilians trying to run across the airport. And in January and February, every night, between 5 and 20 or 30 civilians were killed or injured by these snipers. And the Serb snipers were not particularly careful about who they fired at and they also killed and injured a number of the French soldiers who were trying to round up the escaping civilians to return them.[55]

Perversely, UNPROFOR searchlights provided Serb snipers with the illumination to hit their targets. The structure of the situation meant that the airport—and therefore the UN—became an integral part of a high-intensity and high-stakes smuggling game.

The mass movement of people and goods across the tarmac began shortly after it was handed over to UN forces. Some of the clandestine crossers were simply trying to escape the siege, but most were leaving temporarily to buy goods and smuggle them back into the city.[56] The government-held town of Hrasnica, not far from the airport and outside the siege lines, was transformed into a shopping center; as one local observer recalls, "In Hrasnica every garage was a store. It was the place where Sarajevo came to supply itself."[57] Especially popular were high-value goods such as eggs (pre-shelled and packed in cans), cooking oil, sugar, coffee, and personal hygiene items such as razors and toothpaste. Hundreds of people every night attempted to sneak back and forth across the tarmac in the face of sniper fire and

UNPROFOR patrols, in order to move food, weapons, and other supplies into the city. VIPs—such as the head of the 1st Corps—sometimes
reportedly crossed the tarmac with a ring of bodyguards that served
as a shield against sniper attacks.[58] The tarmac was also the entry
point for many refugees displaced from other parts of the county. The
intensity of the UN's tarmac patrols was erratic—sometimes the
crossers could make multiple trips in the same night, while at other
times a successful crossing might take several days.[59]

Those with sufficient funds could hire a guide to improve their
chances of navigating the airport grounds safely and successfully.
Some of the men under the command of Juka (the underworld crime
figure turned military defender), for example, allegedly organized the
transfer of people across the tarmac in exchange for hard currency. As
a Dobrinja resident living next to the airport noted: "They [Juka's
men] did not ask whether someone is leaving to get food or is running
away from the draft. The only criteria was hard currency." At dusk,
those wanting to exit the city "gathered in front of Juka's HQ, formed
in groups of 10–20 people, and escorted by a guide departed across
the tarmac to Butmir."[60]

The UN soldiers patrolling the tarmac became de facto border
guards, placed in the bizarre and awkward position of enforcing the
Serb siege of Sarajevo. Running across the tarmac is described in the
Sarajevo Survival Guide (a satirical Michelin-style travel guide produced in 1993): "With a financial agreement, one can pass in the first
try," costing between 100–200 German marks. "Different divisions of
the UN force—the Blue Helmets—react in accordance with their national, regional, and personal sense of humor. The French are amused
by our wit. The Ukrainians are made nervous by our stubbornness,
but they can be talked into a deal."[61]

Tarmac runners engaged in various ingenious methods of evasion
and deception. For instance, one crosser would be assigned to trip a
flare to draw UNPROFOR patrols to a particular crossing point while
others would then use the distraction as an opportunity to sneak
through at another point.[62] Those apprehended would also sometimes try to convince the UNPROFOR that they were in fact trying to
enter rather than exit the city—and if their story sounded sufficiently
convincing they would then be escorted to the side where they actually wanted to go. When the UNPROFOR eventually caught on to this

ploy, those caught crossing the tarmac simply started telling the truth—and the UNPROFOR, not believing them, would then take them to the side they wished to get to in the first place.[63]

David Rieff has pointed out that the UNPROFOR soldiers could have turned a blind eye to those crossing the tarmac.[64] Yet it is equally true that they could have been even more diligent in their patrols. As a Bosnian police officer who crossed the tarmac many times during the siege comments, it seemed as if there was an "unstated level of tolerance." He says this was evident, for instance, in the fact that there were holes dug under the airport fencing that the UNPROFOR would rarely fix.[65] A former Bosnian army soldier who was part of a special eight-man unit formed to move arms across the tarmac grounds during the first six months of the siege similarly notes that the UN could have permanently lit up the airport grounds but chose not to—and the darkness was crucial for smuggling and avoiding sniper fire (indeed, tarmac crossings were attempted only at night).[66]

Other individuals who crossed the tarmac multiple times also indicated that UNPROFOR soldiers would occasionally look the other way or could sometimes be talked into letting them go.[67] Muhamed Gafić, a senior officer in a Ministry of the Interior special unit, describes the UN efforts to patrol the siege line at the tarmac: "Officers and soldiers of the UN could close this ring completely, so that even a bird could not fly out, but do they really want to? True, during the dark and foggy nights, they could do this only by forming an uninterrupted human chain, for which they do not seem to have any will. But even in the normal situations, it seems as if they're turning a blind eye."[68]

At the daily press briefings, the UN spokesperson would announce how many hundreds of "intercepts" the UNPROFOR had made the previous night—leaving unstated that countless numbers of people had avoided being intercepted. Going through the daily ritual of recording and announcing these intercept numbers, it seemed, had less to do with measuring actual effectiveness and more to do with publicly signaling that the UN was taking the job seriously and complying with the terms of the airport agreement. After all, many of those caught crossing simply kept trying until they succeeded (with the risk that each attempt exposed them to sniper fire, and indeed many were wounded or killed while crossing).

Much-needed arms and ammunition trickled into Sarajevo via the airport grounds. UNPROFOR soldiers routinely confiscated and destroyed weapons being smuggled across the tarmac, making the movement of such high-value goods particularly risky. If apprehended, those carrying the weapons would typically hand over their goods without protest, not wanting to upset the tacit rules of engagement. However, on particularly desperate occasions, the arms shipments were so valuable and urgently needed that they included an armed escort with orders to shoot if UN troops intervened. On at least one crossing, this allegedly led to a tense standoff with French UNPROFOR soldiers, who eventually lowered their weapons and let the arms shipment through rather than create a bloody incident.[69]

Some accounts indicate that UNPROFOR soldiers also at times colluded in arms smuggling. For instance, UN vehicles driven by members of the French Foreign Legion would sometimes reportedly be used to move arms and ammunition from one side of the tarmac to the other.[70] According to one former Bosnian army officer, he and his men paid French troops to transport eight backpacks filled with ammunition across the airport grounds at a cost of 2,000 German marks per backpack.[71] A former Bosnian government official claims that some crucial war-related materials (including communications systems, detonators, weapons, explosives, anti-armor rockets, hand grenades, rocket-propelled grenades, and bullets) were also moved across the runway with the authorization of the UNPROFOR and UNHCR.[72]

The UN also unintentionally facilitated weapons smuggling across the airport grounds. For example, during the early stages of the siege, Chinese-made anti-tank launchers, known as "Red Arrows," arrived via Pakistan and were carried across the tarmac on stretchers, disguised as wounded soldiers or wrapped corpses.[73] According to one of Bosnia's top army commanders during the war, these weapons were decisive in deterring Serb tank advances into the city.[74] This method was also used to bring in grenade launchers, according to a former soldier involved in the smuggling operation.[75] The fact that the UNPROFOR allowed wounded soldiers to be carried across the tarmac led to other innovative smuggling schemes, including placing meat on stretchers under blankets and hooked up to IV bottles so as to resemble wounded men. The UNPROFOR eventually caught on to this ploy and started inspecting the stretchers.[76]

Weapons materials were also smuggled in via the airport in UN humanitarian aid containers with false bottoms. As explained by one person involved in the covert shipments, the UNHCR regularly transported food to Hrasnica and Dobrinja in containers made at a Sarajevo factory. The aid would be loaded at the airport and unloaded at Hrasnica, and then arms and ammunition would be put into the false bottoms. The "empty" containers would then be sent back to the airport where they would be refilled with humanitarian aid and sent to Dobrinja or the city, at which point the food and the arms were unloaded. The containers would then be returned to the airport, and the cycle would start all over again.[77] Individuals involved in this scheme later said that UNPROFOR troops assisted in the operation and were presumably paid for their cooperation.[78]

According to cargo loaders at the airport interviewed by Sudetic, crates of humanitarian aid arriving as part of the airlift sometimes carried both commercial goods and weapons such as rocket-propelled grenades hidden in cans of baby food stacked in cases. The baby food shipments came from Frankfurt, loaded at the American base at Rhine-Main.[79] It was unclear whether or not UN airlift authorities were aware of such smuggling. According to one former UNHCR airlift official, airlift security was fairly lax until late 1993 when weapons and heroin were discovered in a shipment of sugar from Ancona, Italy. Before this incident, he claims that there were few inspections and oversight of airlift operations.[80]

UN workers were sometimes oblivious to their own collusion in arms smuggling. For example, Rusmir Mahmutčehajić, the former Bosnian Minister of Power and Industry, recounts how in one smuggling operation, a double floor was created in one of the humanitarian aid delivery vehicles to hide arms and ammunition. This vehicle made regular deliveries, entering and exiting the city via the airport grounds for a month before being discovered.[81] Kerim Lučarević, a Bosnian military police commander between 1992 and 1993, also recalls various schemes to smuggle explosives into Sarajevo across the airport grounds via UNPROFOR personnel and humanitarian aid packages.[82] For instance, during the summer of 1992 UNPROFOR troops were making regular deliveries of oxygen in metal cylinders to the local hospital. Thus, cylinders filled with explosives were prepared and mixed in with the oxygen shipments and brought into

Sarajevo together with regular UNPROFOR deliveries. The architect of the smuggling operation, Raif Džigal, reportedly traveled to Zagreb (Croatia) to secure more ammunition, weapons, and oxygen cylinders using "regular papers issued by the Ministry of Health of Bosnia and Herzegovina and came to an agreement with the World Health Organization to fund replacement cylinder valves, certifying, and filling with oxygen and nitro-oxydol."[83] These cylinders were then filled with shells, launchers, and anti-aircraft missiles and delivered to Sarajevo.[84]

But while such schemes to move arms into the city via the airport grounds helped the city endure the siege, it was not enough to break it. Breaking the siege would have required artillery and tanks among other heavy weaponry, which were the most difficult items to acquire on the black market and to smuggle into the city.[85] Thus, even as the city's defenders managed to access enough clandestine weapons supplies to help repel Serb advances into the city, these were limited to only certain types of weapons. The result was to reinforce the siege stalemate.

The airport was also a crossing point for truck convoys entering the city. This was especially important when the so-called UN "blue roads" were opened in the spring of 1994, after threats of NATO air strikes prompted a momentary loosening of the siege noose. The influx of not only official aid but also commercial goods via the blue roads undermined Serb dominance in controlling overland supplies to besieged Sarajevo, while enhancing the position of the Croats. According to Sudetic, Serb leaders moved to shut down the blue routes in late July 1994 not only for military gain but "possibly to regain the market-share their enterprises had lost to the Croats" after the opening of these routes in March.[86] There were also widespread accusations and speculations that shutdowns of the blue routes were provoked by local interests in manipulating and driving up black market prices in the city.

UNHCR airlift workers also developed their own informal, off-the-books methods to keep the aid delivery system running smoothly. Officially, all UNHCR shipments arriving via the airlift had to be approved by the Bosnian Serb authorities. Airlift manifests with lists of items being shipped were therefore automatically submitted to the Bosnian Serb liaison officer at the airport—a task that largely involved making sure the besiegers received their one-quarter cut of all ship-ments. However, some UNHCR deliveries included "sensitive goods" not listed on the manifest. This could include blood for transfusions, blank ID cards, high-value spare parts, and alcohol and tobacco. These shipments would always arrive on the first airlift flight of the morning, typically before 7 AM when the Serb liaison officer on duty at the airport was least likely to pay close attention. On occasion, this required softening up and distracting the officer with chitchat and drinks while the plane was being unloaded—with some UN staff members becoming intoxicated from multiple rounds of whiskey by mid-morning.[87] "The Serbs like to drink," explains one aid worker who spent a great deal of time at the airport. "The way I got a lot of stuff past was that I was a better drinker than them."[88]

Some of the alcohol and tobacco arriving in the undeclared UNHCR shipments of "sensitive goods" would, in turn, serve as bribes at Serb checkpoints to help assure the smooth passage of aid deliveries into the city. Before moving a particularly valuable ship-ment of goods into town, UN staff would first find out who was scheduled to be on duty at the Serb checkpoint to make sure to have their favorite brand of cigarettes or whiskey on hand—and if that par-ticular brand was unavailable, they would not even try to move the goods past the checkpoint that day. One former UNHCR airlift official describes this as an "ethically troubling" dynamic that was neverthe-less necessary given the situation on the ground, including intense and constant pressure from within and outside the city to keep the aid flows moving as quickly as possible. Any problems and hassles at the checkpoint could delay shipments for hours or even days, creating chaos in the aid supply chain. The checkpoint guards thus had enor-mous power—they could facilitate the aid flow or create huge headaches. Small bribes in the form of booze and cigarettes smuggled in via the airlift therefore helped "grease the system," keeping the aid moving.[89] As one aid worker describes it: "You soon discovered the power of American cigarettes and whiskey over there. I'd fly back into Sarajevo, go up to the Serb customs guards—'Hey, how ya' doin', here's a carton of Marlboros in appreciation for the fine job you're doing around here'—and pretty quick, I was able to bring in anything we needed."[90] As part of an effort to tighten the siege in early 1995, Serb general Ratko Mladić replaced the Serb officers at the airport checkpoint. "Until then," writes Sudetic, "the checkpoint had been in the hands of Ilidža police officers whose knack for making profit from their position had been notorious."[91]

Finally, it should be noted that the airport was not only the access point for supplying the city but also provided a neutral meeting point for UN-sponsored negotiations between the opposing sides. The UN was eager to host these monthly meetings, convinced that providing a regular forum for dialogue and keeping the opposing leaders talking would build confidence and help with the conflict resolution process. The formal, front-stage part of the meetings was highly scripted, with each side going through the standard public ritual of denouncing the behavior of the other. During the breaks or after the meeting was formally over, however, the top representatives of the two sides would routinely go behind closed doors, conversing with each other on a first-name basis in calm voices. International observers witnessing this repeated behavior speculate that this backstage activity was to arrange business dealings.[92] One participant in the airport meetings described this dynamic as a surreal experience: "While bombs were falling on the city outside, inside they were drinking and smoking together like old friends."[93]

The airport meetings would sometimes be called off when siege tensions rose. The government cancelled a scheduled meeting, for example, after Sarajevo's Markale marketplace was shelled in February 1994, producing heavy casualties. Bosnian Serb leader Momčilo Krajišnik responded by phoning his counterpart in the Sarajevo government. The staff person who patched the call through from the Lukavica barracks overheard the conversation through the speakerphone. "That night on both televisions," she recalls, "both sides said they had cut off talking to the other one. They were lying. They were still talking to each other. They were dealing and making money continually."[94]

Tunneling under the Siege: Lifeline and Profit Center

The airport tarmac was also the underground crossing point for moving goods and people in and out of the city. UN control of the airport provided cover for Bosnian government forces to tunnel under the tarmac, creating a critical link to the outside world. At the end of

July 1993 the Sarajevo government completed an 800-meter tunnel under the airport, linking Dobrinja and Butmir.[95] The clandestine construction project established a lifeline that passed through the tunnel, exited south of the airport at Butmir, then went on to the government-held outpost of Hrasnica and from there across Mt. Igman to Bosnian-held towns on the Neretva River valley southwest of Sarajevo. From there, mountain roads could be used to reach the Adriatic coast. An average of four thousand people and twenty tons of material went through the tunnel every day. Cabling and a pipeline were also eventually hooked up to bring limited electricity and diesel fuel into the city.[96] Rails were installed in 1994 to carry six mining cars, making it possible to push rather than carry goods through the tunnel. According to estimates provided by the Bosnian Army, almost twenty million tons of food entered the city via the tunnel during the siege, and there were also over one million crossings.[97] If one includes unofficial tunnel traffic, the total amount is presumably much higher.

The entrance to the tunnel was occasionally shelled by Serb forces (including a May 1995 shell that killed eleven people), yet more intensive and regular shelling so close to UN personnel and activity at the airport was inhibited by Serb concerns over potential political repercussions, including the possibility of NATO reprisal.[98] Thus, the UN presence aboveground helped to shield the underground passageway. The UN also facilitated the tunnel traffic by helping to keep Serb forces off nearby Mt. Igman—which would have cut the city off and made the tunnel irrelevant.

UN officials pretended the tunnel did not exist and rejected Serb demands to close it. When Bosnian Serb leaders charged that the tunnel was a violation of the airport agreement, the French UN general Philippe Morillon reportedly consulted with his legal advisers and replied that the space above the airport tarmac was officially under NATO authority, the surface area was under UN authority, and the area twenty centimeters below the surface was under Sarajevo government authority. He allegedly said he had no knowledge of the existence of a tunnel—but commented that the government would be stupid not to dig one.[99]

Access to the tunnel was officially supposed to be restricted for military purposes, but the rules were quickly loosened, allowing it to be used to bring in food and other commercial goods.[100] This had profound consequences. As the *Sarajevo Survival Guide* put it, "The commercialization of the tunnel brought about great changes in the economic life of the city. The tunnel became a place full of people dragging bags with potatoes or eggs. Many tradesmen were allowed to 'rent' the tunnel from the army. Thanks to the tunnel many became rich, but the prices also fell within the city."[101] The opening of the tunnel had major distributional consequences in terms of who would most profit from the siege. It changed the geography of siege profiteering. For this reason, some military commanders who had been profiting from trade elsewhere across the frontlines reportedly attempted to obstruct the tunnel construction. In an October 11, 2004, segment on the history of the tunnel for the Sarajevo television news show *60 Minutes,* the local journalist Zvonko Marić reported that the informants he interviewed claimed that those who attempted to undermine the tunnel construction activities did so out of fear of losing business and profits elsewhere on the line. This report included an interview with Adem Crnovršanin, who was in charge of the crew that dug the tunnel from the Butmir side of the airport runway.[102]

A Dobrinja resident living a block away from the tunnel entrance wrote in his wartime diary on August 4, 1993 (less than a week after the tunnel opened):

> The tunnel entrance looks like the village fair these days. Those who emerge from the tunnel all muddied and sweaty, loaded with backpacks and bags, are awaited by the small traders and re-sellers, who buy everything and take it to the market stands. From all this even the ordinary citizens will benefit because they now can buy things that used to be enormously expensive. . . . The fact that for those several hundred meters one has to go with head bowed and suffer broken foreheads, muddied shoes and dirty water dripping on your face and neck does not prevent masses of smugglers—who in some miraculous way are obtaining passes and permits and are returning with full knapsacks—from making several hundred marks profit just from one passage. The ordinary citizen of Sarajevo is filling the pockets of his local smugglers, those [smugglers] are filling the pockets of Butmir smugglers, those [Butmir smugglers] are filling the pockets of those from Ljubuško, Čapljina, Kiseljak. . . . The circle is not closed there. In this chain there are participating

even some members of UNPROFOR. The ceasing of this war is certainly not suited to many.[103]

Government soldiers moving in and out of Sarajevo via the tunnel were allowed to carry limited quantities of goods in their backpacks for their families, which helped boost morale (cigarettes were particularly popular, given their high value per weight).[104] Soldiers sometimes also doubled as tunnel runners, carrying loads of commercial goods through the narrow passageway. Some reportedly managed to do this while they were officially supposed to be on the frontlines. The same Dobrinja resident quoted above wrote in his diary entry on October 2, 1995, that a neighbor claimed her husband and oldest son were on the frontlines, but that this was a lie:

> [Both] of them were at Butmir, as they were there almost all the time these days. They go there to purchase goods, and then re-sell it here, earning with each passage between 50 and 100 DM. [German marks]. To obtain a permit they needed to bribe the guards, and they were openly bragging about this. The guard's rate was between 10–20 DM. He and his son were short, so they didn't suffer too much running through the tunnel, so often they made two runs per day.[105]

Entire military units were at times allegedly hired to move commercial goods through the tunnel. According to one former soldier, his military commander "rented" his 50–60 person unit to a local businessman to bring in thousands of live chickens through the tunnel over a two- or three-day period. Each soldier carried twelve caged chickens per tunnel crossing. When they were finished with the job, they were nicknamed the "chicken unit." The commander rewarded his men with better food and uniforms. The members of the unit felt privileged and fortunate to have a well-connected commander with regular tunnel access, since they were allowed to bring in extra goods in their backpacks (for personal use or resale) and were given fifteen additional packs of cigarettes in their monthly rations. Businessmen hiring the unit to carry food through the tunnel would also sometimes provide payment in the form of ammunition, which contributed to the defense effort.[106]

The tunnel was a "public secret"—widely known but not officially acknowledged or discussed by government officials. The international aid community eventually came to recognize the tunnel's importance in supplying the city. As a document of the UN's World Food Program observed: "Prices have not risen inordinately during the current suspension of the convoys and airlift—probably due to the uninterrupted use of the tunnel under the airport as a local route."[107]

In addition to basic food staples, luxury items such as alcohol were also brought in through the tunnel. One particularly creative method was to put condoms over the top of cans filled with alcohol. Then the condoms would be filled to disguise the alcohol.[108] According to one account, confiscated alcohol would be poured down two sinks at the entrance of the tunnel—one for hard liquor and the other for wine. There were rumors and suspicions that the two sinks were actually connected to hidden barrels, with the spilled alcohol later repackaged for sale (otherwise, why have separate sinks for wine and hard liquor?).[109] Alija Adamović, who worked on the tunnel digging and maintenance crew, recalls one episode in which a group of thirty wounded soldiers arrived at the tunnel entrance but were told to wait while a shipment of "military equipment" was brought through. He claims that the shipment was actually alcohol, and that two of the wounded soldiers died while waiting to use the tunnel.[110] Other witnesses have also reported having to wait to move wounded soldiers through the tunnel while it was rented out to transport commercial goods.[111] According to Vahid Karavelić, a commander in the 1st Corps of the Bosnian Army, President Izetbegović was upset that so much alcohol was being smuggled in instead of food or arms.[112]

Bringing in fuel through the tunnel was officially restricted because it was a fire hazard. Nevertheless, many tunnel crossers could not resist the temptation to smuggle, since a liter of gasoline bought for a few marks in Butmir could be sold for forty marks in Sarajevo. A soldier smuggling in a small, twenty-liter canister could earn enough money to feed his family for months.[113]

Controlled by the 1st Corps of the Bosnian Army, the tunnel (codenamed "Object D-B") quickly became a major profit center. In the words of the Bosnian family whose house was at the entrance of the tunnel: "May the commanders remember that they have gotten rich by smuggling through our house."[114] The army reportedly claimed 30 percent of all that was transported into the city through the tunnel, with payment in cash or kind.[115] The tunnel was regularly rented out for upward of 10,000 German marks per hour.[116] The hourly rate reportedly depended on the overall level of scarcity in the city and the amount of tunnel time allocated for commercial rather than military purposes (rates dropped as more tunnel hours were made available for non-military purposes and scarcity levels declined).[117] According to sources interviewed by Sudetic, senior Bosnian government officials, including Alija Izetbegović and Bakir Alispahić, allegedly shared in the profits from the tunnel fees.[118]

Only a handful of prominent individuals made fortunes moving large quantities of goods through the tunnel.[119] Alemko Nuhanović, one of the best-known tunnel renters, sometimes angered other tunnel crossers who had to wait for his shipments to move through the narrow passageway. In one incident in late 1994, a medic recalled starting an argument after having to wait forty-five minutes to escort four wounded soldiers through the tunnel while Nuhanović transported a shipment of Coca-Cola.[120] Nuhanović, in turn, complained about having to pay high tunnel fees: "There was food to be found in Kiseljak and Fojnica and some other places and we could even find ways to get it to the tunnel." But "the real problem," he said, was "how to get it through the tunnel and into the town. That's when the payments began. Payments, bribes . . . we thought we must pay everything they asked for because to get things through the tunnel in those conditions was a real feat."[121] On at least one occasion, Nuhanović allegedly also used his tunnel privileges and connections to smuggle people out of the city. In the summer of 1995 he escorted a young woman to the entrance of the tunnel and instructed her to quickly go through while he dealt with the guards. The woman claims that she then bribed the Bosnian guards on duty at the checkpoint on the other side, paying them 400 German marks to overlook the fact that she did not have the proper paperwork to exit the city.[122]

The Sarajevo government tried to tightly restrict who could leave the city through the tunnel. This was partly due to the tunnel's limited capacity and high traffic, but the government also had a strategic interest in keeping a critical population mass—both for the defense of the city and to maintain high levels of international attention and sympathy. Thus, while the flow of arms, ammunition, food, fuel, and

other supplies into the city via the tunnel helped keep the city defended and fed, the flow of people out of the city through the tunnel
was much more restricted. Indeed, it was illegal to leave the city without official permission, and individuals apprehended trying to escape
could face prison terms.[123] Ironically, Serb snipers, roadblocks, and
UN forces at the airport helped to enforce the government's exit controls. Indeed, all sides—the besiegers, the besieged government, and
the UN—shared an interest in forcibly keeping people in the city,
which in turn helped to perpetuate the siege stalemate.

It was precisely due to the tunnel's limited access and capacity
that crossing the airport tarmac remained a popular smuggling route
even after the tunnel opened.[124] This aboveground route was more
dangerous and unpredictable (due to Serb sniper fire and UNPRO-
FOR patrols), but was more loosely regulated and required fewer
connections—though smugglers moving goods into the city by foot
across the runway still had to pay substantial "fees" imposed by
local checkpoint guards in Dobrinja (usually involving handing over
a portion of the smuggled goods).[125]

Trading with the Enemy

The Sarajevo siege stalemate was also sustained by substantial
cross-frontline economic exchange, providing a critical addition (albeit at extremely high prices) to woefully inadequate levels of humanitarian aid. Military hardware also flowed into Sarajevo across the
frontlines, facilitated or even directly sold by those carrying out the
siege. Such black marketeering meant that the besiegers were supplying the besieged, helping to prolong the siege. According to former
Serb leader Biljana Plavšić, "I heard, and later confirmed, that our
folks, even those most highly ranked among us, are selling weapons to
the Muslims. Many times I was in Vogošća and talked to the workers
from our ammunition factory there. They were warning me about the
amoral behavior of selling weapons to the enemy."[126] Plavšić claims
that Karadžić acknowledged engaging in such arms trading when she
confronted him about it at a public meeting.[127] A former senior Bosnian army officer notes that he had a team of people buying arms
from Serbs, and on one occasion bought one million bullets. "I would

have bought them from Karadžić if I had had to. Karadžić had to know about it."[128] An internal Bosnian military memo claims that in June 1992 Karadžić even gave written permission for a shipment of weapons and communications gear across the siege line from Grbavica. The recipient was reportedly the criminal-turned-military-leader Jusuf "Juka" Prazina.[129]

As the siege lines became more settled, stable, and predictable[130]—greatly facilitated by the establishment of a large international presence—a variety of cross-frontline trading routes and relationships developed,[131] built on social (including criminal) networks that transcended ethnic divisions. Highly inflated prices—with markups of as much as 7,000 percent for goods that crossed into the city across the siege lines—provided an enormous economic incentive for cross-ethnic cooperation. Tim Judah notes, "After the first few hellish months of war, Serbian cigarettes and fresh produce such as tomatoes began to appear in the city's markets. These arrived courtesy of the mafia connections of some of the men who were organizing the frontlines."[132] One press report described the cross-frontline dynamic: "By day, Serbian gunmen in the suburb of Grbavica fire mortars and sniper bullets into the Muslim-held quarters of the city, and Muslim soldiers, some under Ćelo's command, fire back. At night, the two forces meet at the bridges spanning the Miljacka River, separating the Serbian and Muslim parts of the city, and conduct a thriving trade."[133] Some of the trade involved barter rather than financial transactions. For example, in 1992, Ćelo Delalić allegedly sent four trucks of beer to Pale in exchange for one truck of fuel for his own car, and Ćelo Bajramović at one point that year traded two Serb prisoners for a cow.[134]

The experience of a young Bosnian Serb man being smuggled out of Sarajevo during the siege illustrates how prewar social networks cut across ethnic divisions to facilitate cross-frontline economic transactions. The man was reportedly taken by car to a designated handoff point at the stadium near the Serb line at Grbavica (a common place for people exchanges) and was then picked up by a car from the Serb side. During the passenger handoff, the two drivers got out of their cars and embraced warmly. It turned out they were brothers-in-law. The sister of the Muslim driver who took him to the line was married to the Serb driver who picked him up. The price to be smuggled out of Sarajevo was about 2,000 German marks.[135]

Frontline trading relationships varied greatly across place and time. The least contested points on the siege line were those where opposing Serb and Croat forces met. One UN report noted that Bosnian Serb forces held their fire along those sections of the Sarajevo front line defended by Croat forces, and that the Serbs and Croats traded cigarettes and food.[136] The Croat military units in Sarajevo were reportedly on good terms with their Serb counterparts, and often disapproved of and discouraged army raids across the line that provoked Serb shelling.[137]

The most important commercial trade route into the city during the first phase of the siege was through the predominantly Croat suburb of Stup, the key doorway of Sarajevo to the west. This involved a transportation network that brought in goods from the Croat-held town of Kiseljak, crossed multiple Serb lines close to Ilidža, and then entered Sarajevo through Stup.[138] The Croatian Defense Council (HVO) was in charge of the Stup line, operating largely autonomously from the Sarajevo government.[139] The Stup HVO refused to be brought under a unified chain of command, with Velimir Marić, the HVO commander at Stup, insisting that he did not take orders from President Izetbegović.[140] The black market business allegedly included the HVO selling fuel obtained from the Sarajevo government to Bosnian Serb forces across the line,[141] and there were numerous accounts of Serbs selling guns and munitions to the HVO and the Bosnian army (reportedly even including a Serb selling Bosnian soldiers a tank for 10,000 German marks).[142] Stup was also allegedly a key route for smuggling people out of the city, especially Croats. Muslims could exit the city via Stup as well, but this involved the additional expense of buying forged Croat identity papers from the HVO—ethnicity, in this sense, was also a commodity that could be bought and sold.[143]

The meeting point for cross-frontline deals at Stup was the HVO-controlled café, the Delminium, described by Sudetic as "neutral territory" where the police from all three sides met and "a watering hole for high-ranking officers from the various militia forces in and around the city." This reportedly included the Serb police officials Tomo Kovač and Momčilo Mandić, as well as Muslims such as Bakir Alispahić (who became the Bosnian Minister of the Interior in June 1993): "Each of them had had intimate links with the Sarajevo underworld for years before the war."[144] Juka and Ćelo Bajramović also allegedly frequented the Delminium.[145] Mirsad Ćatić "Čuperak," a former Bosnian army commander on Mt. Igman, describes a visit to the Delminium during the summer of 1992: "If I didn't see it myself, I would not have believed it. All are here: chetniks [Serb nationalists], ustashe [Croatian nationalists], Army, police, civilians, foreigners. . . . I was sitting in one such 'flock.' All are making some deals. There are no tensions. They know Fadil [Đogo] well." Fadil Đogo, an arms logistician and cousin of Alispahić, had been dispatched to Igman by Alispahić and was responsible for taking Čuperak to the Delminium.[146]

While Croats from Sarajevo could enter Stup, Muslims were prohibited entry without permission from Marić and passing through a checkpoint run by Juka's men. Juka enjoyed a particularly good working relationship with Marić and the Croat forces at Stup in the summer of 1992. When the Bosnian army's General Šiber sent men to investigate the situation in early September 1992, Juka refused to let them pass through the checkpoint. When Juka was shown authorization papers signed by Šiber, he defiantly replied: "What Stjepan Šiber, even Alija Izetbegović can't go through here."[147]

As relations between the Sarajevo government and Croat forces deteriorated in the fall of 1992, Marić's HVO unit was driven out of Stup by the Bosnian army, breaking up the Stup trade route. Indeed, after the war between Croat and Bosnian government forces broke out, few convoys passed through the Croat blockade. According to one Bosnian government official, the only goods that made their way from the Croatian coast during this period originated from companies controlled by Croatia's defense minister, Gojko Šušak. One convoy from Split was allegedly ambushed en route in 1993 because many of the goods were not purchased from a Šušak-controlled company, and because the drivers failed to pay protection money to Šušak and other HVO officers.[148]

Juka and his men also reportedly had close cross-line connections with their Serb counterparts. One of Juka's soldiers, Nermin Uzunović, recollects, "I had friends there [in Grbavica] from before the war; some were even in the police so they used to beat me up." During the siege, "We would talk, they'd say: come on over, but bring no arms. I could trust them—they were fairly influential there. . . . It's not a secret at all: We were in regular contact with their local commanders." He also describes how he went back and forth across the airport tarmac without worrying about Serb sniper fire: "I was crossing over with the agreement of the Chetniks because their line was just by the tarmac; you communicate with the radio-station, then he says 'go' or 'can't go.' But, whenever I'd announce myself it wouldn't matter that their rifles were aimed at me—I'd go and I knew that they wouldn't shoot. I mean, they could kill me, but then they'd have to explain it to their own [commanders]."[149]

Juka once reportedly even boasted to a local journalist that he was able to order specific food items from the Serbs and have them delivered across the frontline. Vehid Gunić, a well-known Sarajevo television producer, wrote in his diary entry for August 15, 1992, about his visit to Juka's headquarters: "I find Juka eating beef goulash. It is obvious that this is not tinned meat, but the real, fresh thing. Where did he get it, I wonder naively." Juka then tells him that he can give orders across the lines. To demonstrate this, he picks up a walkie-talkie and selects a frequency: "Chetnik, this is Juka speaking. By nine tomorrow I need a thousand kilos of young beef. Good meat. Chops. Without gristle. Have you got that?" A voice on the other end responds affirmatively. Juka continues: "I need ten good watermelons and five musk melons. Is that clear?" The voice replies, "We don't have any musk melons." Juka insists, "I need five!" And the voice on the other end replies, "OK, Juka." Astonished at this exchange, Gunić asks: "Where and how will all this get into Sarajevo?" Juka answers vaguely, "We have our channels. There are ways."[150]

Smuggling networks into Sarajevo across Serb lines were reportedly well developed at Ilidža, and this route became particularly critical after the Stup trade route was shut down in the fall of 1992. Serb leaders Krajišnik and Karadžić, in addition to helping to direct the siege, were also allegedly behind two companies, Centreks and Selekt Impeks, involved in selling goods to the besieged city through Ilidža.[151] In one episode, several Sarajevan businessmen from the company Banko Promet were reportedly given permission from Bosnian government authorities to leave the city to purchase goods, but were arrested by the police when they returned since it was illegal to engage in commerce with the enemy. Officially, they were supposed to have purchased the goods in Macedonia, which was hundreds of kilometers away and difficult to reach—even though their government-issued passes allowed them to leave the city for only ten hours. The incident caused much embarrassment when it was made

public.[152] In another incident, a politically well connected businessman attempting to import goods into Sarajevo from Ilidža allegedly
called President Izetbegović claiming that the Serbs at the checkpoint
were demanding 500,000 German marks as payment to let the goods
through. Izetbegović reportedly arranged to give him the money,
but it later turned out that this amount was much higher than the
Serbs were actually demanding (with the businessman pocketing the
balance).[153]

Duško Tomić, a Sarajevan Serb who directed the local charity
called the Children's Embassy, also allegedly purchased large quantities of goods from Serbs and Croats and brought them in via Ilidža.
This necessitated high-level connections on all sides. In one operation,
Tomić allegedly bought nine convoys of food from the Kiseljak-based
company Permaks (which was protected and likely run by Croatian
officials, including Ante Roso and Gojko Šušak) and moved the food
into the city through Ilidža in the first four months of 1993. The deal
reportedly required giving 8 percent of the goods to the Croat HVO,
33 percent to the Ilidža Serbs, and the remaining 59 percent for Sarajevo (the profits of which allegedly went to the Bosnian government).
Tomić's convoys did not always run so smoothly: in November 1993,
one of his convoys, carrying 9,000 tons of food, was reportedly plun-
dered by Serb forces on orders from Tomo Kovač, a senior Serb security official, who then smuggled the goods into the city where they
were sold on the black market.[154]

Another key route for cross-frontline trade that was operational
throughout the siege allegedly began at the cemetery on the southern-
most edge of the Muslim-held town of Visoko. The cemetery was located only a few hundred yards from the Serb line before Ilijaš and
less than a few kilometers from the Croat frontline near Kiseljak.
Sarajevo-bound goods were moved across both Serb and Croat lines
to the cemetery, and from there the transportation routes ran in a
number of directions across various frontlines into the city. The Visoko cemetery connection reportedly began because the Serbs and
Croats wanted to barter goods in exchange for coffins being produced
at the cemetery's workshop. According to Bosnian army officers, the
director of the cemetery developed such a good working relationship
with the Serbs that by 1994 this had become the fastest way to smuggle Bosnian army personnel through Serb lines into the city.[155]

Weapons were also allegedly smuggled into Sarajevo via the cemetery connection, transported across Serb lines concealed in shipments of non-military items such as wood.[156]

Moreover, some sources claim that the cemetery's workers were obtaining military hardware and supplies from the Serbs, in close coordination with the Bosnian logistics base—which also happened to be in Visoko. Serb army officers in nearby Ilijaš and Vogošća told foreign journalists that the logistics base and other military targets in Visoko were deliberately not shelled out of fear that this would provoke the Muslims to fire back with artillery and shells that a Serb officer had sold them at the beginning of the war.[157] More generally, relations across the frontlines at Visoko were at times more cooperative than confrontational. Soldiers from Visoko reported that there was gunfire across the frontline only on weekends when men from Belgrade and Sarajevo would arrive. They claimed that on weekdays, when only the locals were manning the frontlines, relations were sometimes so relaxed that the opposing sides would even play soccer games in "no-man's land."[158] Members of the Canadian UNPROFOR unit stationed in Visoko also reportedly "sold cigarettes, coffee, alcohol, fuel, clothing, and in one case, even weaponry on the black market. Ironically, all of this was happening when the Canadian soldiers were winning worldwide praise."[159]

Strategically located towns near the outskirts of Sarajevo, such as Serb-held Ilidža and Croat-held Kiseljak, turned into bustling cross-frontline black market supply centers. This required a certain amount of cross-ethnic peaceful coexistence and collaboration near the siege lines. Ilidža and Kiseljak profited greatly from black marketeering, especially in the petrol trade. A leading fuel trader was the brother of Momčilo Krajišnik, head of the Bosnian Serb assembly, who reportedly made a fortune by purchasing Croat fuel for the Bosnian Serb army.[160] Much of the smuggled goods from the Visoko cemetery connection discussed above allegedly moved into Sarajevo via Kiseljak and Ilidža.

Prices for goods in Kiseljak varied depending on the number of middlemen involved. For example, beef purchased in Croatia for 1–2 German marks was sold in Kiseljak for 6–8 marks, which would then be sold to distributors in Sarajevo for 20 marks, and end up selling on the street for 50 marks or more per kilo.[161] Kiseljak also supplied both Serb and Bosnian government forces, and each side quietly ignored the clandestine practice from which they benefited. Thus, despite being near the front lines, Kiseljak remained undamaged. Tellingly, the road between Kiseljak and Ilidža was never mined. Kiseljak was also a favorite source of fuel and other supplies for UN personnel and foreign journalists.[162] Cigarettes, for example, were twenty times cheaper in Kiseljak than in Sarajevo. The Ukrainian UNPROFOR troops would reportedly shop in Kiseljak "and then trade the goods at a suitable profit once they had returned to Sarajevo."[163]

Kiseljak was not only a major distribution center for smuggling goods into the city but was also reportedly part of a network for smuggling people out. The profit of these people-smuggling operations was allegedly divided in thirds: one-third for Sarajevo's Muslim police, one-third for Serbs for allowing exit, and one-third for the Croats arranging the Kiseljak connection.[164] Located at the western gates of Sarajevo, Kiseljak was strategically the most obvious place to militarily break the siege from the outside. The town's niche in the cross-frontline trade, however, gave Kiseljak's Croats a financial stake in keeping the siege going.[165]

The Media and Its Dependence on the Black Market

The large media presence in Sarajevo kept the siege story alive for a worldwide audience, which in turn helped sustain international support for the massive humanitarian aid operation. The city's privileged place in the global media spotlight served different interests on all sides. For foreign journalists assigned to cover the war in Bosnia, the siege offered a front-row seat in Europe's bloodiest conflict since World War II—with the downside that many of them rarely set foot outside the city. As the BBC correspondent Martin Bell self-critically observes in his war memoir, "For weeks at a time, during the years of working from Sarajevo, we would venture no further than the airport in one direction and the Presidency in the other. Our measure of Bosnia was approximately the length of a single street in its capital."[166] Nowhere else in the world was the high-drama violence and tragedy of war so accessible. Indeed, Sarajevo's accessibility attracted not only a small army of foreign journalists but also a wide assortment of artists, intellectuals, and celebrities, such as Bianca Jagger and Joan

Baez. This gave Sarajevo a hip, intellectually fashionable profile arguably unmatched in any war zone since the Spanish Civil War. Susan Sontag even came to Sarajevo to direct the play *Waiting for Godot*, which opened to much local and international fanfare. The opening made the front page of the *Washington Post*. One local observer commented that it looked like there were more foreign journalists than locals in the audience.[167]

For the Bosnian Serb leadership orchestrating the siege, the global media attention was disastrous from a public relations standpoint and constrained their military options. Yet as noted earlier, it also conveniently distracted attention away from much worse conditions elsewhere in Bosnia and had the additional advantage of heightening Sarajevo's value as a hostage and negotiating card.[168] The fact that Sarajevo attracted a disproportionate amount of the foreign press coverage of the war was also convenient for Western governments, since it was much easier to demonstrate that they were "doing something" about the plight of Sarajevo than the more dangerous and less accessible war zones in Bosnia. As one British official candidly admitted to a journalist in the spring of 1992: "The last thing we want is pictures from Goražde, we can only just cope with Sarajevo."[169] For the most part, the war in Bosnia was a stubborn annoyance for Western leaders—and dramatic media images of the siege helped to assure that it would not go away. Yet all the media attention on Sarajevo also afforded an opportunity for them to make the city a showcase of humanitarian action, which in turn conveniently substituted for a more decisive and aggressive response to the war. President Clinton, eager to find something positive to say about the situation in Bosnia, even singled out the airlift for praise in his 1994 State of the Union address.

The UNHCR and other aid agencies also benefited enormously from Sarajevo being in the global spotlight, since media coverage of the airlift and aid convoys was essential for political support and financial backing from western governments. Sylvana Foa, a UNHCR press spokesperson, commented, "Television is our lifeline to the politicians who want nothing to do with us or hope that the problem will go away from public consciousness." She bluntly stated: "Without TV coverage we are nothing. Our operations and their impact would die without TV."[170] In the case of Bosnia, most of the television cameras were in (and focused on) Sarajevo.

For Sarajevo's government, sustained media coverage of the siege was essential to its very survival, even if it also proved to be a mixed blessing. As already noted, the disproportionate media attention on Sarajevo came at the high price of obscuring the much more desperate situation in other parts of the country, including large-scale population displacement. Yet the siege media story was crucial in both mobilizing and sustaining international awareness and sympathy, providing a powerful and persistent visual reminder of Bosnian Serb aggression and the overwhelmingly lopsided nature of the conflict. Globally televised images of besieged Sarajevo helped prop up the country's victim status, which in turn shaped international opinion and behavior. Nothing illustrated this more powerfully than the shelling of a Sarajevo breadline in May 1992 and the marketplace shellings in February 1994 and August 1995, with graphic pictures of the carnage projected within minutes via satellite to television screens across the world. These dramatic focusing events not only influenced the course of the long siege but ultimately its ending.

Yet there was nothing automatic about the ability of the foreign press to keep Sarajevo in the global media spotlight. Thus, this needs to be explained rather than simply assumed and taken for granted. Getting the siege story out and sustaining it over an extended period of time required access, infrastructure, and supplies. The opening of the airport dramatically eased access to Sarajevo, with reporters conveniently able to fly in and out on the UNHCR airlift to nearby European cities. An important legacy of the 1984 Winter Olympics was that the city also possessed the physical and technical infrastructure and support services to host a substantial international media presence.[171]

Equally important, but largely overlooked, is that the black market both kept the foreign journalists fed and fueled their vehicles and generators. For example, the black market kept food on the tables at Sarajevo's semi-functional Holiday Inn hotel—the only open hotel in town and the headquarters of the foreign press corps and other visiting "internationals."[172] By August 1993 the hotel housed some 200 journalists. Starting in 1993 it also housed the U.S. Embassy, which occupied one suite.[173] In its "accommodations" section, the *Sarajevo Survival Guide* notes that the Holiday Inn "is well supplied with alcoholic drinks and refreshments," and that the average menu is 50 German marks per person. "Service is decent. At night, the hotel resembles Casablanca."[174]

The hotel's international guests both consumed smuggled goods and supplied scarce foreign currency for the black market. As a former senior UNHCR official observed, "The Holiday Inn survives because of its clientele. The journalists are paid well, many have a generous expense account and they pay in hard currency. The hotel management is therefore able to do deals with check-points to bring in food."[175] The neighborhood of Stup was allegedly an important supply line for Dinko Ćorić, the Croat director of the hotel.[176] The hotel also reportedly developed a trading relationship with Serb-held Ilidža: in early summer 1993 eyewitnesses claimed that refrigerator trucks entered Sarajevo from Ilidža, and waiters at the Holiday Inn said that refrigerator trucks delivered meat.[177] There was also evidence that the highest quality humanitarian aid items were showing up on the tables at the Holiday Inn. As one press account noted, "Soon after the first shipment of UN aid arrived in the city, the reporters were served mackerel and feta cheese—the two most sought after items in the food boxes. It was washed down with bottles of Volvic mineral water, the same brand flown in earlier by a French relief plane."[178] The hotel also relied on black market fuel to run its enormous generator when the electricity was not working (which was much of the time).[179] Among other things, this helped the journalists keep their laptops and satellite phones charged so they could file their stories.

Serb gunners on the surrounding hills could have reduced the hotel to rubble or simply made it too dangerous to stay in. Portions of the building were uninhabitable, and the southern side of the hotel—which faced the nearby siege lines—was heavily damaged. But the hotel was in noticeably better shape than neighboring structures (such as the UNIS towers next door, which were substantially destroyed by incendiary grenades), suggesting deliberate non-targeting. A number of foreigners who stayed at the Holiday Inn have commented on its mysterious survival. The British journalist Anthony Loyd, for instance, speculates that there was either "some tacit understanding within the Serb command that the hotel was the focal point of the media in Sarajevo and should be left untouched or possibly there was a deal to ensure its security."[180]

The Holiday Inn's location, near the siege line along "sniper's alley" and one of the most dangerous and exposed intersections for pedestrian traffic, gave foreign journalists a front-row seat to watch the siege in action. Martin Bell calls it "the ultimate war hotel, like living at ground zero."[181] Originally built to accommodate foreigners visiting Sarajevo for the Olympics, the hotel was well placed to accommodate a small army of foreign journalists. As *Washington Post* correspondent Peter Maass describes it, "The Holiday Inn became a grandstand from which you could watch the snipers at work. A journalist could convince himself on a slow afternoon that he was doing his job by peering through a window at people running for their lives. . . . Watching them was work, not voyeurism. Just ask any of the photographers who found safe spots near a sniper zone and waited for someone to be shot."[182] In his own case, Maass notes, "I could stand at my window, out of the line of fire, and watch more drama unfold in five minutes than some might see in a lifetime. It was all there, within a 200-yard radius of my room at the Holiday Inn, the best and worst of *Homo sapiens*."[183]

While far from offering luxurious accommodations, the Holiday Inn provided basic services and a central location that could make the daily routine of a foreign journalist much more comfortable than one might imagine possible in the middle of a war zone. As Loyd comments, "I felt very cynical toward some of the media in the city. Too many simply walked into the basement of the Holiday Inn each day, drove out in an armoured car to a UN headquarters, grabbed a few details, filled them in with the words of 'real people' acquired for them by their local fixers, and then returned to their sanctuary to file their heartfelt vitriol with scarcely a hair out of place."[184]

Another essential part of the media infrastructure was the city's Radio and Television Building, housing state-of-the-art equipment and facilities. Like the Holiday Inn, it was originally built for the Olympics, providing the city with the capacity to accommodate a large global media presence (and also housed local radio and television stations, which continued to broadcast throughout the war). The building's importance was magnified by the new centrality of the satellite dish in enabling global media reporting. The dish, as one journalist puts it, made Sarajevo "accessible to the outside world."[185]

Another commentator even describes Sarajevo as "probably the first saturation media war of the satellite broadcasting age."[186]

The Radio and Television Building was an enormous concrete block that was one of the city's least attractive but most durable structures, successfully weathering Bosnian Serb fire throughout the siege. The European Broadcast Union installed the latest satellite equipment on the fourth floor of the building, providing the means to instantly project siege images and information to all corners of the planet. A core group of major international media outlets set up a permanent presence in the building, including CNN, ABC, BBC, WTN, Channel 1 (France), and ARD (Germany). Many other media outlets came in and out intermittently. One particularly entrepreneurial foreigner even managed to use the European Broadcast Union's satellite hookups from Sarajevo for live broadcasts to U2 rock concerts while the band was on tour throughout Europe. Projected on to a giant screen on stage, a handful of Sarajevans (typically young, English speaking, and musically inclined) were recruited to talk live via satellite to tens of thousands of cheering U2 fans across the continent—certainly qualifying as the most creative and technologically innovative effort to draw international attention to the city's plight.[187]

Like the Holiday Inn, the building depended on black market fuel to run its generators, given that the availability of electricity was so sporadic and unreliable.[188] As one local television journalist working in the building wrote in his wartime diary: "We have been surreptitiously buying fuel for our generator by night in Čengic Vila [a Sarajevo neighborhood] from the Ukrainian mafia that represents the UN here, so as to keep the programmes going. We have been paying as much as 25 Deutschmarks for a litre of fuel to these carpet-bagging criminals from the Ukraine. . . . It takes as much as five hundred litres of fuel a day for our generator to power one radio programme and a short television programme using ordinary VHS recorders."[189]

In order to tune in to these local broadcasts, Sarajevo residents powered their radios and televisions through various creative means, including the use of car batteries[190] and illegally diverting electricity from government-designated "priority buildings," such as police stations, hospitals, and homes of prominent officials. The government would crack down on "electricity bandits," but the practice was widespread and persisted. A particularly daring "electricity heist" involved tapping into the residence of Prime Minister Haris Silajdžić.[191] One Dobrinja resident wrote in his diary that more than one-third of his street appeared to be receiving "stolen" electricity:

> The electricity was spread from one apartment to another in ingenious ways: through the walls, vents, chimneys, roofs. . . . Soon the streets were adorned with wires like spider webs when electric wires were spread from one building to the next. Even though it appeared to be chaotic, all was under control: those who had electricity were those who Calto [the local military commander] gave his explicit approval or turned a blind eye to.[192]

The fact that the local media continued to operate throughout the siege was important not only for everyday life in the city but also for Sarajevo's external image projection and maintenance of international solidarity and support. Most notable in this regard was the case of Sarajevo's daily newspaper, *Oslobođenje*. As Ed Vulliamy observes, the paper was "showered with international awards for its remarkable gallantry in linking Sarajevans to the rest of the war and the world outside."[193] The newspaper's survival was a powerful symbol of Sarajevo's survival, and its heroic story took on celebrity proportions in the West. The newspaper's senior editors frequently traveled abroad to accept prestigious international journalism awards (on one trip they even met with President Clinton, who expressed his admiration for the paper), and also received thousands of dollars in donations from readers.[194]

Yet the newspaper's internationally celebrated survival on the front stage depended not only on the extraordinary perseverance of its staff, but also on a variety of backstage smuggling methods and channels to secure essential newsprint and fuel. Newsprint was officially barred from the UNHCR airlift since it did not formally qualify as humanitarian aid, but the newspaper managed to covertly acquire it through more informal means. In one scheme, the director of the Koševo Hospital and an Italian aid organization collaborated to bring in supplies of newsprint on the airlift labeled as "packing material." When a senior UNHCR official found out about the false labeling scheme and complained, one of the editors countered: "Are you pleased with yourself for having uncovered such a crime? I am pleased we smuggled it," and then asked, "Shouldn't we be able to publish?" The reply from the UNHCR official was "Yes, but you shouldn't smuggle."[195] Yet the reality of the situation was that publishing required smuggling—an uncomfortable fact that was difficult for this UNHCR official to publicly acknowledge, let alone endorse.

Oslobođenje's impressive accumulation of international journalism awards not only enhanced the newspaper's global visibility and prestige (thus helping to sustain international support and sympathy for the besieged city), but also provided much needed hard currency to purchase fuel on the black market. A minimum of 100 liters of fuel were required daily to run the generator for the five or six hours it took to type and print the paper.[196] As Tom Gjelten points out in his book about *Oslobođenje:*

> The newspaper was able to continue publishing only because it had a cash reserve with which it could buy diesel on the Sarajevo black market. . . . The money came from international awards the paper had won for its perseverance in publishing. During one four-week period . . . the *Oslobođenje* manager spent about $20,000 in prize money on black market diesel, with most of the money going into the pockets of Ukrainian UN soldiers, who were known in Sarajevo as the most reliable diesel suppliers.[197]

Black market dealings with UNPROFOR were also reportedly a source of tension within *Oslobođenje.* One editorial board member moonlighted as a manager of a local bar called Mon Cheri, where he sold whiskey, beer, and sodas clandestinely supplied by Egyptian and Ukrainian UNPROFOR soldiers. One of the editors disapproved of this, fearing that the side business could create problems for the newspaper with the higher-ups in the UN command with whom it was important to maintain good relations.[198]

Indeed, the newspaper was dependent on UNPROFOR troops not only for black market fuel, but also on more senior UNPROFOR officers who admired the determination of its editors and were therefore willing to subvert the rules by discreetly supplying newsprint and fuel. As Gjelten notes, "Were it not for sympathetic UN officials who quietly classified newsprint as humanitarian aid and authorized clandestine deliveries of diesel fuel to the printing plant, *Oslobođenje* could not have continued publishing."[199] For example, during the summer of 1993, one of the editors appealed to the Belgian UNPROFOR general Francis Briquemont for help, explaining, "We can't earn enough to buy the fuel on the black market." The general responded by delivering a "top secret" gift of two tons of fuel.[200] Thus, the newspaper kept its generator running through a delicate combination of informal UNPROFOR generosity and sympathy on the one hand, and UNPROFOR corruption and black market profiteering on the other.

Foreign journalists and their local staff also relied on the black market to fuel their vehicles. Again, numerous accounts indicate that the UNPROFOR played a particularly important clandestine supplier role. According to one reporter working for a major foreign news agency during the war, the agency's Sarajevo office depended heavily on black market fuel provided by UNPROFOR, typically purchased at 30 German marks per liter, and that the same was true for the rest of the foreign press corps in the city. "Thankfully," the reporter says, "nobody at the main bureau desk ever asked us where we bought fuel for our vehicles. The answer would have caused discomfort and embarrassment." It would have been an awkward problem for the news service "to be publicly viewed as contributing to the black market." Yet, as the journalist puts it, by providing fuel for the international media to cover the siege, the black market "lifted the cloud of darkness over Sarajevo."[201] This helped to bring the city's plight to the world's attention, which in turn helped mobilize and maintain political support for continued relief aid. While the foreign press corps wrote stories about black marketeering in the city, including growing evidence of UNPROFOR complicity and corruption, they rarely openly implicated themselves as part of the consumer base. An exception is Rieff, who acknowledges that "most journalists, including myself, bought black market gasoline from complaisant UN Protection Force soldiers of various nationalities."[202]

The Money Letter Smuggling System

Journalists and other internationals in Sarajevo supplied the black market with hard currency not only by buying smuggled food and

fuel and paying salaries to local workers, but also by regularly carrying money-filled letters into the city from the Bosnian diaspora community. Foreigners (and locals with blue cards) routinely smuggled
letters for Sarajevo residents and their friends and family members
abroad, with many of the in-bound letters filled with cash (which
would then be used to purchase black market goods for household
survival). Many of the individuals sending money letters to friends
and relatives in Sarajevo had fled the country in the first few weeks
and months of the war, and were scattered across Europe, North
America, and elsewhere. Their exodus was understandably resented
by many of those who remained in the besieged city. Yet by leaving,
they became a crucial source of hard currency and an essential part of
the city's external support system. According to one Sarajevo-based
reporter, a norm soon emerged that it was unacceptable for a journalist to refuse a request to take a letter in or out of the city. Similarly,
there was allegedly an unspoken collective agreement among the
journalist community not to draw public attention to the large influx
of money letters. Only when UN officials started opening the letters
in late 1993 did they come to realize just how much money was trick-
ling in to Sarajevo via the journalists traveling on the UNHCR airlift.[203]

When the UN cracked down by limiting the number of letters and
amount of money that individuals could carry, some reporters responded by smuggling letters inside their flak jackets, removing the
heavy metal shielding and stuffing the empty spaces with letters. One
journalist who regularly used this method stitched the compartment
shut to hide the contents.[204] At other times, the journalist would simply put cash in the luggage and officially declare it as belonging to the
press service. Once in Sarajevo, the journalist would then use the office satellite phone to call abroad for the list of recipient names and
amount to be delivered. This typically involved 40,000 to 70,000 German marks per trip.[205]

The letter-smuggling system was remarkably well developed, reportedly involving a large portion of the foreign press corps that regularly traveled back and forth to Sarajevo. One press office allegedly
even provided a self-service letter drop-off and pick-up box for local
residents. Friends and family members abroad would send letters to
Sarajevo in care of the agency's regional bureau in a nearby country.

Journalists would then smuggle these letters in on their frequent return trips to Sarajevo.[206] This system was reportedly not unique to this
particular foreign news agency. For instance, the same letter forward-
ing service was provided at the headquarters of a leading European
television news service, which, as one former employee described it,
became a "depot" for Sarajevo-bound money letters.[207]

Local journalists did not have the same travel privileges as their foreign counterparts, but those who did manage to travel internationally
similarly engaged in money letter smuggling. For instance, as noted
earlier, *Oslobođenje* editors often traveled to Western Europe and North
America to receive journalism awards. One editor recalls: "Returning
to Sarajevo from my trips abroad, I would carry bundles of letters with
tens of thousands of marks and dollars sent by friends and relatives
from America, Canada, Croatia for people whom I did not even
know." UNPROFOR inspectors at the airport officially restricted the
number of letters one could carry to five, and baggage was restricted to
one piece weighing a maximum of twenty kilograms. But, he notes, "I
always had letters and a few pieces of baggage which I managed to
'smuggle' in with some help from foreign colleagues flying with me to
Sarajevo or thanks to some flexibility on part of the UNPROFOR
police—usually its Scandinavian members—who would pretend that
they did not notice how heavy my suitcases were."[208]

Many Sarajevans also regularly brought money-filled letters into
Sarajevo as a result of the traveling privileges that came with working
for the UN, international non-governmental organizations, or foreign
press agencies. One local woman working as an interpreter for UN-
PROFOR, for example, smuggled in 100,000 German marks on one
trip, and another woman employed by the UNHCR brought in a similar amount on multiple trips abroad.[209] Other locals with travel privileges included high-ranking government officials who could travel
via the UN-controlled airport as part of formal diplomatic delegations. For example, one of the members of the Bosnian presidency recalls making between ten and fifteen foreign trips on official government business during the siege. Each time he returned he carried a
large number of letters filled with cash, but he was never frisked by
the UN officers at the airport. The radio station would then announce
names of people who should come to his office, and his assistant would
then distribute the letters to the recipients when they showed up.

He estimates that he personally brought in a total of 500,000 German marks this way, and that the flow of money letters was the most common mechanism for Sarajevo residents to receive hard currency from abroad.[210] A few small banks with an affiliated office abroad managed to open in Sarajevo midway through the siege, providing another mechanism for friends and family abroad to send money to their loved ones in the city, but use of this channel was inhibited by extremely high transactions fees (sometimes as high as 50 percent of the sent amount).[211]

The "good Samaritan" letter smugglers helped the city's population survive—but also enriched black market war profiteers. After all, for many Sarajevans, receiving assistance from friends and relatives abroad through these informal financial mechanisms was the only way they could afford to buy goods on the black market at such inflated prices. When the war began, many of the city's residents had some hard currency savings stashed away at home ("mattress money"). But for most, these savings were depleted as the siege persisted. Thus, a fresh influx of hard currency was essential for sustaining Sarajevo's thriving black market—a substantial amount of which arrived via the money letter smuggling system.

On rare occasions, city residents also received care packages from friends and family abroad, delivered via various religiously based charity organizations (such as Caritas, Adra, and Merhamet). But money was not usually sent this way, since many of these packages were lost en route or arrived opened and with missing items. Senders would at times creatively hide money within the packaged goods, but this was a high-risk strategy. In one case, for instance, the sender hid 1,000 German marks so well within a jar of lard that the recipient didn't find out about it until after he had sold the lard for 100 marks.[212]

The Smugglers' Markets and Cigarettes as Currency

The most visible side of Sarajevo's underground economy was the bartering and selling of smuggled goods and other items at the public markets that sprung up in various neighborhoods. The largest and best known was a crowded covered hall in the center of town called the Markale. The quantity, quality, variety, and prices of goods shifted dramatically from day to day depending on the permeability of the siege. German marks were the preferred currency, though much of the trading involved barter. Many of the goods sold at the market had uncertain and shadowy origins, but the trade was tolerated as an important contributor to the city's survival. Local residents both despised and depended on the market. As one journalist puts it, "Detested though it was, the market had become the lifeblood of Sarajevo's economic life under siege."[213] One resident describes a shopping trip in early January 1993: "Yesterday I was in the Markale market. At least two thousand people were milling about in that small area. The stalls are manned by some bums with pistols in their belts and some kind of accreditation. Smugglers with accreditation?"[214]

At the market stalls one could typically find humanitarian aid items, including food staples that never reached the intended recipients. For instance, as one local resident noted, "A few days ago butter appeared in the market. I still haven't heard of anyone I know receiving butter in their aid rations even though the package had UNHCR markings."[215] Another observer comments that some items at the market "obviously had been smuggled from U.N. bases in Sarajevo. The best loot came from the French base in Skendarija; you could occasionally find a can of pate de foie gras or a bottle of Beaujolais."[216] Other goods, especially clothing, appliances, and other nonperishables, included items that had been looted from local stores at the start of the war. Many local residents shopped at Markale and other public markets for goods not provided in the aid rations, such as coffee, cigarettes, and personal hygiene items.

In her wartime memoir (based on a compilation of letters and diary entries), Elma Softić comments: "The black market is thriving. Everyone dabbles in it. I, for instance, go to the market and trade cigarettes for cotton batting [a cheap substitute for sanitary napkins] or else I sell the cigarettes (mind you, I don't stand in the marketplace: instead I do it more elegantly—I give them to someone else to sell in exchange for a 20% cut) and then I buy facial cream, which costs, on average, 4DM [German marks]." Noting the popularity of the market, Softić points out, "Of all the people I know, my parents are the only ones who have not as yet bought, let alone sold, anything on the black market."[217]

Some of the UNPROFOR barracks also became a marketplace of sorts. For example, a foreign journalist witnessed an old man approach a French soldier with a black velvet jeweler's pouch. "This is no good," said the soldier. "The price is too high. But you can't sell this here. This gate is for coffee. Go to the gold gate—it's around the back."[218]

Cigarettes were so valued in wartime Sarajevo that they became an alternative form of currency. This was also the case in German P.O.W. camps during World War II (except that in the camps, unlike in Sarajevo, the main cigarette supplier was the Red Cross). In his personal account of the economic organization of a P.O.W. camp, an economist explains the utility of cigarettes: "Although cigarettes as currency exhibited certain peculiarities, they performed all the functions of a metallic currency as a unit of account, as a measure of value and as a store of value, and shared most of its characteristics. They were homogenous, reasonably durable, and of convenient size for the smallest or, in packets, for the largest transactions."[219] These same convenient characteristics also made cigarettes a viable currency in wartime Sarajevo. As Softić writes in her diary, "Everything is traded for cigarettes and cigarettes are traded for everything."[220] One liter of milk could be traded for a pack of cigarettes—described as "the best exchange between babies and smokers known in history."[221] One foreign journalist in Sarajevo put such high value on cigarettes that he called them "the lucky charms of war, more useful than a flak jacket."[222]

The Bosnian government distributed cigarette rations as a form of salary, ranging from soldiers on the frontline all the way up to members of the presidency. These cigarette rations, in turn, could either be consumed to calm nerves and satisfy addictions or traded for food and other smuggled goods at Markale and other public markets. Soldiers in the 1st Mountain Brigade, for example, were paid one pack of cigarettes per day (with cigarettes delivered every ten days), and ten packs could be sold for 100–150 marks.[223] Individual cigarettes also came in handy as a substitute for small bills, which were in short supply. For example, when buses were running, drivers would give out cigarettes when they did not have small bills for change.[224]

Smokers were at a clear disadvantage in this exchange system (having to consume rather than exchange cigarettes for other items), but smoking also inhibited hunger and calmed nerves. The psychological importance of cigarettes is starkly illustrated in a passage from a local journalist's wartime diary: "My neighbor Zulfo is depressed because there are no cigarettes, and is contemplating suicide. I gave him a packet of cigarettes as a Bajram [Muslim holiday] gift and re-stored his self-confidence."[225]

Cigarettes were supplied via smuggling, but also locally via the Sarajevo tobacco factory. With cigarettes functioning as currency, the tobacco factory essentially played the role of a government mint. Well stocked before the siege with tobacco meant to supply the entire region, the factory was officially designated a priority building and managed to operate throughout the war, maintaining about 20 percent of its pre-war production capacity. When the paper for rolling and packaging cigarettes was depleted, the factory resorted to using paper from one hundred tons of books as a substitute.[226] As a high-value local product rationed out by the government to both civilian and military personnel, cigarettes provided many Sarajevans with a dependable supply of currency that made smuggled goods and other black market items far more affordable than would otherwise have been the case. Factory officials were also suspected of supplying cigarettes to black marketeers.[227] Some soldiers also reportedly used their cigarette rations to barter for food with their Serb counterparts across the front line.[228]

Finally, for those who could afford it, black market food and drinks were available at the various restaurants, cafes, and bars that sprang up in the city during the siege. The privileged clientele were a mix of locals and internationals. One former UNPROFOR member describes the scene at the Boemi restaurant:

> Down a flight of stairs and suddenly we were in a different world—a restaurant called Boemi. Plush red carpets, tables set in alcoves, waiters in bow ties, a musician and soft lighting. The menu too was impressive—mixed grill, pancakes, good wine from Serbia and from Mostar. Hard currency buys anything in Sarajevo. I was shocked by the contrast between life above and below ground. Above people were being butchered in the streets by an unseen hand, scavenging for food and cowering in their dirty flats. Below, in Hades, you could sip fine wine and fill your belly.[229]

"Ninety percent of it all comes from the UN," a waiter at the restaurant told a foreign journalist. "It is mostly black market between the UN soldiers and our people."[230] The *Sarajevo Survival Guide* lists a handful of restaurants that opened in the city since October 1992, with food that included veal and hamburgers. "How the food actually gets there is kept as the biggest professional secret. Silent are both those who order and those who deliver. And those who eat."[231] One restaurant, the Hedgehog, even served squid during some of the worst months of the siege, despite the fact that the city was nearly 100 miles from the Adriatic coast.[232] The owner of another restaurant, the Bazeni, paid $4,000 per month to get a "priority use" designation from the government, a status intended for essential facilities such as hospitals. "In wartime it is forbidden to sell alcohol, but if you are a priority enterprise, it's no problem," explained Fuad Čolpa, the owner. "And if you don't serve alcohol you don't have any business."[233]

The business of survival in wartime Sarajevo was based on the interdependence between the highly visible formal (front-stage) and less visible informal (backstage) sides of the siege, including the incorporation of the UN-led aid effort into the economy and smuggling across the frontlines that was structured, conditioned, and facilitated by the large international humanitarian and media presence in the city. Sarajevo's formal and informal accessibility and permeability made a prolonged siege stalemate militarily viable, economically profitable, and politically sustainable for some key actors on all sides. And as discussed in the next chapter, these siege conditions also created an enormous opportunity for abuse, corruption, and a reconfiguration of power within the city—which largely took place backstage, away from the global media spotlight.

The Sarajevo airport. Photo reproduced with permission of the Historical Museum of Bosnia-Herzegovina.

Unloading humanitarian aid at the Sarajevo airport. Photo reproduced with permission of the Historical Museum of Bosnia-Herzegovina.

UNHCR humanitarian aid convoy truck, Sarajevo. Photo reproduced with permission of the Historical Museum of Bosnia-Herzegovina.

The Markale market, Sarajevo, January 1994. Photo reproduced with permission of the Historical Museum of Bosnia-Herzegovina.

Bosnians wait to cross the street, behind armored car, for protection from snipers, Sarajevo, 1995. Photo reproduced with the permission of Ron Haviv/VII.

Bosnian soldiers on the front lines around Sarajevo, 1994. Photo reproduced with the permission of Ron Haviv/VII.

CHAPTER 4

THE SIEGE WITHIN

The siege of Sarajevo was actually two sieges: one external, the other internal. The internal siege was made possible by the external siege, and helps to explain how the interests of some players within the city were served by the siege conditions even as the majority of the population suffered. The siege provided an opening and cover for the abuse of power and a rationale for tolerating such abuses; it created an enabling environment for SDA party leaders to extend and consolidate their political power and marginalize opponents and competitors; and it created enormous economic opportunities for theft, war profiteering, and redistribution of wealth while most of the city's residents struggled to simply survive. As a former senior Bosnian government official laments, "If the people had known ahead of time what kind of criminality and profiteering would be involved during the siege they would not have opted to fight."[1]

Focused on the external side of the siege, the UN-led humanitarian mission in Sarajevo largely overlooked its less visible, internal side. The foreign press also shied away from scrutinizing it, most of the time preferring to stick to the simpler and more palatable front-stage narrative of external aggressors versus internal defenders. Rieff has described this as a "sin of omission": "Those of us [foreign journalists] who were convinced of the rightness of the Bosnian cause tended to underplay the corruption of Bosnian political elites who, throughout the war, even in Sarajevo, were making fortunes off the conflict, doing private deals with the Serbs, and placing family members, friends, and mistresses in cushy jobs abroad."[2] President Izetbegović, for example, reportedly sent family members to Croatia and Turkey, and part of his family allegedly even managed to stay in Serb-occupied Grbavica well into the siege without being harmed.[3] The local press was also inhibited from focusing too much critical attention on this side of the siege. For example, *Oslobođenje* at one point aborted plans to publish a two-page profile on "crime and public safety."[4]

Thus, while the persistence of the external siege and the dramatic footage it generated propped up Sarajevo's global image as a victim (which it certainly was) on the front-stage, less noticed was that the city was also being victimized and exploited from within by some of its protectors and leaders. This happened in multiple ways at multiple levels, often backstage away from public view.

Criminal Defenders as Predators

The city's criminal defenders, while initially celebrated as patriotic heroes, were increasingly stealing from and terrorizing those they were supposed to be defending.[5] Consider the case of Juka. In addition to defending the city, Juka and his men robbed, extorted, abused, and raped civilians, and looted warehouses and shops.[6] Criminals such as Juka were using their government-supplied accreditations to rob storage facilities and shops. When the police would attempt to stop them they would simply show their accreditations and claim they were taking the goods for the army's needs.[7] As the situation deteriorated, General Stjepan Šiber pleaded with Juka, showing him a thick file documenting his men's crimes and saying it was bad for the army's image. Another senior government official told Juka that the French UNPROFOR officers were saying that there is no Bosnian army but only smuggling gangs.[8] Such appeals apparently worked on at least one occasion: a former government minister confronted Juka about stealing gasoline by shaming him, accusing him of aiding the enemy and appealed to his patriotism by asking him to help protect and ration the supplies. The official speculates that Juka complied because the accusation and appeal did not come from a military superior, since Juka did not recognize military authority above his own.[9] In particular, Juka viewed Bosnian General Sefer Halilović as a rival, and on one occasion interrupted a press conference held by Halilović and other top military officers, yelling from the floor, "You bastards! Why haven't I been invited?"[10]

Halilović finally issued an order for Juka's arrest in October 1992, after which Juka and many of his men fled Sarajevo to take up positions on nearby Mt. Igman, where he could control the most important access road in and out of the city. Juka set up new checkpoints that allowed him to take large cuts of aid and other goods moving into the city. Defiantly sitting atop Mt. Igman surrounded by his most loyal soldiers and prized Dobermans, Juka promised to ride into Sarajevo on his white horse to break the siege and liberate the city. Instead, the Bosnian army drove Juka and his men off Mt. Igman in late January 1993. Juka subsequently switched allegiances and joined the Croat HVO forces (where he was allegedly paid 500,000 German marks by Mate Boban [HDZ leader] to be christened and even change his name to Jole Boban).[11] Thus, in less than a year, Juka went from being labeled a "war hero" to a "traitor." Yet even after being pushed out of the Sarajevo area and joining the HVO in 1993, Juka managed to maintain close business ties with his old criminal colleagues, such as Ćelo Bajramović, inside the besieged city.[12] In 1994 Juka was found shot to death on the side of a road in Belgium.

Sarajevo's criminal army leaders not only ignored the chain of command but often flaunted their disdain for it. One soldier, for example, recounts that General Divjak issued papers for his transfer out of Zulić's unit, but upon receipt of the transfer order Zulić simply used the forms signed by Divjak as toilet paper.[13] The formal chain of command was largely a fiction, especially during the first year-and-a-half of the siege. For instance, the 1st Corps commander formally had authority over Mušan "Caco" Topalović's unit. A local platoon leader thus asked him to instruct Caco to release an elderly Croat refugee from trench-digging work. The commander simply replied that this was an impossible request, since he had no real leverage or control over Caco. The platoon leader then turned to more informal channels, asking his contacts in the Sarajevo underworld to make the necessary arrangements with Caco.[14]

Caco's soldiers routinely abducted people from the city's streets and took them to the frontlines to dig trenches. This included the family members of senior government officials and army generals.

One night in late 1992, a soldier in Caco's unit was instructed to guard "prisoners" in a basement near the front line, but while standing guard he came to realize that those being detained were actually local residents who had been forced to dig trenches (the soldier subsequently deserted, and fled Sarajevo with the help of a guide across the airport tarmac).[15] Some of those press-ganged into trench digging never returned, in some cases allegedly because Caco's men coveted their apartments. Their bodies were reportedly disposed of in Kazani—along with hundreds of other victims of Caco's men, many of them local Serb civilians—an illegal gravesite in a cleft of Mt. Trebević.[16] Ramiz "Ćelo" Delalić's soldiers also used the threat of trench digging as a means to extort money from targeted individuals. The soldiers would routinely collect "donations" from local citizens, usually between 2,000 and 5,000 marks. If the person refused or could not pay, they would be sent off to dig trenches.[17]

The government's increasingly fragile and uneasy relationship with the city's criminal defenders was also put to the test in late September 1993 when Ćelo Bajramović was hit with a small-caliber bullet while leaning against the plate-glass window of a local cafe. The bullet was lodged in a valve near his heart. The Sarajevo government, desperate for Ćelo not to die in a local hospital due to threats of retaliation by his men (who took over the hospital unit and turned it into an armed camp), begged the UNHCR to negotiate with the Serbs to allow Ćelo to be medically evacuated to Italy for emergency heart surgery. Radovan Karadžić allegedly signed the letter authorizing Ćelo's evacuation. (After recovering in an Ancona hospital, Ćelo reportedly attempted to return on an airlift plane, but a UN official noticed his name on the passenger list at the last moment and alerted the authorities not to let him board. He eventually made it back to Sarajevo on his own.)[18]

Tensions between Sarajevo's criminal military leaders and central government authorities escalated during the summer of 1993, and at one point Caco's men took hundreds of hostages and surrounded the presidency building to protest the arrest of Senad Pecar, one of Caco's lieutenants. Among the hostages was General Rasim Delić's son. When he attempted to escape, he was returned to Caco by Egyptian UNPROFOR soldiers who apparently thought he was an escaped Serb prisoner.[19]

The Sarajevo government finally moved to crack down on the most notorious criminal army gangs in the fall of 1993. The city's military

dependence on criminals had gradually diminished with the formation of a professional army, and the gangs were an obstacle to further
military professionalization and consolidation. Their persistent re-
fusal to integrate into the formal military command structure and
their increasingly blatant lawbreaking had become a serious challenge to government authority, and had also become an embarrassment to Sarajevo's leaders who wished to maintain international sympathy and support. Public tolerance for their activities had also
diminished as their lawbreaking became more brazen. As a former
Bosnian army general recollects, there was a "thin line between patriotism and criminality, and some didn't see the line as real."[20] "The last
straw," he says, "was when they broke into the funeral company
home, Pokop, and stole the equipment used for burying the dead."[21]

On October 26, 1993, the government launched a police action that
paralyzed the city, with officials broadcasting stay-at-home warnings to
local residents.[22] The targets of "Operation Trebević 2" were the 9th motorized and 10th mountain brigades and their respective commanders,
Ćelo Delalić and Caco Topalović. Eighteen people were killed, including Caco. Hundreds of members of the two targeted brigades were
detained during the sweep. The action was applauded by the internationals working in the city, a rising number of whom had experienced
thefts of their vehicles, equipment, and other belongings. "It is high
time they acted," a senior UN official said. "It's a wild west out here. If
the Bosnian government can't maintain order a few kilometers around
the presidency they can't expect to maintain international credibility."[23]

The crackdown was actually much more limited and selective than
it first appeared. Most of the detained soldiers were quickly released,
and many of those who remained in custody had the charges against
them reduced from "armed mutiny" to "insubordination." Caco's
lieutenant, Senad Pecar, who had been arrested the previous summer,
was promoted to brigade commander following Caco's death. And
one of Caco's personnel officers, Timur Numić, even became director
of the SDA party headquarters.[24]

Caco's popularity in some sectors endured beyond his death and
even the war, with some 20,000 Sarajevans attending his November
1996 funeral ceremony and passing his wrapped body above their
heads for a dozen or more blocks through the heart of the city. Dis-
mayed and alarmed by the government's approval of the funeral,

retired Bosnian army general Jovan Divjak wrote President Izetbegović: "I cannot understand why, in the days when you are making
superhuman efforts to preserve Bosnia as it is, you organize the funeral of those who inflicted the greatest harm." He asked Izetbegović:
is this funeral not "a sign to all of those who have violated the laws?
A sign that they can come pillage the houses, steal cars and the belongings of others with impunity?"[25] In his memoir, Divjak describes
Izetbegović 's approval of the public funeral ceremony as the "glorifi-
cation of a gangster"—a gangster who, unlike himself, had previously been able to enter the president's office whenever he wished.[26]
Divjak had originally denounced Caco's crimes in a letter to the general staff and the President on May 27, 1993—more than four months
before Caco's arrest.[27]

Efforts to prosecute crimes committed by the city's criminal defenders provoked mixed feelings. In a spring 1993 court case bringing
criminal charges against eleven soldiers (accused of murdering five
civilians, looting apartments, auto theft, and stealing $100,000 worth
of tires, VCRs, and stereos), prosecutor Ismet Hamzić explained his
unease: "Without these thugs, I wouldn't even be here to talk about
this case," he said. "People like them stopped the Serbs." Some of
those involved in the court case complained that there was government pressure to protect the defendants.[28]

Political Corruption, Abuse, and Opportunism

The siege within the siege was not restricted to renegade military
units but extended more deeply within the state apparatus. Munir
Alibabić, the Central Security Service Director during much of the
siege, argues that Sarajevo was robbed by its own government
under the shield of patriotism. Alibabić and others charge that Caco
was eliminated not because he was an out-of-control commander
but because he had become a political liability for President Izetbegović and his inner circle: Caco knew too much and could implicate
political leaders as accomplices in his dirty work. While small fish
were rounded up in the anti-crime sweep, larger crimes were never
properly investigated or solved. According to Alibabić, the standard
excuse for lack of investigations was always the same: the defense of

the city was the all-consuming priority, with those officials using this excuse most often the same ones who were accumulating cars, companies, shops, restaurants, and coffee houses. The Ministry of the Interior, Alibabić charges, had become a small SDA-dominated group of profiteers, with senior officials increasingly operating more like businessmen than policemen.[29]

A particularly notorious case was allegedly Bakir Alispahić, who was not only a loyal ally of Izetbegović and a member of the Executive Committee of the SDA,[30] but also used his official position to protect and engage in a wide variety of shady business dealings—some of which were well known by the authorities even before he was appointed as Minister of the Interior in June 1993.[31] One scheme, for example, reportedly involved an attempt to smuggle in 550,000 German marks worth of goods in trucks painted white with UN markings, with a police escort provided for the trucks as they entered the city. In another incident, Alispahić himself was reportedly arrested with several truckloads of alcohol, but was quickly released after intervention "from above."[32]

Investigations and charges against party members were allegedly discouraged because of their party allegiances. For example, investigations into Caco's criminal behavior, including the murder of many Serb civilians in the city, were reportedly blocked with the excuse that the party could be compromised.[33] In this view, the political leadership remained silent and tolerated Caco's criminal behavior and that of many others until they had outlived their usefulness and became disposable. As a former soldier in Zulić's unit puts it, the criminal leaders were "chewed up and spit out" when no longer needed.[34] Earlier complaints and warnings about crimes and abuses, including a four-page letter in May 1993 from General Divjak to Izetbegović, had reportedly fallen on deaf ears. And indeed, shortly after Alibabić sent President Izetbegović an eight-page report detailing illegal activities within the Ministry of the Interior, including Alispahić's dealings, he was relieved of his duties without explanation, demoted, and transferred to another desk with little responsibility.[35]

Former Bosnian general Sefer Halilović and others charge that a particularly large-scale form of organized theft was the systematic misuse and diversion of financial donations from abroad for the defense effort. The collection of hundreds of millions of dollars in international assistance—from the Bosnian diaspora and from sympathetic Islamic countries such as Iran and Saudi Arabia—was carried out by a few party loyalists in the central government handpicked by Izetbegović, giving them extraordinary financial power with no oversight or accountability.[36] Halilović claims that most of these foreign donations stayed in private accounts and were never used for their intended military defense purposes. While it is obviously impossible to know the exact amounts involved, it is clear that the structure of the situation invited abuse: the covert nature of importing arms and soliciting clandestine external financial support provided a cover and opportunity for corruption, theft, and profiteering.

Those who cultivated and maintained covert external funding links, such as Deputy Minister of Defense Hasan Čengić (appointed by Izetbegović to be the chief foreign fundraiser and weapons buyer), enjoyed an unrivaled privileged status. The Sarajevo government's heavy reliance on smuggled arms from abroad empowered some individuals while marginalizing others, giving key players an incentive to nurture this dependency.[37] One former senior Bosnian official recollects how his efforts to push for greater military self-reliance were systematically blocked: "I wished to get around the embargo with local production of arms. We had great resources in Bosnia to do so." But, he said, "every time I tried to set up a factory, I was undermined. The oligarchy of Izetbegović and Silajdžić did not want their monopoly of external purchases interrupted. The money came from Saudi [Arabia] or Iran and only the central government could arrange these purchases. Local production would have undermined the money flow."[38] One former official, who held a variety of top positions in the Sarajevo government during the war, laments that there was not a greater effort to foster local weapons production, and claims that it was actively discouraged by well-placed individuals in the government who found it easier to travel abroad and shake hands with donors to raise money for covert arms imports. Indeed, in one factory in Bosnia, he says, domestic production of rifles was deliberately shut down, with the government opting instead to buy the same model rifle at a much higher price on the international black market. He now suggests that a "public accounting of where all this money went would be good for the country," noting the total lack of transparency in international fundraising and arms purchasing during the war.[39]

External dependence on smuggled arms also had important political ramifications. President Izetbegović played up his ties to Islamic countries and ability to secure their covert financial support to make the case for extending his term as head of the presidency. Mirko Pejanović, a member of the presidency during the war, notes that it would have been inconceivable to extend Izetbegović's term in office in non-wartime conditions, and that Izetbegović was eager to stay in power.[40] Indeed, when the issue of rotating the presidency was raised during the war, Izetbegović allegedly insisted that he should remain in office because no one else was as well known and connected in the Islamic world and that this was vital for the war effort.[41]

Not only were covert military supplies increasingly controlled by individuals closely tied to the SDA party leadership, but the growing influence of the SDA contributed to the Islamicization of the army, eroding Bosnia's (and especially Sarajevo's) traditional multicultural and multi-religious character.[42] This was reinforced by the highly controversial arrival of some 3,000 Mujahidin fighters[43] from the Middle East and North Africa, whom the Bosnian government did not actually need for the military effort but were part of the political price of becoming dependent on covert funds and arms from Islamic countries. Often entering Bosnia via Croatia in the guise of "humanitarian workers" funded by Islamic charities, the arrival of these foreign combatants added ammunition to the Serb propaganda campaign that they were defending Christian civilization against Islamic fundamentalism. The Mujahidin fighters were also responsible for some of the worst atrocities on the Bosnian government side. The degree to which they were invited in and embraced or grudgingly tolerated by the Sarajevo authorities is unclear and continues to be hotly debated. Their lingering presence after the war (despite formal orders to leave)[44]—facilitated by the questionable provision of Bosnian citizenship and passports—fueled fear and speculation in some quarters that the country was becoming a beachhead for Islamic extremism.[45] The imported fighters were mostly active outside of Sarajevo in Central Bosnia, but reportedly engaged in a military offensive launched from Mt. Igman that included a firefight with UNPROFOR troops at the airport.[46]

As the war wore on, the Bosnian military was also increasingly politicized—turning into a party army and subordinated to the political goals of the SDA.[47] Consequently, according to one study of the evolution of the Bosnian military, "major military operations would be undertaken less for strategic reasons than for the sake of the regime's political ambitions or to improve its political standing."[48] This included a poorly designed and implemented military offensive in Sarajevo in June and July 1995 that cost the lives of some 400 Bosnian soldiers.

More broadly, the siege conditions provided an enabling environment for a new SDA-connected elite to emerge and consolidate power, built around the Izetbegović family and its inner circle of party loyalists. According to Sudetic, this included Senad Šahinpašić (who had helped Alija Izetbegović form the SDA and had long had a close relationship with the president's son, Bakir Izetbegović), the family of Alija Delimustafić (the former Bosnian Minister of Internal Affairs), and Alemko Nuhanović (a meat seller from Višegrad).[49] In a February 1994 SDA meeting, Izetbegović made it clear that loyalty and obedience to the SDA would be prioritized over competence and qualifications. Non-party members in ministries and state companies were increasingly pushed out and replaced by favored SDA members. As one senior Bosnian government official who was sacked during the war explained it, "Everyone who wasn't obedient was gotten rid of. Instead of organizing people, they were only hoping for help from abroad."[50]

The opening of the so-called UN "blue roads" in the spring of 1994, which enabled a flood of commercial goods into the city across the airport grounds for a number of months, helped to consolidate and expand the economic position of Sarajevo's most politically connected entrepreneurs. Prices fell and supplies increased, bringing much needed relief to the city's population. But a handful of SDA-protected merchants were the main economic beneficiaries. Small independent competitors were increasingly pushed aside. According to one former Bosnian government official, Sarajevo's new elites "used the military units stationed in Dobrinja and Hrasnica to block access to the city for goods shipped by small private businessmen who did not have political protection." Specifically, he charged that "the commander of the Bosnian army brigade in Hrasnica, Fikret Prevljak, had been close to Bakir Alispahić for years before the war. Prevljak, clearly with the approval of his superiors, imposed a road toll of 500 German marks on many of the trucks plying the road over Mt. Igman, the 'feeder' for the blue route into the city." He also claimed that Prevljak "used his men to plunder trucks hauling goods that did not belong to businessmen who enjoyed Izetbegović's protection."[51]

Politically and economically empowered by the siege conditions, Sarajevo's emerging new elites accumulated substantial "start-up funds" for future business ventures and would be best positioned to take advantage of the postwar reconstruction process. The siege environment thus enabled a radical reconfiguration of the city's social power structure, leaving a lasting legacy well beyond the lifting of the siege.

Obstructing Access to Water

Some of the dynamics of the "siege within the siege" are strikingly illustrated by the frustrated and delayed efforts to increase the desperately needed supply of water to Sarajevo's residents. It was no surprise that water access was drastically curtailed by the Serb authorities (who controlled the city's most important prewar sources of water). What was a surprise was that that water access was also impeded from within. Nothing symbolized the city's miserable existence more than the image of exhausted Sarajevans carrying plastic jugs of water while braving Serb sniper fire and mortar attacks. Hundreds of city residents were killed or injured while engaging in the endless pursuit of water. Finding, waiting for, and carrying water for their families defined the daily routine of many of the city's residents—providing continuous and highly visible evidence for a global audience that the civilian population was a victim of Serb aggression. Sarajevo had only a handful of small streams of potable water not controlled by the besieging forces. The brewery in central Sarajevo had its own deep wells, and tanker trucks transported water from the brewery to other parts of the city. Other common wells were also dug, and tap stands were set up where people would stand in line for hours to fill their containers.

In 1993, Fred Cuny, a widely respected American disaster relief expert, launched a bold and ambitious project to set up an emergency water treatment system in Sarajevo. If fully operational, the system would provide running water to most of the city's population during at least part of the day.[52] The idea was to filter the Miljacka River, which ran through the city, into the existing water system. Backed by the philanthropist George Soros and the International Rescue Committee, Cuny and his colleagues managed to ship to Sarajevo two emergency water treatment systems aboard C-130 transport planes. This required overcoming extraordinary technical, logistical, and political obstacles—including moving massive, steel-plated modules past the Serb liaison officer at the Sarajevo airport. The shipping manifest, which the Serb authorities had to approve ahead of time, simply read "Water filters." Brian Stears, an aid worker who specialized in moving items past the Serb airport authorities—sometimes by outdrinking them—explains how it worked:

> The Serbs didn't have a clue—probably figured it was some little piece of machinery—so they signed off on it. And then the planes come in and they're these enormous fucking tanks that fill a whole plane, and they're going, "What the hell is that?" But at that point their higher-ups had already approved them and the guys out at the airport weren't going to countermand their superiors, so we just loaded them up and got them into the city before anyone could say anything.[53]

The first water treatment plant was finally completed by the end of 1993, set up in a road tunnel that provided cover from Serb shelling.[54] But to Cuny's great surprise and dismay, the Sarajevo government proved to be more of an obstacle than the Serb authorities. City officials refused to give approval to turn the system on, arguing that the water was unsafe to drink. Cuny then had the water tested, not only by a laboratory in Croatia but also by the World Health Organization and by U.S. Army bioenvironmental engineers in Germany. All the tests concluded that the water was safe. Yet the government still stubbornly refused to turn the system on. In frustrated defiance, Cuny one night quietly opened the valves anyway, releasing water into the city's pipes—with no negative health effects for those families that suddenly had running water coming out of their home taps.

City officials quickly intervened to shut the system down, continuing to insist that the water was not safe to drink. In one document, Cuny wrote that, in a meeting "during the heaviest day of shelling in Sarajevo in six months," with "bullets literally pinging off the windowsill," Bosnian government officials demanded more stringent water-testing regulations than anything in the United States.[55] Cuny explained some of his frustrations with the Bosnian government authorities:

> They claim one reason the system is not safe is because we do not have a first stage settling tank to clear the water before it enters the system. We have explained repeatedly that in a pressure treatment system, it is not needed. They also claim that because the system is manually operated instead of automatic, it is dangerous, yet they cannot define what the danger is. At one point, they told us they would not allow the system to be turned on until we painted the inside of the tunnel but could not explain what relationship that had to water quality.[56]

As a financial backer of the project, Soros also attempted to intervene, pleading with Bosnian authorities to give the go-ahead. "I remind you that the sympathy of the world is with Bosnia," wrote Soros in a February 11 letter to Bosnian prime minister Haris Silajdžić. "Any hint that the government is forcing its people to carry water under fire when they could be getting it safely at home could seriously damage its image."[57] Soros even made a personal visit to President Izetbegović. The delays nevertheless persisted.

There are a number of potential explanations—involving both front-stage and backstage dynamics—for the Sarajevo government's unexpected obstructionism. A cynical front-stage explanation is that Bosnian government officials resisted and delayed turning on the taps because the globally televised images of the desperate and dangerous quests for water by ordinary Sarajevans would disappear—and such heart-wrenching imagery was an important public relations tool in maintaining international sympathy and support. A plausible backstage explanation is that turning on the taps would remove a source of black market revenue. As the *Washington Post* reported, "Government agencies that trucked water to dry parts of the city received a fuel allocation, part of which they sold on the black market for $100 a gallon. If water started flowing through the taps, the lucrative fuel allocation would dry up."[58] The aid workers John Fawcett and Victor Tanner, who were closely involved in the water treatment project, also point to other admittedly speculative but plausible backstage explanations. First, "there were portions of the city administration involved in selling water from the Brewery and they saw the plant as undercutting their business." Second, "the Brewery was receiving diesel fuel from the UN in order to run pumps pulling up water from its deep wells. It was rumored that as the monitoring of this diesel was so weak, that the Bosnian government was using some of it to run machinery to produce weapons."[59]

Under growing international pressure, including prominent negative press attention, the Sarajevo government reluctantly decided to allow the system to function at minimum capacity—but still cautioned residents to use the water for non-drinking purposes only (such as flushing toilets). The government's obstructionism continued through 1994. Only when the Serb leadership significantly tightened the siege noose in late April 1995 did the Sarajevo authorities finally embrace the water filtration system as an essential part of the city's survival strategy, keeping it on twenty-four hours a day (eventually providing 80 to 90 percent of Sarajevo's potable water).[60] Ironically, some of same government officials who initially blocked the water project were now not only publicly promoting it but trying to project the impression that they had supported it all along.[61]

The "siege within the siege" is both the murkiest and most controversial dimension of the Sarajevo war years. It remains the subject of heated and bitter debate in the local media and political circles long after the war has ended. It is all too easy to get caught up in the mystery, intrigue, and conspiracy theories that characterize much of this debate. The point here is not to find a "smoking gun" or add further fuel to this politically charged fire, but rather to show how the external siege conditions enabled these opportunistic and predatory backstage dynamics that were insufficiently scrutinized at the time. In the end, much of this behind-the-scenes story will likely remain unknown, lost in the shadows and confined to the realm of speculation.

CHAPTER 5

LIFTING THE SIEGE

T he siege of Sarajevo was finally lifted in October 1995 with a cease-fire that brought a conclusion to the Bosnian war. The Sarajevo government delayed implementing the cease-fire until natural gas and electricity service were restored to the city—giving Croat and Bosnian forces five more days to take Serb-held territory near Prijedor and Banja Luka in western Bosnia.[1] Although the fighting stopped with the cease-fire and subsequent signing of the U.S.-brokered Dayton Peace Agreement in November, the city was not entirely reopened and reintegrated until March 1996. At that time, central road networks were fully reconnected, and Serb forces withdrew from the neighborhood of Grbavica (setting fires, looting, and stripping the high-rise apartments bare as they departed, including the removal of wiring, doors, and window frames), as well as the suburbs of Ilidža and Vogošca. Complete control of the city was a key victory for the Sarajevo government in negotiating the Dayton accords—and was bitterly opposed by many Bosnian Serb residents in these areas, large numbers of whom left along with the Serb troops. The last UN aid flight left Sarajevo in January 1996, marking the conclusion of the longest-lasting airlift in history. Given the remarkable longevity of the siege, how and why was it finally lifted? Much of the answer can be found by tracing the interaction between the formal (front-stage) and informal (backstage) mechanisms that brought an end to the conflict.

Front Stage: Triggering NATO Air Strikes

The Sarajevo government was never able to break the siege militarily, and its failed efforts to do so late in the war generated heavy casualties. Many speculate that the ill-fated military offensive in June 1995 had more to do with local politics and international signaling than with breaking the siege.[2] But while Sarajevo remained bottled up and under siege, a decisive shift in the military balance on the ground elsewhere in Bosnia in favor of the Bosnian army placed Serb forces on the defensive for the first time, helping to create the political conditions for a negotiated settlement. Sarajevo was not the main battleground during the final phase of the war, but the city played a key role in prompting NATO air strikes ("Operation Deliberate Force"), which in turn helped to tip the military balance. Tracing the interplay between front-stage and backstage behavior helps to explain this decisive shift.

The trigger for the NATO air strikes came on August 28, 1995, when a mortar shell fell on Sarajevo's Markale marketplace, the central outdoor market for selling and bartering smuggled goods and other items. The bombing killed thirty-eight people and injured more than eighty others. Within minutes, foreign television crews arrived at the scene to broadcast graphic images of the carnage across the globe. While similar bombings had taken place in the past, this time Western leaders were looking for a legitimizing trigger and rationale to take more decisive military action against Serb positions encircling the city. The gruesome images from the marketplace bombing provided the opening for the launching of air strikes that had already been well planned out.

The backstage and front-stage action were closely linked. Backstage smuggling provided the goods drawing the crowds to the marketplace, and the front-stage bombing of the marketplace provided the carnage attracting the cameras. And the high visibility of the international military response to the marketplace bombing in turn enabled the Bosnian army to take advantage of its less visible clandestine accumulation of arms in violation of the UN embargo. Washington was a key player on both the front stage and the backstage: it took a formal, lead role in initiating and sustaining the air strikes while also informally encouraging and perhaps even facilitating arms smuggling to Bosnian government forces.

The launching of the air strikes—at that time the largest military operation in NATO's history (involving more than 3,500 sorties and dropping more than 1,000 bombs)—was particularly visible because Sarajevo-based foreign media crews were close by to record the blow-by-blow action. As the journalist Tim Ripley noted, "In the Television Station and at the Holiday Inn, camera teams were feeding the images out live around the world."[3] Lieutenant Colonel Steve Stengel, who was involved in the first daylight mission over Sarajevo, recalls: "My lead [pilot] fired the AGM-65 Maverick missile that was picked up by the television cameras. We were not even on the ground before we were featured on the *BBC* news."[4]

Those charged with carrying out Operation Deliberate Force were well aware that they were performing for a global audience and that Sarajevo was center stage. Explaining the aggressive use of close air support, Wing Commander Ken Cornfield comments: "We wanted to show the Bosnian Serbs we were aware of a number of targets in the city and demonstrate to the world, via the media, that the operation was centered on Sarajevo."[5] The air strikes were also about projecting an image of international strength and cooperation, notes Brigadier General Dave Sawyer of the U.S. Air Force: "By having a lot of activity around Sarajevo, we were sending a message to the world that the UN and NATO were working together."[6]

But Operation Deliberate Force was not only about signaling and image projection. The air strikes on Bosnian Serb positions (including the targeting of communications, ammunition, and heavy weapons) around Sarajevo—reinforced by artillery support from the heavily armed British and French Rapid Reaction Force that had been deployed on Mt. Igman—meant that the Bosnian Serb leadership based in nearby Pale could no longer use the city as a hostage and political negotiating card. The balance of military power in Sarajevo thus shifted for the first time, with important repercussions for the wider war. As Ripley observes, "This meant that they [Bosnian Serbs] could not apply leverage on the city to compensate for their defeats in western Bosnia. . . . Denied their usual revenge tactics, the Bosnian Serbs had no option but to fight it out with the Croats and Muslims to the south and west of Banja Luka."[7]

Scaling back of humanitarian operations during the last months of the war was a prerequisite for the NATO bombings. The UN policy of consent was no longer operationally viable. The tightening of the siege meant that the Sarajevo airlift, for example, had to be shut down from April 8 to September 15, 1995. As Adam Roberts points out, "A more robust policy of decisive enforcement action only became possible in Bosnia after the humanitarian aid programme had practically stopped in mid-1995 due to Bosnian Serb actions."[8] This seemed to contradict the UN Security Council's assertion that "the provision of humanitarian assistance in Bosnia and Herzegovina is an important element in the Council's effort to restore international peace and security in the area."[9] Indeed, far from the humanitarian aid effort enhancing international leverage and influence during the war, it had the opposite affect. In Sarajevo, Robert Donia notes, "when the besieging forces deprived the city of essential services and aid, UN civilians and military officials frequently granted concessions in exchange for Bosnian Serb nationalist promises to permit the resumption of international aid. The Serb nationalists masterfully manipulated the humanitarian concerns of international officials, knowing that the city's dependence on aid delivered under UN escort provided a chokehold to be tightened at any time."[10] Thus, bringing an end to the war was only possible once aid delivery was no longer viable and prioritized above all else by the UN and Western governments.

By the spring of 1995 the UN's humanitarian mission in Sarajevo and elsewhere in Bosnia had become increasingly difficult to sustain. This was most starkly apparent during the UN hostage crisis in May, in which some 300 UN personnel (mostly French peacekeepers) were used by the Bosnian Serbs as human shields, chained to the doors of ammunition bunkers in Pale and the Mt. Jahorina communication sites. Karadžić and other Serb leaders apparently made a handsome profit by videotaping the incident and selling the footage to the global media. The televised images, which attracted worldwide attention, humiliated the UNPROFOR and outraged French president Jacques Chirac.[11] Although the hostage crisis was soon resolved, it reaffirmed the growing sentiment that the UN's humanitarian approach to the siege and wider war was untenable and indeed had become an embarrassing symbol of international impotence. In other words, the initial global cheers for the UN's humanitarian effort had increasingly turned to jeers, generating a growing performance crisis for the UN and its Western government backers.

This was dramatically reinforced when Bosnian Serb forces sacked the eastern enclave town of Srebrenica (making a mockery of its designation as a UN "safe area") in July 1995 and then proceeded to systematically kill over 7,000 Muslim men and boys. The global fixation on Sarajevo and the absence of a large international presence in Srebrenica meant that the besieged town remained offstage and out of the spotlight during most of the war. But the sheer number of deaths jolted Western leaders, shamed the UN, and further tarnished the image of the Bosnian Serbs in international public opinion.[12] International tolerance for "ethnic cleansing" in Bosnia had reached a tipping point in the summer of 1995, drawing Western leaders to endorse the kind of military action they had so carefully avoided since the start of the war. At the same time, the balance of military power on the ground had shifted decisively.

Backstage: Shifting the Military Balance by Evading the UN Arms Embargo

NATO air strikes in late August 1995 helped to bring the war to an end, but this high-profile display of force was effective only in conjunction with Bosnian and Croatian military offensives on the ground. A major shift in the military balance during the last phase of the war, deliberately kept out of sight of the media cameras, was an essential condition for a negotiated settlement in the fall of 1995. As the former Croatian army general Martin Špegelj points out: "What was finally decisive in ending the war was the emergence, to general astonishment, of a strong army of Bosnia-Herzegovina."[13]

A crucial part of the Bosnian army's unexpected strength was growing access to smuggled weapons in violation of the UN arms embargo. In this sense, ironically, it was the very failure of the embargo that helped to bring the war to an end. Rather than stopping the bloodshed, the embargo helped turn the conflict into a protracted war of attrition in which the Sarajevo government was denied access to heavy weapons and forced to rely on smuggled light arms. For much of the war, the embargo privileged the already heavily armed Bosnian

Serbs. Over time, however, the cumulative effect of circumventing the embargo helped to tip the military balance in favor of the Bosnian army (which already had a manpower advantage). Thus, the subversion of an arms embargo designed to inhibit and contain conflict contributed to the ending of conflict. Indeed, Bosnia as a state survived partly by evading the UN arms embargo.

No country dared make a unilateral front-stage move to formally defect from the arms embargo, but informal defection backstage made the embargo increasingly porous, especially after the U.S. brokered alliance between Croatia and the Bosnian government in the spring of 1994. In the international politics of the UN embargo, the formal, front-stage action was about image management, keeping up the appearance of unity within the so-called "international community" and reaffirming a commitment to multilateralism. Meanwhile, much to the dismay of many senior UN officials and European leaders, the informal, backstage activities of the United States and other key actors such as Iran and other friendly Islamic states quietly subverted the embargo. One Dutch intelligence analyst notes that the UN was partly responsible for prompting these behind-the-scenes clandestine moves:

> The fact is that Bosnia was officially admitted to the United Nations as the 177th member state. It is strange then that the Security Council did not draw the logical conclusion that a new state may take measures for defence against an armed attack. The embargo curbed the legal arms trade, but did nothing to reduce the demand for, and supply of, arms, and only displaced it onto illegal circuits.[14]

The UN arms embargo, first imposed in September 1991, had placed the Sarajevo government in a highly disadvantageous military position long before the war even started. Virtually self-sufficient militarily, neighboring Serbia was the least vulnerable to the arms embargo. Similarly, the Bosnian Serb nationalists, aided by the armaments left behind when the JNA formally withdrew and by clandestine supply channels to Serbia, were minimally affected by the embargo and therefore had the most to gain from it.[15] The Sarajevo government, on the other hand, was poorly armed. American intelligence reports indicated that the Bosnian military forces had only two tanks and only one or two armored personnel carriers in 1992, while Serb forces possessed 300 tanks and 200 armored personnel carriers. Bosnian military forces had two dozen artillery pieces compared to 600–800 on the side of the Serb forces.[16]

Moreover, the Sarajevo government was geographically heavily disadvantaged. Most weapons imported into the almost entirely landlocked country had to be smuggled through Croatian territory. Thus, the embargo made an already difficult situation even more so. Accessing external arms supplies would have to be done through covert channels, which included paying exorbitant "taxes" in the form of Croatian transit fees (the standard trans-shipment fee was about 30 percent, with payment in kind).[17] Equally important, dependence on the black market limited the types of equipment available, since heavy weaponry, such as armor and artillery, was particularly cumbersome and difficult to smuggle in (and which the Croats were most reluctant to facilitate).[18]

The mechanisms for evading the arms embargo ranged from small independent entrepreneurs at the bottom of the trade to large-scale state-sponsored smuggling at the top. In the first year of the Bosnian war, there were reports of a "virtual cottage industry of small-scale freelance [arms] smuggling."[19] More elaborate and organized smuggling operations soon emerged. President Izetbegović toured the Middle East in October 1992 asking sympathetic countries for covert assistance. Funds were also collected from the growing Bosnian diaspora, which helped to purchase black market military equipment and supplies.[20] Iran reportedly sent covert arms shipments to Bosnia as early as September 1992, and by 1993 countries such as Brunei, Malaysia, Pakistan, and Saudi Arabia were providing arms and other supplies. Partly motivated by a desire not to be upstaged by its rival Iran in covertly aiding Bosnia, Saudi Arabia allegedly provided $300 million to access weapons via the same clandestine network of traffickers and operatives that was created a decade earlier by the Saudis and the United States to supply the anti-Soviet insurgents in Afghanistan. One Saudi official claims that the U.S. role in this scheme "was more than just turning a blind eye to what was going on. . . . It was consent combined with stealth cooperation."[21] Saudi sources claimed that covert U.S. involvement was crucial because Saudi Arabia lacked the "technical sophistication" to carry out the operation by itself

(American officials immediately denied such allegations when they appeared in press accounts).[22]

According to a number of reports, a key broker for black market weapons deals for the Bosnian government was an obscure organization called the Third World Relief Agency (TWRA).[23] The TWRA was allegedly used as a front to funnel $350 million to the Bosnian government between 1992 and 1995, at least half of which was apparently used to purchase and smuggle weapons.[24] Most of the money reportedly came from Middle East countries, including Iran and especially Saudi Arabia. Donations also came from Turkey, Sudan, Brunei, Malaysia, and Pakistan.[25] The United States allegedly knew about the TWRA's operations starting in 1993. "We were told [by Washington] to watch them but not interfere," recalls a senior Western diplomat. "Bosnia was trying to get weapons from anybody, and we weren't helping much. The least we could do is back off. So we backed off."[26] Austrian and German authorities also allegedly looked the other way. Mohammed el-Fatih, the Sudanese director of the agency, had acquired a diplomatic passport in March 1992, making it possible to move large quantities of hard currency without worrying about police inspections. The TWRA also allegedly sent substantial amounts of cash to Croatia to pay off Croatian officials for their acquiescence in shipping arms through their territory, and was reportedly involved in smuggling money into Sarajevo on UNHCR planes.[27]

Headquartered in Vienna, the TWRA had offices in Sarajevo, Budapest, Moscow, and Istanbul. Hasan Čengić, the top Bosnian government official charged with negotiating clandestine arms deals, was on the advisory board of the TWRA. In a major smuggling operation funded by the TWRA in September 1992, Soviet-built cargo planes reportedly landed in Maribor, Slovenia, from Khartoum, Sudan. The cargo—120 tons of assault rifles, mortars, mines, and ammunition originally from surplus stocks of Soviet weapons in East Germany—was labeled as humanitarian aid. From Maribor, the weapons were allegedly transported by chartered Russian helicopters to Tuzla and Zenica in Bosnia, stopping at the Croatian port of Split to refuel. Another operation reportedly involved $15 million in light weaponry, smuggled into Bosnia from Croatia via Malaysian and Turkish UNPROFOR troops. The director of TWRA fled Vienna and moved to Istanbul in 1994 when he discovered that an investigation was underway implicating him in money laundering and arms smuggling. In 1996, the Bosnian government awarded the former head of the TWRA a gold medal for his agency's "relief work."[28]

The TWRA's operations predated the opening of a direct arms smuggling channel between Iran and Bosnia (via Croatia) in May 1994. Iran had reportedly been supplying arms to Bosnia since early in the war, but after the U.S.-brokered Croat-Bosnia Federation in the spring of 1994 it became significantly easier to smuggle in weapons via Croatian territory. At an April 28, 1994, meeting with U.S. Ambassador Peter Galbraith, Croatian president Franjo Tudjman inquired about the U.S. stance on the Iran–Bosnia smuggling pipeline. Galbraith allegedly replied that he had "no instructions" from Washington on the matter, which was interpreted as tacit approval. The first shipment of arms from Iran—bringing in sixty tons of explosives and military equipment—reportedly arrived in Zagreb on May 4. Many of the subsequent flights arrived at the Croatian island of Krk, with the weapons supplies then moved to the mainland by helicopter.[29] Air shipments of arms and ammunition reportedly averaged eight per month, with 30 percent taken by Croatia as a trans-shipment fee. According to CIA estimates, arms shipments to Bosnia from Iran reached approximately 14,000 tons, worth about $150–$200 million.[30] By early 1995, Iranian cargo planes were reportedly arriving in Zagreb three times per week.[31]

Some arms shipments also managed to bypass Croatian territory, thus avoiding the heavy Croat tax. A number of reports claim that arms were flown at night directly to Tuzla in February 1995 using C-130 cargo aircraft. The origin of these "black flights" has never been confirmed, with much speculation that the United States was directly involved or subcontracted the work out to private cargo companies.[32] Many UN officials were convinced that Turkish aircraft were involved, making deliveries from Northern Cyprus.[33] The clandestine flights took place when there were either no Airborne Warning and Control System (AWACS) planes monitoring Bosnian airspace or when there were AWACS with U.S.-only crews.[34] Within the UN there was much hand-wringing and finger-pointing at the United States, with some disgruntled UN officials leaking information about the mysterious flights to the media in an effort to publicly shame and embarrass Washington.[35]

Despite the Bosnian government's growing capacity to smuggle in arms, dependence on black market channels had significant limitations and drawbacks. As the *New York Times* editorialized in November 1994:

> Even though Bosnia is now smuggling in enough weapons to turn the tide, formally lifting the embargo is important because it would allow in the tanks and other heavy weapons the Government's side still lacks. It would also give Bosnia's political authorities more control over which units get the new arms. . . . A procurement system based on smuggling directs arms to those commanders who have the best underworld connections. Lifting the embargo would also free Bosnia from reliance on radical weapons suppliers like Iran and Libya that have few inhibitions about circumventing UN rules.[36]

Nevertheless, critics who argued that the embargo should be lifted to "level the playing field" were opposed by those who thought that this would simply "level the killing field," escalating the conflict. As the Chief Political Officer of the UNPROFOR in Sarajevo, Phillip Corwin, argued: "Any signs of lifting the embargo will encourage a wider war, and a wider war will mean more refugees. The main reason the European powers are in the former Yugoslavia in the first place is to prevent refugee flows to their countries."[37] Many international officials also feared that a formal lifting of the embargo, which the U.S. Congress was increasingly pushing for, would be interpreted by the Bosnian Serbs as a de facto declaration of war—which would, in turn, derail humanitarian operations and sharply increase the dangers and risks to UNPROFOR troops on the ground.[38] This was yet another illustration of how the UN's humanitarian mission in Bosnia inhibited a more forceful international response.

At the same time, a side effect of the UN-led humanitarian mission was to unintentionally provide a cover for smuggling arms to Bosnian government forces. Covert arms shipments were sometimes disguised as UN aid, hidden within the large quantities of legitimate aid entering by land and air. Discoveries of such camouflaged arms shipments were embarrassing for the UN, and added to Serb propaganda claims that the UN was aiding the Sarajevo government.[39] Moreover, some UNPROFOR troops directly participated in arms smuggling schemes, both in Sarajevo (as discussed in the previous chapter) and elsewhere in Bosnia. For instance, according to one report, Turkish and Malaysian soldiers were involved in smuggling light arms; Bangladeshi troops were engaged in large-scale selling of ammunition to the Bosnian military; and the UNPROFOR battalion from Malta ordered 4,000 mortar shells—yet possessed only four mortars.[40] Bosnian government forces also reportedly managed to buy some arms supplies from Serbia, circumventing not only the embargo but also ethnic animosities.[41]

The stalemated international politics of the arms embargo—with Russia and major European powers supporting and the United States increasingly opposing it—meant that the embargo remained in place even as Washington officials quietly encouraged evasion. While avoiding the diplomatically risky move of unilaterally lifting the embargo on the front stage, the Clinton White House adopted a policy stance of not only non-enforcement (i.e., turning a blind eye) but also possibly informal facilitation in arming the Bosnian government backstage.[42] The clandestine channeling of arms to Bosnia from Islamic countries was enabled by the fact that the UN depended on U.S. intelligence to monitor the embargo.[43] European and UN officials grumbled about U.S. covert complicity, but were partly pacified by the fact that Washington did not publicly flaunt its disregard for the embargo. Leaders on both sides of the Atlantic had an interest in not making too big a fuss over the issue. During his 1992 electoral campaign, Bill Clinton stated: "I think we have to consider whether or not we should lift the arms embargo now on the Bosnians since they are in no way in a fair fight with a heavily armed opponent."[44] Once in office, however, Clinton quickly backpedalled, avoiding a confrontational public stance that would strain transatlantic relations. Thus, while privately encouraging the evasion of the arms embargo, the Clinton White House publicly opposed the mounting calls in the U.S. Congress to lift the embargo. Such a unilateral public move, the White House argued, "will drive the UN force out of Bosnia and oblige the U.S. to send in ground forces, as part of NATO, to assist in that withdrawal. It will divide NATO and increase American responsibility for the outcome of the war in Bosnia."[45]

With a rising influx of smuggled weapons, especially after the U.S.-brokered alliance of convenience between Croat and Bosnian government forces, the military balance took a decisive turn in 1994–95. "Time is on Bosnia's side," remarked a military insider who participated in a smuggling scheme that shipped 200 tons of Chinese weapons via Croatia to Bosnia (disguised as humanitarian aid in a convoy of thirty-eight trucks) in the summer of 1994. "With further similar transactions, one day Bosnia will take the war to the Serbs."[46] From April to August 1994, *Jane's* calculates that 1,500 tons of ammunition and arms (such as grenade launchers and anti-tank missiles) were covertly shipped to Bosnia—worth an estimated $250 million.[47] Iran was the Sarajevo government's leading supplier late in the war, reportedly providing more than 5,000 tons of arms between May 1994 and January 1996—privately encouraged by the United States even as some officials worried about creeping Iranian influence in Bosnia and as the Tehran government was routinely denounced publicly in Washington policy circles as a sponsor of terrorism.[48]

While international attention focused on Bosnia, neighboring Croatia quietly built up its military capacity in violation of the UN arms embargo, reportedly spending between $1.5 and $3 billion on smuggled weapons (largely from Cold War stockpiles sold by corrupt officials in Eastern Europe).[49] Successful evasion of the embargo was also evident in the outfitting of the Croatian army. As one press report put it:

> The revamped Croatian army is a far cry from the poorly armed soldiers who barely held on to their new independence four years ago while losing one-third of their land to the Serbs. . . . Today the elite Croatian soldier is armed with a German Heckler and Koch HKG3A3 7.62mm assault rifle made under license in Pakistan. He wears a camouflage U.S flak jacket, manufactured in Canada, with pockets for six magazines and hand grenades. He walks in black leather U.S. combat boots.[50]

Croatian forces also received substantial training and advising from a private Virginia-based firm, Military Professional Resources International (MPRI)—which, according to one press report, was "interpreted in diplomatic circles as a strategy by Washington to approve contracts in sensitive areas using private but trusted personnel."[51]

Ironically, the UN indirectly helped fund Croatia's covert arms purchases. As Ripley notes, "The rent paid in cash by the UN for its

Croatian bases went straight into the arms buying budget."[52] Indeed, Croatia charged such enormous landing fees for Bosnia-bound UN humanitarian aid flights that UNHCR airlift officials increasingly preferred to use the Italian and German air bases.

Zagreb reportedly helped to build up the Bosnian army's fighting capacity through clandestine assistance to the 5th Corps in the Bihać area. In the later phase of the war, Zagreb covertly facilitated the funneling of twenty million German marks per month to the 5th Corps. The funds were allegedly laundered through a variety of European banks and then delivered by helicopter to Bihać. In addition, Croatia allowed the 5th Corps to set up its own arms procurement operation out of Zagreb. Arming the 5th Corps also reportedly involved buying off corrupt Serb officials. According to Ripley, "A major part of the 5th Corps subsidy from Zagreb was spent bribing Serb officers to allow helicopter and aircraft over-flights," noting that it was only from August 1994 on that Serbs started to shoot down Bihać-bound aircraft.[53] The 5th Corps also bought a substantial amount of arms directly from the local Serb population west of Bihać, and bribes to Serb officers also enabled black market convoys to transit through the Krajina to Bihać in July 1995.[54]

In coordination with Croatian forces, the Bosnian army went on the offensive in the summer of 1995, quickly regaining large swaths of territory lost at the beginning of the war. Bosnian Serb–held territory shrank to 50 percent of the country by the end of September. These military offensives were the largest military operations in Europe since 1945. On the defensive for the first time and with little prospect of turning the tide, the strategic calculus of the Bosnian Serb leadership shifted, creating space for a final negotiated solution.[55] As Richard Holbrooke, the chief U.S. architect of the Dayton Peace Agreement, writes in his memoir, "The shape of the diplomatic landscape will usually reflect the actual balance of forces on the ground. In concrete terms, this meant that as diplomats we could not expect the Serbs to be conciliatory at the negotiating table as long as they had experienced nothing but success on the battlefield."[56]

Mounting press reports of covert U.S. encouragement—particularly in giving a "green light" to the Iranian arms pipeline—would in 1996 be used as political ammunition by President Clinton's domestic opponents, who hoped to use it to tarnish and embarrass the administration in an election year. This culminated in congressional hearings and a lengthy report from what was dubbed "The Iranian Greenlight Subcommittee." This was essentially a political move on the front stage to try to turn the administration's backstage behavior into a political scandal. Mark Danner wrote in anticipation of the scheduled congressional hearings: "In the coming weeks, citizens will watch as that late twentieth century American art form, the full-dress political scandal, enters its decadent phase. Panelled committee rooms, indignant congressmen, stubborn administration witnesses—all the familiar trappings will be on display."[57]

Holbrooke publicly defended the administration's backstage moves: "We were quite aware of the risks" in allowing Iranian arms and trainers into Bosnia "and didn't like them," he said, calling the decision "the least bad of lousy choices." Without the smuggled arms from Iran and elsewhere, Holbrooke bluntly stated, "the Bosnian government would never have survived the winter of 1994–1995 and we never would have gotten to Dayton. It's as simple as that."[58] In his memoir, Holbrooke points out that the covert arms shipments from Iran (and other Islamic countries) to the Sarajevo government were established early on in the war, predating the Clinton administration, "with the clear knowledge of American Embassy and U.N. officials in Zagreb, and were even mentioned in newspaper stories at the time."[59] In reprinted passages from a memo he wrote to Warren Christopher and Anthony Lake shortly before Clinton took office in January 1993, Holbrooke describes these as *not-so-secret* secret shipments."[60] In other words, the backstage action was not so hidden from view on the front stage, yet few at the time wished to draw too much attention to it and create political awkwardness and embarrassment. And ultimately, this proved crucial in bringing the war to an end and lifting the siege of Sarajevo.

CHAPTER 6

AFTERMATH

The clandestine political economy of war left a deep imprint on the postwar reconstruction process in Sarajevo and throughout the region.[1] In the aftermath of the conflict, Bosnia emerged as a regional hub for the smuggling of people and goods, very much exploiting and building on wartime informal trade channels and networks. As was the case during the war years, the ability to transcend ethnic grievances was nowhere more evident than in the underworld of smuggling. While bridging ethnic divisions was the new mantra of many Western-sponsored reconstruction projects,[2] black marketeering was not quite what international donors and officials had in mind. At the same time, the clandestine economy continued to be harnessed to fund competing ethnic nationalist agendas bent on subverting the creation of a viable multi-ethnic state. Thus, criminal and political agendas were closely intertwined.

The Dayton Agreement was part of the problem. It ended the bloodshed, but also created a weak and fragmented state structure (based on two formal entities, the Federation and the Republika Srpska, and ten local cantons) that facilitated various forms of criminal enterprise. Moreover, the massive postwar international presence in Bosnia, especially in Sarajevo, contributed to the clandestine economy by becoming part of the consumer base—most notably and controversially as a core clientele at many of the new brothels employing trafficked women and girls.

The Criminalized Aftermath of War

The postwar challenge in Sarajevo and throughout Bosnia was far more complex than simply recovering from the physical scars of the conflict. The black market dealings and smuggling channels that proved so essential to the Bosnian war effort at the same time contributed to the criminalization of the state, economy, and society—with serious repercussions for reconstruction. In January 2000, the U.S. Special Representative to Bosnia told the Legal Affairs and Human Rights Committee of the Council of Europe: "War-time underground networks have turned into [political] criminal networks involved in massive smuggling, tax evasion, and trafficking in women and stolen cars."[3] In the case of postwar Sarajevo, for example, entrenched political corruption—based on close relationships of loyalty and trust between nationalist politicians, the security apparatus, and criminals that were forged during war—slowed the rebuilding of the city, eroded public trust in government, and impeded political reform efforts.[4] In short, criminalized war problems soon turned into politicized crime problems.

A decade after Dayton, the per capita GDP of Bosnia was still only 50 percent of the average for Southeast Europe and below 50 percent of prewar levels.[5] More than half the country lived below the poverty line, and some 20 percent of the national income was based on the remittances from the hundreds of thousands of Bosnians living abroad (many of whom had been displaced by the war). The official unemployment rate was over 40 percent. But while Bosnia's formal, aboveground economy struggled to recover, the informal, underground economy flourished—generating substantial revenue and employment and becoming part of the basic survival strategy for many in the face of bleak economic prospects. In 2002, the World Bank estimated that the underground economy represented between 50 and 60 percent of Bosnia's GDP.[6] Some critics charged that the World Bank and other international financial institutions were contributing to the problem: at least in the short term, the sweeping market-based reforms they aggressively pushed as a condition for loans and reconstruction aid were contributing to economic dislocations, with some sectors of the population turning to the clandestine economy as a coping mechanism in the absence of an adequate social safety net.[7]

At the same time, such a sizeable clandestine economy presented an obstacle to creating effective state institutions and establishment of the rule of law. Much of the country's imports arrived as contraband across minimally policed borders, providing consumer goods at a discount but enriching smuggling organizations and corrupt border officials and depriving state institutions of desperately needed tax revenue.[8]

Political and economic agendas closely overlapped in the clandestine economy, illustrated in a June 2002 corruption scandal in the Republika Srpska, in which the finance minister and head of the customs service were forced to resign and twenty-seven customs officers were suspended after it was discovered that customs agents had been bribed to drastically undervalue imported goods. The bribes not only lined the pockets of corrupt officials but allegedly also went to help fund the SDS party and the security detail for Karadžić (who went into hiding to avoid extradition to the Hague War Crimes Tribunal).[9] The scandal illustrated that criminal enterprise in postwar Bosnia was "not just a continuation of business by criminal means but an extension of politics by other means."[10] Resources from the clandestine economy were strategically used to empower rival nationalist state building projects, producing state deformation more than state formation or state destruction. As Amra Festić and Adrian Rausche argue, nationalist political parties utilized the clandestine economy— including "financial revenues from diverted public funds, customs and tax fraud, money laundering, and other illegal schemes"—to sustain power and subvert the post-Dayton constitutional order.[11]

The highly fractured nature of the political authority structure created by Dayton contributed to the problem, inviting massive rent-seeking and making coordinated border controls and collection of customs duties extremely cumbersome and difficult. For example, by creating interethnic borders within the country with little inter-entity cooperation on law enforcement matters, Dayton made it possible for law evaders to avoid the reach of the law by simply moving back and forth across entity lines.[12]

Dayton set up a purposefully weak and fragmented state apparatus that would be difficult to maintain without sustained international presence and oversight. Thus, what was initially supposed to be a limited, one-year international administrative intervention after the war turned into an uneasy and repeatedly extended quasi-colonial trusteeship under the supervision of the Office of the High Representative (OHR), headquartered in Sarajevo.[13] While the OHR was often resented locally and criticized internationally,[14] more than a decade after the war it was not entirely clear that the local power brokers actually wanted it to leave—after all, they had done well in the postwar years, and there was little assurance that the highly dysfunctional Dayton political system would be sustainable on its own.

Sarajevo's privileged international status in wartime Bosnia continued into the postwar era, reflected in an influx of foreigners and donations to turn the city into the centerpiece of reconstruction. As was the case during the war, the disproportionate focus on Sarajevo masked a harsher reality in much of the rest of the country. And in Sarajevo itself, all of the outward markings of rebuilding a hip, cosmopolitan European city—trendy cafes and restaurants, fashionable shops, reasonably safe streets, bustling downtown pedestrian walkways, and a popular annual international film festival drawing celebrities from across the globe—provided a deceptive veneer of normalcy.

The most visible side of Sarajevo's reconstruction process— repairing war-scarred buildings, clearing mines from roads, and the presence of thousands of international advisers, monitors, police trainers, NATO peace enforcers, and NGO representatives—was paralleled by a less visible though equally important side, involving smuggling, corruption, and aid diversion. A core objective of the Western-sponsored rebuilding effort was establishing a "free market democracy."[15] The sobering and uncomfortable reality, however, was that the main beneficiaries of the rush to introduce elections shortly after the war were the same nationalist political parties that had been in power before the war, and that the most viable and entrepreneurial market activities were in the illicit sectors of the economy.

The Criminalized New Elite

For most Bosnians in the aftermath of the conflict, participating in the clandestine economy was part of an everyday household survival strategy. But for the privileged few with the necessary political connections, the clandestine economy helped to provide the basis of initial wealth accumulation and an alternative ladder for upward social mobility. Black market entrepreneurs were amongst the leading beneficiaries of the war, emerged from it as a *nouveau riche* criminalized elite, and continued to utilize political connections and smuggling channels built up during wartime. Thus, war not only involved military confrontation but also socioeconomic transformation. As part of this transformation, many who lived on the margins of society experienced a rapid rise in status that would have been inconceivable in peacetime. War, in short, was a highly effective mechanism for criminalized social advancement. As described by one Sarajevo journalist, "The rabble have lined their pockets, and behave as though everything they now claim as their own had belonged to their grandfathers. They don't deserve to be called a 'new class,' since even that requires a certain tradition; but I have no doubt that they will soon become just that. Who asks the wealthiest Americans nowadays what their forefathers did?"[16] A former local commander similarly comments, "We know that there are people, because we know them personally, who didn't have a pair of decent shoes before the war, and today they have 4–5 million marks and entire buildings in their property. On the other hand, there are people who had a lot before the war, and have nothing today."[17]

Key players in the acquisition and distribution of supplies during wartime emerged as a powerful new elite with close ties to the government and ruling political parties. While the creation of new elites was part of the transition process throughout post-Communist Eastern Europe and the former Soviet Union,[18] in Bosnia the process was distinct in that it was dramatically accelerated by and took place under conditions of embargo busting and war profiteering. In contrast to East Central Europe where the old nomenklatura/political elite converted political capital into economic (and sometimes criminal) capital, in the case of Bosnia, criminal capital accumulated during a criminalized war was converted to political capital after the war.[19]

In Sarajevo, the city's social structure was turned upside down: at the same time as many of the most educated professional technocrats fled abroad, many who were previously on the margins of society experienced rapid upward mobility thanks to their wartime roles and political connections. The daily Sarajevo newspaper, *Oslobođenje*, lamented during the siege that "before our eyes, the new class is being born in this war, the class of those who got rich overnight, all former 'marginals.' "[20] A law professor at the University of Sarajevo observes that while new elite formation during transitions elsewhere took years and even decades, in Bosnia it happened overnight, with small fortunes made during the war by simply smuggling in a shipment of cigarettes or fuel.[21] Robert Donia writes that in postwar Sarajevo, "the operators of the organized Sarajevo underground are among the wealthiest and best protected of Sarajevo's new elite."[22]

A legacy of the war was the criminalization of the city, as power and influence shifted during wartime to those most connected in the shadowy world of clandestine transactions.[23] While physical destruction was the most visible legacy of the siege, the city's political and social transformation was the most consequential and long lasting. Profiting from the besieged city's war economy provided the material basis for creating and consolidating the power of new elites closely tied to the dominant nationalist Serb, Croat, and Muslim parties. As Chuck Sudetic describes it, the commercial flows into Sarajevo during the war "helped to create a monied ruling elite—read: mafia—at the top of each of the nationalist parties that dominate Bosnia's political life."[24] These elites shared political power at the start of the war, but lacked wealth. The siege thus provided an effective vehicle for initial capital accumulation, which in turn placed the new elites in the most advantageous position to profit from the peace. This included the privatization of state-owned companies, internationally funded reconstruction projects to rebuild the city, and the general liberalization of the economy promoted by international financial institutions as a condition for continued aid.[25] In this regard, the shady dealings involved in the privatization of the Sarajevo Holiday Inn (which had been made famous by wartime media reporting) came to symbolize the problem of postwar corruption in Bosnia.[26] Similarly, just as wartime humanitarian aid provided opportunities for local diversion and profiteering, so too did the more than $5 billion in international assistance to Bosnia from 1996 to 2003. In 1999 the *New York Times* reported that as much as $1 billion in aid had been stolen.[27]

Moreover, local war profiteers on all sides of the conflict, including many politicians and military commanders, were shielded from pros-

ecution thanks to a sweeping amnesty law. When international officials pushed for an amnesty law for draft dodgers and deserters, local
politicians opportunistically expanded the amnesty to include such
crimes as illegal commerce, tax evasion, and illegal use of humanitarian aid. The time period covered by the amnesty was from January
1991 to late December 1995. The starting date, more than a year before
the outbreak of the Bosnian war, closely corresponded to when the
nationalist political parties (SDA, HDZ, and SDS) gained power.
Some of the politicians who pushed for the amnesty law had investigations and indictments pending against them.[28] Thus, illicit wealth
accumulation during and immediately prior to the siege was effectively legalized. The OHR in Sarajevo, tasked with overseeing the
post-conflict implementation of the Dayton Peace Agreement, did not
block the broadening of the amnesty because it technically did not
violate the Dayton terms.[29]

Some of those who profited the most from the Sarajevo siege recast
themselves as legitimate new elites. For example, the local journalist
Gojko Berić writes:

> Thirty-five year old Alemko Nuhanović passes for one of the
> richest people in Sarajevo today. Alemko is the owner of a score
> of shops in the city, a hotel, a distribution centre and wholesale
> warehouses in Zenica and Tuzla. He is now creating an indus-
> trial meat-processing business. Everyone in Sarajevo knows that
> this war profiteer is backed by someone very powerful; even, it
> is suggested, the General Staff of the (now Bosniak) Army. I re-
> call a scene from Sarajevo during the time of the siege: Alemko,
> in uniform and wearing a gunbelt, standing on a lorry full of
> bread and throwing it to a huge crowd of people scrambling to
> get a loaf or two. Now, when a journalist asks him how he ac-
> quired his wealth, Alemko says, "Allah and the poor know
> that!"[30]

Another prominent Sarajevo example is the Bosnian wartime
Deputy Minister of Defense, Hasan Čengić, who reportedly lived
modestly before the war as an Islamic clergyman but during the war
was appointed as the president's chief foreign fundraiser and weapons
buyer. After the war, Čengić allegedly ran a family-run regional busi-

ness empire. In March 2004, the independent political weekly *Dani* placed Čengić at the top of its list of the ten most influential people in Sarajevo.[31] For highly placed logisticians such as Čengić, the covert nature of importing arms and soliciting clandestine external financial support from Islamic countries (with little or no paper trail) provided an ideal cover for corruption and profiteering.[32] In his wartime diary, retired Bosnian army general Šiber noted that Čengić was nicknamed "the money God."[33]

On the Bosnian Serb side, Momčilo Mandić (a deputy minister for the Bosnian Interior Ministry in Sarajevo shortly before the war, who lived on a moderate civil servant salary) emerged from the war as one of the wealthiest men in the region. In 2003, the U.S. State Department charged that Mandić was "a major funding source for Radovan Karadžić through Mandić's control of an elaborate network of criminal enterprises engaged in embezzlement, business fraud, fictitious loans, and various other activities." This included use of a Mandić-owned bank (Privredna Banka Sarajevo) and a Mandić-owned company (ManCo Oil Company) to support Karadžić and his security detail.[34] Mandić's black market business skills during the war were reportedly most apparent in supplying arms, oil, and other goods. His initial wealth was allegedly created by stealing from the Sarajevo Ministry of the Interior treasury (150,000 German marks) shortly before the war started, was expanded by the wartime robbery of warehouses and manipulation of humanitarian aid, and was then completed with his dominant position in oil smuggling, banking, and fictitious loan schemes in Republika Srpska.[35] Mandić also reportedly removed and later sold thousands of blank Bosnian identity papers, such as driver's licenses and passports (Bosnian identity papers were highly valued during the war because they provided refugee benefits to their carriers and often led to a refugee or immigration visa to a Western country). His political positions (as a Deputy Minister of the Interior and then Justice Minister in the wartime Bosnian Serb leadership) provided an ideal cover for the accumulation of illicit wealth.

With international financing, the Sarajevo-based national court of Bosnia was partly established to investigate and prosecute people such as Čengić and Mandić, but the vast majority of funds were devoted to prosecuting war crimes rather than organized crime cases. While the section of the court devoted to war crimes was lavished with international resources and attention, the less glamorous and more mundane work of the organized crime section took a back seat—even though organized crime cases were easier to prosecute than war crime cases and often involved the same individuals.[36] Frustrating prosecutors was the fact that about 90 percent of the organized crime convictions between late 2003 and mid-2006 were revoked, revised, or modified for the betterment of the defense.[37] Witnesses were reluctant to come forward due to a general lack of public trust and confidence in the legal system. With a low probability of conviction, defendants had little incentive to plea bargain—denying the prosecution a powerful tool commonly used in Western courts.

Many indictments were filed in the national court, but the system was quickly clogged, especially with war crime cases. Although those indicted were no longer untouchable and immune from scrutiny, many of them no doubt calculated that they could simply wait it out—expecting Western governments to eventually lose interest and the international funding for the court to dry up. Indeed, some court personnel in mid-2006 predicted that the United States would in the not-too-distant future simply declare victory and pull out even though the court itself had only been up and running for a few years. As one lawyer at the court put it, "Some small fish will be convicted, which will be given a positive spin as evidence of local 'capacity building.' It's a facade."[38]

Sarajevo as Transit Point for Migrant Smuggling

In the late 1990s Bosnia became a human cargo trans-shipment point for illegal entry into the European Union, with the Sarajevo airport serving as the central connecting hub. Thus, the airport's key wartime smuggling role extended into the postwar period, but this time as a stopover for migrants heading west. The International Organization for Migration estimated that 40,000–50,000 irregular migrants (from countries such as Turkey, Iran, Tunisia, China, Bangladesh, and India) transited through Bosnia in 2000, most of them arriving on regular flights to the Sarajevo airport from Istanbul.[39] The absence of a visa regime with the main countries of origin made it possible for the transiting migrants to simply declare they were tourists, showing a round-trip ticket and sufficient funds to support themselves. After a short stay at local hotels known to be accommodating to migrants (such as the Hotels Alemko, Palais, Orijent, and Sinovi Drine), smugglers would reportedly arrange ground transportation toward the Croatian border and on to Western Europe.[40]

Bosnia's new niche in the migrant smuggling business was partly a legacy of the war. For instance, the routing of thousands of Iranian migrants through the Sarajevo airport in the immediate years after the war was a direct consequence of the close wartime ties between Bosnia and Iran.[41] Until December 2000 Iranian passport holders did not need a visa to enter Bosnia because the Sarajevo government was grateful to Iran for its assistance during the war. Chartered flights from Tehran regularly landed at the Sarajevo airport and returned virtually empty. For instance, in the first eleven months of 2000, more than 12,000 Iranians arrived at Sarajevo airport, but only about 1,000 left via the airport. Pressed by Western officials, the Bosnian government finally imposed a visa requirement on Iranians at the end of the year.[42] The number of "tourists" arriving in Bosnia from Iran subsequently plummeted.

The Sarajevo airport nevertheless continued to serve as a stepping-stone for smuggling migrants into Western Europe.[43] As one *BBC News* report described the scene at the airport in April 2001: "Large batches of young men from Turkey and Tunisia appear several times weekly in the arrivals hall of Sarajevo Airport, nervous and shuffling, their futures in the less-than-reliable hands of people-smuggling gangs who whisk them away into taxis."[44] Ian Johnston, a British police officer working with the State Border Service at the Sarajevo airport, acknowledged in early 2001 that "on the average flight, 90 percent of the passengers are not here as genuine tourists."[45]

Introducing a visa requirement for Turkish citizens was contemplated but rejected after the proposal was opposed by the Ankara government.[46] There were 14,083 Turkish citizens (predominantly Turkish Kurds) who arrived in Bosnia via the Sarajevo airport in 2000, but only 4,117 of the passengers returned. This prompted suspicions that the airport was being used as a way station for those seeking clandestine entry to the EU. Following more intensive scrutiny of travelers arriving in Sarajevo, Air Bosna (the national Bosnian airline) introduced a stopover at the Tuzla airport for Sarajevo-bound flights from Turkey. This, in turn, provoked accusations by the UN that the airline was deliberately aiding migrant smuggling. "We have done nothing illegal," protested the director of Air Bosna, Omer Kulić. "When we introduced landings in Tuzla, we were simply responding to market demands." Pressured by the UN, the Tuzla landings were subsequently shut down, and the number of monthly passengers from Turkey dropped sharply, from 1,500 in early 2001 to only 398 in August of that year.[47]

The UN mission in Sarajevo claimed in January 2001 that the Bosnia route was taken by about 10 percent of the estimated 500,000 smuggled migrants entering Western Europe. Werner Blatter, the UN official responsible for refugee movements in Sarajevo, tried to put a positive spin on the situation, arguing that Bosnia's new status as a migrant smuggling hub was a sign of the country's growing attractiveness and stability: "Six years ago [during the war], no one in their right mind would have come through here."[48]

Sex Trafficking and Peacekeeping

Shortly after the end of the war, Bosnia also became a major destination for the trafficking of women and girls to work in the many brothels springing up across the country—with the large international presence providing a core part of the customer base.[49] In the wake of Dayton, thousands of peacekeepers, UN staff, private contractors, and NGO personnel arrived in Bosnia—with as many as 20,000 foreigners in Sarajevo alone. This influx of "internationals" not only contributed to the legal economy (for example, by renting apartments and hiring local staff and translators) but also to the illegal economy—including as a core clientele for the brothels that were opening up across the country.[50] A senior official with the UN High Commission for Human Rights in Sarajevo estimated that foreigners made up about 30 percent of the brothel customers, but were the source of approximately 70 percent of the brothel revenue since they spent more than locals.[51]

Trafficking patterns in Bosnia followed peacekeeper deployment patterns. As Sarah Mendelson notes, "Many experts point to the locations and names of the bars as evidence that traffickers not only target but also respond to the demand of international peacekeepers. While SFOR [stabilization force, NATO's peacekeeping force] was stationed in Bosnia, activists claimed that one could drive through Bosnia and know which international contingent had responsibility for the region by the names on the brothels."[52] Many of the women and girls working in the brothels were trafficked into the country for forced prostitution from Eastern Europe and the former Soviet Union.[53] By October 2002, the UN Mission in Bosnia suspected 227 nightclubs and bars of involvement in trafficking. The proliferation of brothels corresponded closely with the arrival of peacekeepers, and their apparent decline similarly corresponded with the departure of many peacekeepers in 2003.[54]

A number of investigative reports indicate that local police were directly and indirectly complicit in the sex trafficking and brothel business—for example, as guards, clients, informants, and partial owners of the brothels.[55] Foreign police officers, serving as monitors with the International Police Task Force (IPTF), were reportedly part of the clientele. In one case, David Lamb, a former senior IPTF human rights officer, described the delivery of women to IPTF monitors in Sarajevo:

> There were allegations from victims that they were taken to an apartment where the Pakistani [IPTF monitors] lived and had to give sexual services to them [in January 2001]. One time a Pakistani monitor drove [two] trafficked women in a U.N. car to a hotel in Sarajevo and provided them to the "chief" of the Pakistani contingent. The women called him the chief. . . . At the time of the allegations, the senior Pakistani officer was in Sarajevo and served as the chief of the internal investigations unit.[56]

One U.S. Special Forces officer responded when asked if he would share information with the IPTF: "They were the best customers. It was just common . . . knowledge. . . . You knew which houses were the brothels and it was pretty common to see an IPTF or someone else in the U.N. community at these places."[57] One American IPTF officer allegedly even bought a woman from a Sarajevo brothel for 6,000 German marks or less. According to IPTF human rights monitor Kathryn Bolkovac, "One [U.S.] monitor bought a woman in Ilidža. He was repatriated. He was duty officer with me and told me about the woman he bought. . . . He admitted to me that he did this. He had her for a few months at least."[58] Bolkovac was fired by Dyncorp, the U.S. company contracted to support and supply U.S. military and civilian police personnel in Bosnia. She sued the company, claiming that she was fired for blowing the whistle on trafficking.[59]

Bolkovac was not the only person implicating Dyncorp personnel in trafficking. A report by the Criminal Investigation Division (CID) of the U.S. Army noted that a source had notified CID "that several U.S. government contractors [approximately five] were involved in white slavery. Sources stated that several members of Dyncorp, who live off base, purchased women from local brothels and had them live in their residences for sexual and domestic purposes. Source stated that the individuals purchased the women from local 'mafia' and when tired of the women would sell them back."[60] Dyncorp sent home five employees at SFOR installations in 1999 after accusations surfaced that they were involved in purchasing women. Ben Johnson, a former Dyncorp employee, testified that the company tolerated and overlooked the buying of trafficked women, and named eight Dyncorp workers who he claimed had admitted purchasing women and girls. Johnson made these charges in a formal statement on file with CID in Bosnia. Johnson also stated in testimony before the U.S. Congress in April 2002 that Dyncorp employees would "even take [the trafficked females] on [to] locked-down military installations because the [UN] vans will not get searched if you drive them on post."[61] Dyncorp laid Johnson off, stating in the official letter of discharge that Johnson had brought "discredit to the Company and the U.S. Army."[62]

Bosnian law enforcement authorities complained to Human Rights Watch investigators that they had no authority to go after NATO contractors, given their immunity from arrest, detention, and prosecution (part of a much larger problem of insufficient accountability of international actors in Bosnia).[63] As one local police officer explained in March 2001: "When we find a foreigner is involved, this is the biggest problem for us. We can't do anything against them—they are above the law. On the video [filmed outside the nightclubs], the number plates [have the letters] CP. These are the contractors' jeeps. I'd like someone to help with this. You can't do anything about this. If we could prioritize, this is one of our main problems."[64]

Sex trafficking and the proliferation of brothels went largely unnoticed until the late 1990s. As a former Human Rights Watch investigator notes, until the local press began to report on the problem in early 1999 the issue remained "unacknowledged, unreported, and unnamed."[65] As the trafficking issue became increasingly reported on in the media—and therefore increasingly embarrassing for international officials in Bosnia—the UN's special representative in Bosnia, Jacques Paul Klein, announced tough new rules and enforcement initiatives, including the creation of the Special Trafficking Operation Program (STOP), a specialized anti-trafficking unit.[66] One observer notes: "The STOP teams typically smashed down the door of a brothel, entered with great flourish (on occasion, with television cameras in tow), and then asked if the females present had been trafficked."[67] Some eighty raids during the last three months of 2002 bordered on the theatrical, with STOP teams targeting the same bars and picking up and interviewing the same women, over and over again.[68] One official of the Organization for Security and Cooperation in Europe (OSCE) characterized STOP as "a great PR exercise. It looked like the UN was fighting trafficking."[69]

In one highly touted STOP raid, UN officials boasted that 177 women had been "liberated," and applauded Bosnian law enforcement cooperation. Klein proclaimed that the operation "clearly demonstrates to all of us that police training has paid off; professionalism has been enhanced; and the ability to work constructively together, regardless of entity or ethnic origin, is possible." Yet as reported by Human Rights Watch, all but thirteen of the "rescued" women simply vanished shortly after the raids, and local NGO experts claimed many of them were back at the brothels.[70] Nevertheless, the high-profile raids were a public relations success story for Klein, generating positive media coverage. At the same time, the raids drove the trafficking problem further backstage—and therefore more out of public sight and the media eye.

One perverse and unintended consequence of the STOP raids was to give corrupt police even more power to abuse their positions. For instance, one local law enforcement officer, who served as the area's STOP team leader, apparently tipped off brothel owners of impending raids in exchange for free sexual services. Similarly, according to Celhia de Lavarene, the director of STOP, the chief of police in Kiseljak tipped off brothel owners in exchange for free sex: "We interviewed a lot of women and they told us that the chief of police goes to the bars and warns the owners."[71]

A public scandal broke out in the fall of 2000 when it was revealed that some of the IPTF monitors participating in the raids had been customers at one of the targeted brothels. On November 14, 2000, twenty-five IPTF monitors, backed up by peacekeeping troops, raided three brothels. Thirty-five women and girls were released who stated they had been trafficked for forced prostitution. The women were then driven to Sarajevo to be interviewed by UN officials. One official who interviewed them later told Human Rights Watch: "SFOR and IPTF brought the girls to Sarajevo, and then the girls pointed out that the guys driving them had been their clients." One of the women indicated to IPTF investigators that the men "were in white cars with U.N. on it."[72] In the ensuing scandal, six IPTF monitors were sent back home.

Quickly repatriating international personnel was standard operating procedure for the UN. Rapid repatriation also made it impossible for the accused to serve as witnesses in investigations. Klein publicly pledged to hold international personnel accountable, but in practice, investigations were rarely pursued very far or deep. In one case, an internal affairs officer told his supervisor that he had a "shovel" and requested instructions on "how deep to dig." The response was to "only scratch the surface."[73]

The UN Mission in Bosnia, it seemed, was more concerned about its public image than about following through with investigations of abuses. For instance, according to Human Right Watch, the UN accepted the resignations or repatriated only those IPTF monitors whose names were disclosed in local media reports.[74] A number of analysts commented on the UN's muted response to allegations of UN personnel involvement in trafficking-related crimes, and suggest that this partly reflected fear that public scandals and embarrassments would undermine the ability of the UN to attract and maintain peace-keeping recruits.[75]

The Arizona Market: Peace through Illicit Trade?

Bosnia's postwar clandestine economy involved (indeed depended on) substantial cross-ethnic collaboration. As discussed earlier, dense interethnic social ties in prewar Bosnia (including criminal ties) facili-

tated black marketeering across ethnically divided frontlines in wartime. And in the immediate postwar era, the ability to overcome ethnic
divides was arguably nowhere more advanced than in the clandestine
economy.

The most impressive evidence of this was Bosnia's "Arizona Market," an expansive open-air black market bazaar that emerged in the
spring of 1996 near the headquarters of some 4,000 peacekeeping
troops and the "Colorado" and "Las Vegas" brothels. A few hours
drive from Sarajevo in northeast Bosnia, the sprawling market sprung
up in an area that once was a NATO-enforced checkpoint and "zone
of separation" between Serb, Muslim, and Croat forces. As described
by a spokesperson for the Brčko District OHR office, "It was a safe
spot so locals themselves began to exchange cows and other goods."[76]
Tomo Tomšić, a market landowner, explained the initial impetus: "If
we hadn't traded with each other, we would have starved, and it was
easier to be involved in a black market than to plow a field."[77]

By 1999, as many as 25,000 shoppers were visiting the Arizona
Market on a single weekend, with the state losing an estimated $30
million in tax revenue every year from goods sold at the market.[78] It
also reportedly became a hub for bringing in illegal migrants, prostitutes, and drugs from Asia and the former Soviet bloc to Western Europe.[79] By late 2000 it had mushroomed into a complex of about 2,000
plywood and steel shacks spread out over some thirty-five acres.
About 20,000 people owing their livelihoods to the Arizona Market
(named for NATO's designation of an adjacent highway). The largest
building at the market was the "Acapulco Night Club," housing some
forty prostitutes from Moldova, Ukraine, and Romania (and frequented by nearby U.S. and Russian peacekeepers).[80]

A large sign erected in the midst of the Arizona Market read: "Our
thanks to the U.S. Army for supporting the development of this market."[81] The Pentagon provided some $40,000 of the start-up costs. As
retired Major General William Nash explains:

> We cleared a side of the road, took a few mines away and put
> some gravel down and allowed these shacks to be built to start
> some commerce, and the reason the commerce was there was
> because it was near a checkpoint so the area was secure so Serbs,
> Croats and Bosniacs could all come and do business without

fear of ethnic violence from their respective police forces or armed forces because it was in the zone of separation and guarded by the NATO force, Americans. . . . Over the years the Arizona Market has had an up and down existence with some issues of black marketing, trafficking in literally drugs, sex, and rock and roll.[82]

Colonel Greg Fontenot, the NATO force brigade commander for the northeastern section of Bosnia, recalls that his troops not only encouraged the development of the Arizona Market, but provided some of the initial protection: "As the market grew, our troops had to take steps to prevent shakedowns by nearby police and to stop a string of car-jackings in the area." Meanwhile, he acknowledges, "we were becoming aware that people were selling pirated CDs and jackets, and there seemed to be some even more unsavory kinds of commerce." As he explained it, "unregulated capitalism is a pretty rude sort of activity."[83] Fontenot notes that he "would walk through the market at least once a day, and our Civil Affairs troops were also there, in uniform, as well as at the nearby checkpoint. . . . But we did not regulate what was sold in the market and we stayed out of most day-to-day decisions."[84] When the Bosnian government at one point dispatched thirty police to take control of the Arizona Market, they were blocked by NATO troops and armored vehicles and returned to Sarajevo.[85]

International officials at first enthusiastically promoted the Arizona Market as a way to generate local entrepreneurship, economic revival, and cross-ethnic interaction. "The market was encouraged," explains Michael Montgomery of the Brčko District office of the OHR. "One way to move forward in the post war years was to use business as a foundation. To use an American phrase, the market was in 'everyone's interest.' "[86] A USAID study reached a similarly upbeat conclusion: "At the Arizona market, stall owners and patrons come from all of Bosnia's ethnic groups and even cross borders from neighboring Croatia and Serbia to sell goods and find deals. . . . On a daily basis, Bosniaks [Muslims], Serbs, and Croats interact, socialize, exchange information and sometimes discover how similar they really are."[87]

The Arizona Market was indeed a business success story (so much so that it was featured in a Harvard Business School case study),[88] but not quite in the way international officials had in mind. The bustling market turned into a smuggler's paradise, where one could find among other, common-use goods, untaxed cigarettes and alcohol, illegal drugs, stolen cars, and guns. As described in one press report, at the Arizona Market "locals demonstrate the sort of disregard for the forces of law and order (and taxation and regulation) that would have made the pioneers of the American West proud. . . . Arizona has become a byword not just for business but also for crime."[89]

The Arizona Market soon became an embarrassing symbol of postwar lawlessness and the failure to regulate the hundreds of border crossings into Bosnia. In 1999, the UN's Jacques Klein charged that the market was run by hardliners promoting ethnic division, and he pushed (unsuccessfully) to have the entire area bulldozed.[90] In 2001, High Representative Wolfgang Petrisch similarly argued that the market was a vice that should be eradicated.[91] Other international officials, however, called for a more tolerant attitude. Acknowledging that the Arizona Market had certain problems, the American NATO force colonel in charge of the area pointed out that Times Square in New York City—with its own pimps and prostitutes—was also far from perfect.[92]

Trying to put a positive spin on the situation, some observers depicted the Arizona Market as a successful example of interethnic cooperation, pointing to the fact that Serbs, Croats, and Muslims mingle peacefully through commercial exchange on what once was bitterly contested terrain. One area of the market was in the Muslim-Croat Federation, and the other was in the Republika Srpska. Shortly after the war ended, an American military commander in the area hailed the market as a model of tolerance and reconciliation.[93] Similarly, Major Chris Riley, the local NATO spokesperson, defended the market, arguing that "anything that normalizes relations is valuable, and trade is as normal as it gets."[94] One seller at the market, an ex-soldier, had a somewhat different perspective: "I am quite ready to sell brandy to Serbs in the morning and shoot them in the afternoon," adding, "There were plenty of people who did this during the war."[95]

Individual fortunes were made through cross-ethnic collaboration in keeping the Arizona Market supplied. For example, Bosnian Muslim Sadinet ("Sido") Karić was nicknamed the Arizona Market's "smuggling king," specializing in the illegal importation of textiles from Turkey and Hungary. Transcending ethnic divisions, his business dealings were reportedly made possible by political connections spanning across the Bosnian Federation, the Republika Srpska, Serbia, Bulgaria, and Turkey. Karić and some of his associates were arrested in 2003 on smuggling and money laundering charges as part of a broader law enforcement operation in Bosnia.[96] But even as the contraband trade at the Arizona Market was based on cross-ethnic cooperation, investigators found that revenue generated by the market was also used to fund ethnic nationalist causes.[97] Thus, even as international officials optimistically promoted the classic liberal economic argument that peace could be fostered through trade and economic interdependence, the jury was still out on whether durable peace could also be sustained through illegal trade and a clandestine form of economic interdependence.

Unable or unwilling to shut the Arizona Market down, the OHR launched an ambitious initiative to try to clean up and regulate it. By early 2002, all 2,500 stalls and shops were licensed and had to pay taxes. An Italian company, Italproject, was hired to transform the Arizona Market into a modern shopping center and run it for twenty years—representing Bosnia's single largest foreign investment (about $125 million). This included adding infrastructure such as running water and a sewage system. The brothels, which had drawn media attention and given the place a reputation as a center for prostitution and sex trafficking, were shut down with much fanfare.[98]

But while stall owners were registered and paying taxes and criminal activities were much less visible, buying and selling smuggled goods (brought in across Bosnia's highly porous borders)[99] remained part of the lifeblood of the market. The Arizona Market had matured without entirely erasing its shadier side. As explained by Jan-Eric Boo, a Swede serving as the European Union's Advisor for Major Organized Crime in the Brčko District Police: "This place has two faces: one good, legal part, providing work and income to the District; and another one, darker, which lies under the surface, with criminal activities. We are hoping to support a good cause and to make it win over a dark one."[100] In this sense, the Arizona Market—its peculiar development and multiple faces—represented a microcosm of the political economy of postwar Bosnia and international efforts to engineer its transformation.

International interest and engagement in Bosnia and the wider region has shifted during the past decade from war-fighting to crime-fighting concerns. Indeed, it has become one of the few issues sustaining Western attention, turning policing initiatives such as tighter border controls and anti-trafficking campaigns into a key funding mechanism.[101] International officials have increasingly blamed crime and corruption for obstructing reforms and undermining the reconstruction process and have pushed new initiatives to curb them. Yet it is highly problematic and much too convenient to simplistically label Bosnia (and the western Balkans more broadly) as an "organized crime problem" that can be handled narrowly and one-dimensionally through more aggressive crime control measures. Because of its sheer size, diversity, and highly politicized nature, the clandestine economy defies simple definitions and prescriptions. Rather than simply reinforcing the common tendency to either condemn or ignore the clandestine economy and its relationship to post-conflict reconstruction, what is needed is greater recognition and understanding of its considerable complexity, ambiguity, and embedment within larger political and economic problems in the aftermath of war.

CHAPTER **7**

EXTENSIONS

Much can be learned about the Sarajevo siege experience and its broader relevance by comparing and contrasting it to other cases across time and place. Although a detailed account is beyond the scope of this book, some brief sketches provide useful comparative insights, revealing substantial variation in levels of internationalization, degrees of permeability, and ultimate outcome. For instance, a particularly important difference between Sarajevo and the other besieged Bosnian enclaves was that places such as Srebrenica were far more difficult to access, inhibiting substantial international presence and attention. With Sarajevo in the spotlight on center stage, the other enclaves were often treated as sideshows, profoundly shaping local siege dynamics. Extending the analysis to historical and contemporary siege patterns beyond Bosnia, from Leningrad in World War II to Grozny and Falluja in more recent years, offers further analytical leverage. These sub-national and cross-national comparative cases illustrate what Sarajevo could have become but did not. Srebrenica was massacred, Leningrad was starved, Grozny was leveled, and Falluja was turned into a free-fire zone. How and why did Sarajevo avoid a similar fate? Examining these comparative cases helps to provide an answer.

Srebrenica

Outside of Sarajevo, the Bosnian towns and villages that withstood the initial Serb military offensive in the spring of 1992 developed their own distinct siege dynamics and war economies, powerfully conditioned and constrained by geographic circumstances, accessibility, and international attention. As in Sarajevo, none of the other besieged enclaves (designated by the UN as "safe areas" in 1993 even though they were never safe) survived on humanitarian aid alone,[1] thus necessitating more informal supply mechanisms—including varying amounts of smuggling and cross-frontline trading.[2] In the case of the eastern enclave of Srebrenica, this helped the population stubbornly endure years of siege conditions but was not enough to avoid being brutally sacked. While Sarajevo became militarily stronger over time, the opposite was true in Srebrenica,[3] where arms smuggling remained anemic, the small UNPROFOR contingent succeeded in partly disarming the town, and international attention and concern never added up to a credible military deterrent.

An exhaustive independent investigative report on Srebrenica mandated by the Dutch parliament described the encircled enclave as a "large prison" or a "large concentration camp."[4] Sporadically accessed by humanitarian aid convoys (only three UNHCR convoys managed to reach Srebrenica during the first year of the war), the town's desperate residents—more than 80 percent of them refugees—resorted to other survival measures. This included the so-called *Torbari* (the "bag people") raiding parties that broke through the thinly policed siege lines to steal food and other supplies from nearby Serb villages. These swarming hit-and-run operations, involving thousands of hungry Muslim refugees, terrorized and massacred Serb civilians and burned down buildings.[5] The plundering also reportedly infuriated Bosnian Serb leaders, particularly General Ratko Mladić, which many have suggested created a grudge and vendetta that he used as a pretext to not only overrun the town but kill thousands of its inhabitants late in the war. With a limited international presence and being largely inaccessible to foreign television crews,[6] the minimally defended enclave was particularly vulnerable. Not unlike in Sarajevo, its residents were doubly trapped—first by the besieging Serbs, and second by their own municipal authorities who arrested those caught trying to sneak through Serb-held territory to Tuzla and elsewhere.[7]

Srebrenica would have been in even more desperate shape without a trickle of black market goods, much of which arrived via smuggling from the Tuzla area to the north and Žepa to the south. UNPROFOR observation posts witnessed significant amounts of smuggling between Srebrenica and Žepa.[8] Naser Orić, the Bosnian army commander in Srebrenica, noted the Žepa-Srebrenica smuggling connection in an interview: "Smuggling, there was some. . . . There were six or seven thousand inhabitants of Žepa, and they reported three times as many, and that is how they had food [from humanitarian supplies]. Then they would sell the surplus." Orić also pointed to the role of UNPROFOR: "From the Dutch [Srebrenica-based UNPROFOR], you couldn't buy anything, not a gramme of salt. But the Ukrainians [Žepa-based UNPROFOR] were such that they would sell everything. They would only keep their slippers if necessary."[9]

Indeed, selling off their own supplies on the black market sometimes created awkward and tense situations for the Ukrainian UNPROFOR soldiers in Žepa. At one point they contacted their battalion base in Sarajevo, claiming that they had exhausted their supplies. Their superiors replied by advising them to go buy them back from the Bosnians.[10] The Ukrainians were allegedly a key source for a wide variety of goods, ranging from toothpaste and razor blades to food, coffee, and cigarettes. Those local smugglers making the nightly trek between Žepa and Srebrenica strapped containers with thirty liters of fuel to their backs; others loaded the containers on horses.[11]

The Bosnian Serb forces surrounding Srebrenica sometimes tolerated the smugglers, especially those carrying small amounts of supplies on their backs (many were burden bearers drawn from Orić's military work brigades), but as the use of horses became more common the smugglers were often ambushed. These Serb ambushes would, in turn, reduce supply and increase black market prices—leading the Dutch Srebrenica report investigators to suspect possible collusion between profiteers in the enclave and the besieging Serbs. Dutch UNPROFOR troops also attempted to interdict smugglers arriving from Žepa because the smuggled items included weapons and ammunition (and as a UN-designated "safe area" in 1993, Srebrenica was officially supposed to be demilitarized).[12]

The black market role of Žepa's Ukrainian "Blue Helmets" is noted in numerous accounts. This reportedly included serving as a convenient intermediary for trading between the besiegers and the besieged. For example, the Dutch Srebrenica report observes, "Despite the tremendous restrictions in freedom of movement, there was a constant stream of goods, primarily between Srebrenica and Žepa where the Ukrainian battalion acted as the link in the trade between Serbs outside and the Muslims inside the enclave."[13] Thus, as in Sarajevo, the Ukrainian contingent of UNPROFOR was a major black market player—but their location in Žepa presented a significant geographic hurdle for Srebrenica's smugglers.

There was also reportedly some direct trading across the frontlines in Srebrenica, often between people who knew each other before the war. According to the Dutch Srebrenica report, "On the frontlines 'unofficial' contacts between Serbs and local Muslims took place on a regular basis," and that this "occasionally led to direct trading activities with the Bosnian Serbs."[14] This was particularly evident in the southern end of the enclave, where the "Serbs there earned a great deal of money by supplying goods to Muslim traders." Observing such dealings apparently added to the growing cynicism, hostility, and sense of detachment among the Dutch UNPROFOR troops: "It was incomprehensible for them that parties traded with each other during the day only to use the items they had traded to go after each others' blood in the evening and at night."[15]

Authorities on all sides officially imposed penalties for "trading with the enemy," but the dramatic markup in black market prices for items such as salt, coffee, and oil provided a powerful incentive to engage in the risky trade.[16] This was reportedly true not only for local smugglers but also humanitarian aid convoy drivers, who allegedly snuck in high value items to sell at inflated black market prices.[17] As in Sarajevo, tobacco was a particularly prized commodity, with prices in Srebrenica even higher than in the capital.[18] And as in Sarajevo, tobacco also served as a form of barter currency. Although the German mark was the favored form of hard currency, the exchange value of food and other items was reportedly based on cigarettes.[19]

Sustaining Srebrenica's black market necessitated smuggling money into the enclave, which was done through a variety of mechanisms. According to the Dutch Srebrenica report, aid workers and

UNPROFOR soldiers were sometimes asked, while back at home on leave, to return with money designated for certain Srebrenica residents. Reportedly, this often involved large amounts of cash, even reaching more than 100,000 German marks, which could be hidden, for instance, in food packages and other items. Cash smugglers were typically paid a certain percentage for their services.[20]

Smuggling and black marketeering helped to sustain Srebrenica under dire conditions, but as in Sarajevo it was also a source of abuse, corruption, and profiteering that increasingly alienated the local population. "In a sign of cynicism and despair," noted one rare press report in January 1994, "people here have renamed a main road Profiteers' Street, in recognition that black marketers control much of life here."[21] In a 1995 letter to Bosnian general Delić, Bosnian general Jašarević wrote:

> The increasing mistrust felt by the citizens of Srebrenica for the civilian and military leadership was encouraged by the unequal allocation and manipulation of goods provided by humanitarian aid. Naser Orić and municipal officials Osman Suljić, Adem Salihović, and Hamdija Fejzić were linked to this. There is information indicating that these men smuggled humanitarian aid, weapons, oil, et cetera, and that they collaborated with members of UNPROFOR and even with the aggressor in their smuggling activities.[22]

Discrepancies in access to scarce aid and other supplies was sometimes glaring. A Dutch colonel posted in Srebrenica recalled: "Once I attended a banquet at the mayor's place that was like a four or five-star banquet while the rest of the population was really suffering."[23] Corruption and profiteering not only alienated Srebrenica's civilian residents but also contributed to the souring of relations between the Dutch UNPROFOR battalion and local leaders, in particular, the military commander Naser Orić. William Shawcross writes that "the Dutch saw Naser Orić, the Muslim leader of Srebrenica, as a murderous gangster who terrorized the refugees and profited greatly from the horror of the enclave—and from the Western aid that was delivered."[24] Orić was equally unpopular with some of the international aid agencies in Srebrenica. A staff member of the NGO Médecins Sans

Frontières (Doctors Without Borders) wrote in March 1994: "The king of the place is without competition Commander Naser [Orić]. . . . Without his official consent, nothing can be done in this town! . . . He controls the black market, the prostitution and Opština [the municipal authorities]."[25]

Part of Orić's power allegedly derived from control over the distribution of humanitarian supplies. This was aided by the fact that the UNHCR, which had no Srebrenica-based personnel during much of the war, had even less influence over local distribution than it did in Sarajevo. As in Sarajevo, skimming aid and falsely inflating the number of recipients helped to both feed soldiers and supply the black market.[26] The municipal authorities also reportedly attempted to control the selection of local staff working for international aid agencies, creating a crisis in relations that eventually prompted the majority of the agencies to substantially scale back their Srebrenica-based operations.[27]

Orić (a former policeman, bouncer, and bodyguard of Slobodan Milošević) and his men (some of whom had prewar criminal records)[28] ruled Srebrenica with an iron fist, filling the power vacuum created when the majority of the town's prewar political and economic elites fled to escape the fighting. The large influx of refugees, the miserable siege conditions, and the extreme scarcity of supplies created a fertile environment for corruption and abuse of power. In this regard, Srebrenica experienced an internal siege not unlike the "siege within the siege" in Sarajevo.

At the same time, Orić was widely respected and praised for his defense efforts, especially in the first phase of the war when he led the effort to push out Serb forces and create a viable military unit out of a rag-tag crew of local recruits. The Canadian UNPROFOR unit commander told the Dutch Srebrenica report investigators that Orić was an exceptional military leader, and that Orić took good care of Srebrenica's residents.[29] Such mixed descriptions of Orić—ruthless warlord and Robin Hood figure—mirror some of the characterizations of Sarajevo's criminal defenders. The main difference, however, is that in Sarajevo, local characters such as Juka and Caco were only in charge of sections of the siege lines in the initial phases of the war, whereas in Srebrenica, Orić and his men were in charge of the entire town throughout the war.

The Bosnian Serb army further tightened its stranglehold on Srebrenica from mid-February 1995 on, so much so that the siege was extended to include blocking supplies to UNPROFOR. The Dutch UNPROFOR commander warned that the humanitarian situation was rapidly deteriorating, even noting that "smuggling routes have been closed."[30] This observation seems to acknowledge the importance of smuggling in sustaining the enclave, and that the Serb forces had the capacity and will to shut this informal survival mechanism down.

When Srebrenica fell in early July 1995, Orić and his closest commanders had already left the enclave months earlier on orders from the Bosnian army (for "consultation and training"). There has been widespread speculation in the Bosnian press that the Sarajevo government made a strategic decision to sacrifice Srebrenica, a town that was never considered militarily viable.[31] Similar speculation regarding deliberate abandonment of Srebrenica has surrounded UN and Western government decision making, particularly the decision to turn down repeated Dutch UNPROFOR requests for NATO air strikes to repel the Serb military offensive.[32] Some 2,000 Serbs, backed by armor and artillery, overran the largely undefended town. A small quantity of anti-tank missiles had been smuggled in, but the defenders apparently did not know how to use them. The town's defenses were further undermined by the fact that UNPROFOR routinely confiscated any weapons it came across as part of a larger effort to disarm UN-designated "safe areas."[33] As the Serb forces advanced, the Dutch UN peacekeepers sat on the sidelines, naively believing the Serb assurances that Srebrenica's residents would not be harmed.

Following the sacking of Srebrenica, some of the Serb soldiers wore UN helmets and drove around in UN vehicles stolen from the Dutch to lure escaping residents into ambushes.[34] In a matter of days, over 7,000 men and boys were killed—by far the worst massacre of the war. As information about the magnitude of the deaths began to spread—aided by satellite images of mass graves—the shock and horror captured the world's attention, briefly drawing the spotlight away from Sarajevo. Only after it fell was Srebrenica no longer the obscure enclave it had been throughout much of the war. But Sarajevo was ultimately a beneficiary: the scale of Serb atrocities in Srebrenica strengthened international resolve to intervene more forcefully later that summer in the form of NATO air strikes around the capital city.

When the journalist Chuck Sudetic later asked Yasushi Akashi (the UN Special Representative for the Former Yugoslavia) whether he and General Bernard Janvier (UN force commander in the Former Yugoslavia) had taken into account repeated Serb warnings that they had a vendetta against Srebrenica's Muslim men, Akashi replied that this had never crossed their mind. Sudetic writes, "As I got up to leave, he [Akashi] volunteered an insight into his feelings about Srebrenica and perhaps why the vendetta did not enter into their thinking. 'Oh, those men of Srebrenica,' he said, 'such thieves, such a black market, such a mafia.' "[35] Thus, it seems that the criminalization of Srebrenica also facilitated its dehumanization in the eyes of at least some key UN decision makers.

Orić moved to Tuzla after the war, where his business interests included running a nightclub and a riverfront restaurant. Orić discouraged critical scrutiny: in 1998, a Tuzla lawyer criticized Orić in public and was subsequently kidnapped and beaten by Orić's men. As one municipal official put it, Orić "had some unpleasant enforcers," including some "who you wouldn't want to meet on a dark night."[36] In August 1998, after Orić's name appeared on a U.S. list of local organized crime leaders, police stopped Orić and his pet tiger following a meeting in Mostar with Ismet "Ćelo" Bajramović and others. The police reportedly found Orić in possession of a stolen jeep and unlicensed weapons.[37] In April 2003, Orić was arrested by NATO troops in Tuzla and transferred to the War Crimes Tribunal in The Hague. Having served his time in detention while awaiting trial, Orić was released as soon as the proceedings ended in the summer of 2006 (most of the charges were dismissed). On his return to Bosnia, Orić received a hero's welcome at the Sarajevo airport—greeted by thousands of well-wishers, including Ćelo and his entourage.[38]

Leningrad

The highly internationalized and criminalized siege of Sarajevo offers a striking contrast to classic siege-style warfare associated with traditional military engagements. This is illustrated by briefly looking at the nearly three-year siege of Leningrad by German forces during World War II, which took place in a radically different world-historical context lacking anything resembling CNN and satellite dishes, UN "Blue Helmets," and NGO aid workers. Leningrad was part of a global war, but the siege itself was not globalized. Sarajevo, in contrast, was part of a local and regional war but the siege itself was the most globalized in history.

In contrast to Sarajevo, the war economy in Leningrad was a more mobilized command economy, involving greater regulation and centralization. The siege had a criminalized dimension, but this was far less consequential for overall siege dynamics than in Sarajevo. For example, the besieged city in 1941–44 developed a localized trade in black market goods, concentrated in a marketplace called Haymarket, which had been a center of illegal trade and prostitution in the pre-Bolshevik period. The post-revolution communist government had cracked down on the illicit market, though it still operated under close official scrutiny. When the German blockade on the city in September 1941 drastically curtailed supplies, Haymarket once again became a center of economic exchange. By the first winter of the siege, "it became the liveliest place in Leningrad."[39] Those who ran the market became local war profiteers, as desperate families offered valuables such as Bekker pianos for bread or dog meat.[40] In this regard, Haymarket played a role not unlike that of the Markale marketplace in central Sarajevo.

Leningrad, like Sarajevo, also experienced serious problems of theft, looting, and abuse and manipulation of ration cards.[41] In both places, individuals with privileged access to supplies, such as warehouse workers, were in a particularly tempting position to engage in skimming and diversion. But while these sorts of crimes were prevalent in both cities, crime control was much harsher in Leningrad—including frequent use of the death penalty for crimes such as stealing ration cards.[42]

In dramatic contrast to Sarajevo, black market entrepreneurs in Leningrad did not have cross-frontline networks to access large quantities of smuggled food and other supplies. Virtually cut off from the outside world, food was extremely scarce—so much so that, unlike Sarajevo, starvation was common. Indeed, starvation was directly and indirectly the cause of death for the great majority of those who did not survive the siege.[43] Using a classic siege strategy, the German blockade was designed to starve the city into submission. In Sarajevo, in contrast, the besieging Serbs could manipulate, divert, and limit food supplies but not entirely block them without provoking international intervention. In Leningrad the hunger situation was so severe that there were accounts of cannibalism, allegedly including the illicit sale of human flesh meat patties at Haymarket.[44] Criminal proceedings were initiated against hundreds of people for engaging in the crime of cannibalism.[45] Domestic animals had largely been eaten by the end of December 1941, and by February only five police dogs remained in the Leningrad police department.[46] In Sarajevo, many people abandoned their dogs and other pets when they could no longer feed them, but they were not so desperate to resort to eating them.

Leningrad's black market was largely based on barter exchange, with bread and vodka the most common currencies.[47] Although there was also substantial bartering in Sarajevo during the siege (with cigarettes serving as the most popular alternative form of currency), black market exchange was more monetized than in the Leningrad case. The large international presence in Sarajevo and formal and informal links to the outside world assured a supply of hard currency.

A key similarity between Leningrad and Sarajevo is that the ability of the two cities to survive was significantly aided by a vital supply line that bypassed the besiegers. While Sarajevo relied on the lifeline that ran via the tunnel under the airport tarmac, Leningrad had its "Road of Life" across the frozen Lake Ladoga, which during the winter months provided access for Russian-supplied goods. This supply route is credited with having saved the city from total starvation and destruction.[48] Nevertheless, more than a million Leningraders lost their lives during the siege—"the greatest demographic catastrophe ever experienced by one city in the history of mankind."[49]

In sharp contrast to Sarajevo, the rise of criminal actors into leadership positions was absent in the case of the Leningrad siege. Many Haymarket traders were the "robbers, the thieves, the murderers, members of the bands that roved the streets of the city."[50] These criminal actors had less of a symbiotic relationship with the authorities than was evident in Sarajevo, but were largely left alone because they provided a useful service. Soldier patrols in Leningrad did not interfere with Haymarket, restricting their role to searching individuals for stolen ration cards (if a stolen card was found, the person was shot on the spot).[51] Unlike Sarajevo, where criminals took on leadership roles in the defense of the city, the role of criminal actors in Leningrad did not extend beyond what was a highly confined and localized black market. Instead of negotiating with criminal actors in leadership positions, as was the case in Sarajevo, the military in Leningrad had to confer with the Communist Party on military decisions because it had organized and maintained the city's defense.[52] In Leningrad, the People Militia Army was formed along with several factory worker detachments to help defend the city.[53] Sarajevo did not have this streamlined authority in place when the siege began, thus enabling a more informal and criminalized environment in which criminal combatants could operate with substantial autonomy. Importantly, Leningrad was also the center of Russian military production in World War II, limiting the need to smuggle in arms.[54] Sarajevo, by comparison, was not as starved for food, but was starved for military supplies and relied heavily on smuggling channels for their acquisition.

Grozny

Cross-national secondary comparisons not only help identify what is and is not distinctive about the Sarajevo experience but also shed light on the counterfactual question: what would have happened in Sarajevo had a massive international humanitarian response not been viable or not been chosen? One possible answer is that Sarajevo would have become more like Grozny (the Chechen capital that was leveled by Russian forces during the recent Chechen wars), or alternatively, that the attempt to turn Sarajevo into another Grozny would have provoked a much stronger international military intervention to lift the siege in the absence of a humanitarian substitute. In either case, an extended siege stalemate would not have developed.

Grozny (and Chechnya more broadly) was a highly criminalized conflict zone. Illegal arms transfers (mostly stolen or bought from Russian troops) to insurrectionist forces, the illegal extraction and smuggling of oil, and organized criminal businesses such as kidnapping were essential ingredients in sustaining the 1994–96 Chechen war, with Grozny as the epicenter.[55] Anatol Lieven comments that the Chechen rebels "had no formal military discipline or hierarchy, and

I knew for a fact that several of the groups and their commanders doubled as criminal gangs."[56] Lieven acknowledges that this made him—as well as Russian intelligence—greatly underestimate the rebels' fighting will and capacity. This partly mirrors the Sarajevo experience, where criminal combatants played a surprisingly decisive role in the early defense of the city and defied initial Serb expectations of a quick victory. Russian forces eventually took Grozny, but not without suffering heavy casualties, and were ultimately driven out.

The second war in Chechnya, which began in September 1999, arguably resembled a criminal business as much as a war, involving large-scale profiteering from looting, hostage-taking, arms trafficking, and illegal oil trading. The Russians even turned to a convicted embezzler, former mayor of Grozny Beslan Gantemirov, to lead a mercenary militia, prompting one observer to label it a war of "crooks against terrorists."[57] Gantemirov had allegedly embezzled much of the funds targeted for the reconstruction of Grozny after the first Chechen war. Lieven observed that "Gantemirov and his men have deep criminal links with leading figures on the side of the Chechen armed resistance. In part, this is precisely what makes Gantemirov useful to the Russians: he can use his contacts both to penetrate enemy groups, and to persuade their leaders to cut a deal and surrender."[58] This proved to be a mixed blessing, however. In one case, for example, it included providing safe passage and perhaps even a guarantee of future immunity "for leading gangsters/guerilla commanders on the Chechen side—some of whom promptly launched attacks on Russian forces elsewhere in Chechnya. These men appear to include some of the leaders of the very worst kidnapping gangs, whose attacks on Russian and western citizens between 1996 and 1999 helped bring about the present war."[59]

But while Grozny and Sarajevo both had highly criminalized war economies, the former was far more predatory and far less accessible to international actors. Sarajevo's wartime accessibility and permeability helps to explain why it did not suffer the same fate as Grozny, which was eventually reduced to rubble by Russian forces.[60] "Basically, they [the Russians] just blew the place to pieces," comments one of the few Western reporters to enter Grozny. He contrasts the level of destruction to that of Sarajevo: "In Sarajevo there were times when we thought it was a bad day if a few hundred shells fell on the city. During the second half of the battle for Grozny the Russians sometimes fired over 30,000 shells a day into the southern sector. It was an area less than a third the size of Sarajevo."[61] Much of the city was flattened. Unlike in Sarajevo, however, most of Grozny's residents were able to flee the city—making such relentless bombardment less lethal than would otherwise have been the case.

The international humanitarian presence in Grozny and elsewhere in Chechnya was virtually non-existent. With humanitarian missions in conflict areas across the globe in the 1990s, including in Bosnia, Kosovo, East Timor, and parts of Africa, Chechnya stood out as the most notable exception. For example, the UNHCR, the International Rescue Committee, the International Committee of the Red Cross, and the France-based Doctors Without Borders—all prominent organizations that operated in wartime Bosnia—did not have any expatriate workers in Chechnya by the fall of 1999 when the second war was escalating.[62]

Their absence was not only due to the fact that Russian authorities limited and discouraged external scrutiny and involvement but also because criminalization of the Chechen war economy had reached such extreme levels that it inhibited any significant on-the-ground international presence. This took a particularly dangerous and violent form: widespread organized kidnapping for ransom, including targeting international actors such as aid workers and human rights monitors.[63] In 1996, six Red Cross workers were murdered just outside Grozny, and in 1998 a regional UNHCR director was taken hostage.[64] Extreme physical risks greatly restricted international monitoring and assistance in Grozny and throughout Chechnya. Indeed, Fred Cuny, the most celebrated aid worker in wartime Sarajevo, later disappeared in Chechnya. More than four years later, a group of Chechens offered Cuny's body for ransom to his relatives.[65]

To illustrate the dangers of working in the Chechen conflict zone, the anthropologist Steve Sampson reprinted an e-mail message sent to him in 1998 by a colleague:

> Steve, I am sure that I am not the first one to tell you this but DO NOT GO TO CHECHNYA. I was working in Daghestan, I had 4 of my colleagues taken hostage in Chechnya. It was 106 bad days. Then I had this good friend [Marc] who said he had 'special

arrangements' [to remain safe] and did not care. He got caught. He managed his way out, but had 2 fingers cut. Then I met with [John,] who thought he was outside the sphere of the Chechen bandits' operations. He is still in a basement, after 9 months. One other thing. When my colleagues got caught, they were taken from the Daghestan border, through all Chechnya, crossing all checkpoints without any problems. We are not talking here about isolated groups of bandits but rather organized crime networks with strong relations with political circles. It became obvious to me when I had to deal with the case.[66]

Media access was also far more difficult and cumbersome than in wartime Sarajevo. While the Russian government imposed few controls on the media during the first Chechen war, the negative Russian and international press attention prompted a much tighter leash on media access during the second war. This included "a strict system of accreditation and escorts. At times there was a complete ban on reporters in Grozny or anywhere near Russian military forces."[67] Moreover, there were considerable personal risks that inhibited media coverage. As explained by one reporter, "The kidnapping of journalists explains why the Russian bombardment of town and villages since the war restarted last month has received so little attention in the Russian and international media."[68] Thus, the combination of both frontstage dynamics (Russian restrictions) and backstage dynamics (the high risk of kidnapping) severely impeded external access.

Partly as a consequence of the extreme dangers and limited accessibility of the Chechen war zone, the brutal Russian siege of Grozny did not face the same international scrutiny as the Bosnian Serb siege of Sarajevo. If Sarajevo's siege economy had been equally predatory and included large-scale robbing and kidnapping of international actors, there would likely have been a massive and rapid exodus of foreigners from the city—leading to a very different siege dynamic. Most likely, Sarajevo would either have become another Grozny, or the attempt by Serb forces to turn Sarajevo into another Grozny would have provoked a stronger and earlier international military intervention to lift the siege. In either case, a long siege stalemate would not have developed. Although journalists and other foreigners in Sarajevo were sometimes robbed, the local authorities managed to not let this get too out of hand. For instance, when UN and other aid worker vehicles were stolen within the city, complaints to the government could result in tracking down and returning the vehicle[69] (though in one case an aid worker's truck already had a new paint job and a machine gun mounted on the back).[70] Thus, in Sarajevo, unlike Grozny, the large international presence was incorporated into and became part of the siege economy rather than simply being targeted and driven out by it. Sarajevo's siege economy had a parasitical and accommodating relationship with the external interveners, whereas in Grozny it was far more predatory. Moreover, the predatory nature of the Chechen war economy persisted in the aftermath of the siege, maintaining a high level of insecurity for local residents, impeding reconstruction, and inhibiting external involvement.[71] In 2003, the United Nations described Grozny as the most destroyed city in the world.[72]

Falluja

The battles for the Iraqi city of Falluja in 2004 provide another contemporary case with useful comparisons to the Sarajevo experience, particularly in regard to the role of the media. As was the case in Bosnia, siege warfare has been a major component of the conflict in Iraq—nowhere more strikingly evident than in Falluja in the aftermath of the U.S. military invasion and toppling of the Hussein regime. Falluja (a city of some 250,000 people, mostly Sunnis, thirty-five miles west of Baghdad) soon became a center of insurgent activity and anti-American violence and resentment. Strategically located on Highway 10, Falluja had long been a hub on a key smuggling route bringing in illegal goods from neighboring Syria and Jordan.[73] During the years of UN sanctions following the first Gulf War, the smuggling trade in Falluja boomed, encouraged by the regime in Baghdad. The U.S. arrival brought an end to much of this illicit business, to the dismay of many locals. After the U.S. invasion it became a conduit for bringing weapons and foreign fighters into Iraq. The deteriorating situation in Falluja represented a growing challenge to U.S. efforts to pacify and stabilize Iraq. The fate of the city would prove to be a turning point in the war.

The first siege of Falluja was prompted in late March 2004, when four American private security contractors were ambushed and killed in the city by an angry mob of men and boys. The bodies were dragged through the streets, burned, and mutilated, with two of the bodies hung on a bridge for public display—all captured on camera and televised to a global audience. Responding to these gruesome images, the United States promised immediate and forceful action to punish the perpetrators. The U.S. response was touted as a police action—dubbed "Operation Vigilant Resolve"—but took the form of a military siege. "It's 17th century tactics," noted Staff Sergeant Michael Ventrone. "It's under siege."[74]

In early April, U.S. Marines and two battalions of Iraqi forces surrounded Falluja. Tanks and armored Humvees were deployed to block road and highway access, and dirt-filled barriers and rows of razor wire were used to seal off the city. The U.S. forces entering Falluja a few days later, which began with a two-battalion attack, met fierce resistance. As the United States intensified the offensive, including use of tanks, artillery, helicopter gunships and air strikes, so too did international criticism and local outrage. The escalating siege reinforced an image that the United States was an invading force bent on occupation, and stories and pictures of mounting civilian deaths had a catalyzing effect in mobilized Iraqi (and broader Middle Eastern) sympathies for Falluja and generating new recruits for the insurgency. In this regard, Al-Jazeera played a key role, reporting on the casualties and destruction from within the city (especially from within the hospital) while the Western media remained embedded with U.S. military forces.[75]

Thus, just as Sarajevo turned into a front-stage public relations disaster for the besieging Serb forces, so too did Falluja for the besieging U.S.-led forces. In both places, the presence of the media in the city played a key restraining role. But in Falluja it was the non-Western media—especially Al-Jazeera—that was decisive in the public relations battle. As the *New York Times* described the situation: "The Arab media, the only journalists who could operate safely in town without being embedded—or kidnapped—were broadcasting every bombed-out mosque, every shell-shocked family. Because of them, Falluja was turning into a rallying cry for the entire Arab world—another Palestine."[76] U.S. forces also attempted to play the role of humanitarians providing relief aid and facilitating evacuations, but the performance did little to convince local and international audiences. One media story even made use of the Sarajevo analogy to criticize the U.S.-led siege, stating that Falluja "has become this war's Sarajevo."[77]

Despite U.S. efforts to seal off the city, the siege leaked like a sieve. As in Sarajevo, humanitarian aid shipments into Falluja generated concerns that this was providing a cover for smuggling. As the *Washington Post* reported, "The Marines' decision to allow relief and medical traffic in and out of the city, made partly as a humanitarian gesture and partly to quell growing criticism of their offensive, has also inadvertently created opportunities for their adversaries to smuggle in weapons and fighters. In the past several days, Marines and Army military police have found antiaircraft guns hidden in a cargo truck full of grain and grenade launchers hidden in ambulances."[78] Other reports indicated discovering weapons and would-be fighters hidden in aid convoys.[79] Moreover, early on in the fighting, U.S. troops and roadblocks were overwhelmed by a convoy of thousands of Iraqi sympathizers—both Sunni and Shiite—carrying relief aid to Falluja from Baghdad.[80] "We know a lot of people are hurting inside the city, but a lot of relief is going to the other side," lamented one U.S. soldier.[81]

By the end of April, U.S. forces withdrew from Falluja, placing security in the hands of a militia—the "Falluja Protection Army"— headed by former Iraqi military officers. Abandoning the front stage to the Iraqi militia in an effort to defuse the anti-American backlash generated by the siege, U.S. troops retreated to less visible positions on the city outskirts. In reality, Falluja remained largely in the hands of insurgents for the next six months, providing a base of operations to plan and carry out clandestine attacks elsewhere in Iraq. Kidnapping became a growth industry in the city—according to one account, the typical ransoms were $5,000 for a truck driver from nearby Baghdad, $15,000 for a truck driver from neighboring Jordan, and $50,000 for an employee of a large corporation.[82] The U.S. withdrawal further emboldened the insurgency—what began as a dramatic show of force to signal U.S. resolve quickly turned into a symbol of weakness.[83]

On October 14, the U.S. military again began to surround Falluja, but with a far larger force and a changed operational environment. The vast majority of the city's residents had fled before the final U.S. military offensive in early November. At that point, any males between the ages of fifteen and fifty-five attempting to leave the city were detained.[84] Large numbers of insurgents nevertheless managed to slip away, evading the military cordon around the city (a pattern that would repeat itself in other urban areas when U.S. troops went on the offensive).[85] Many insurgents joined forces with their counterparts in the nearby city of Ramadi, where, according to one press report, "Marines here say they have found it impossible to seal off either the highway or the desert smuggling routes between the two cities."[86]

During their final offensive to take Falluja, U.S. forces also kept humanitarian aid convoys and non-embedded independent journalists from entering the city. The first priority of the U.S.-led forces was to quickly capture the Al-Falluja General Hospital—which had provided so many of the horrific media images of civilian casualties during the April siege. Importantly, the American-led besiegers benefited from substantially reduced Arab media coverage—the Al-Jazeera Iraq bureau had been shut down by the interim government and thus had difficulty accessing the city.[87] With Falluja largely emptied of its population and media coverage (particularly television news) virtually non-existent, the regional and international reaction was far less intense than the previous April—even though the intensity of the attack and the resulting damage were much greater.[88] More than half of the city's 39,000 homes were damaged, and some 10,000 of those were destroyed or left uninhabitable.[89] A *New York Times* reporter described Falluja after the siege as "a desolate world of skeletal buildings, tank-blasted homes, weeping power lines and severed palm trees."[90] The final U.S.-led military push to take the city also took place immediately after the U.S. presidential elections were over—avoiding potential political fallout from a negative domestic backlash. Thus, the siege of Falluja was far less constrained the second time around, as evident by the overwhelming use of force.

The civilian casualties in Falluja prompted at least one comparison to Sarajevo: "Reports last night referred to victims being buried in graves in Falluja's municipal soccer stadium, in a grim echo of the siege of Sarajevo."[91] But Grozny was in some respects the more appropriate comparison, given that in the end, both cities were sacked with few constraints in the use of force and little international monitoring. In the media-saturated and humanitarianized capital city of Sarajevo, in dramatic contrast, the siege was drawn out for over three and a half years precisely because it was more permeable and the overwhelming use of force by the besiegers would have provoked more forceful international intervention. While Sarajevo certainly suffered enormously, it escaped the gruesome fate of Srebrenica, the large-scale starvation of Leningrad, and the extreme levels of destruction that characterized Grozny. The global visibility and accessibility of Sarajevo, made possible through both formal (front-stage) and informal (backstage) mechanisms, perpetuated the siege—but in the end also saved the city.

CONCLUSIONS

Siege warfare tends to be associated with epic historical battles, from Carthage in ancient times to Leningrad in the modern era.[1] Indeed, as one urban geographer reminds us, sacking cities and killing their inhabitants "was the central event in pre-modern war."[2] Yet as evident across the globe—from Sarajevo to Grozny to Falluja—sieges have stubbornly persisted. One former U.S. army strategist even boldly proclaims that "we may be entering a new age of siege warfare."[3] More broadly, armed conflict has become increasingly urbanized,[4] given that a majority of the world's population is now concentrated in cities.[5]

Siege-style warfare has not only endured but been transformed, reflecting broader global economic, technological, and political changes in recent decades. While almost all wars now take place within rather than between states, local sieges are often internationalized, linked to the outside world through both formal and informal mechanisms, ranging from satellite dishes and humanitarian aid convoys to diaspora funding channels and arms trafficking networks. But the internationalization of sieges is highly uneven. Not all are on center stage: some are extremely difficult and dangerous to access (as in the case of Grozny), some are treated as mere sideshows (as evident in Srebrenica, until its sacking), and in all cases some of the most important action takes place backstage.

Revisiting Sarajevo

This book has focused on a particularly prominent contemporary case: the 1992–95 siege of Sarajevo, the longest and most internationalized siege in modern history. The tortuous, globally televised battle for the Bosnian capital came to represent the entire post–Cold War experience of ethnic conflict, UN hand-wringing, Western paralysis, questionable humanitarianism, and a mushrooming global relief aid industry.[6] Like the Rwandan camps in Goma, ex-Zaire, Sarajevo became an embarrassing symbol of Western failure and incompetence, prompting Hollywood movies and a myriad of journalistic polemics. Outrage over events in Sarajevo, one could argue, helped pave the way for more robust international military intervention in Kosovo at the end of the decade, and contributed to the United States turning away from UN-led multilateral conflict resolution initiatives.

The main purpose of this book has been to help explain the remarkable longevity of the Sarajevo siege. As I have stressed, the internationalization of the siege, which aimed to end the conflict, in practice ended up perpetuating it. Indeed, the internationalization of the siege helped create and cement an interdependent relationship between key players amongst the besiegers, the besieged, and the external interveners. Many observers have argued that the Sarajevo siege (and the wider war in Bosnia) was prolonged by international intervention, particularly the large-scale delivery of humanitarian aid. But as I have shown, the specific mechanism through which this was accomplished goes well beyond the one usually described. It was not only the official aid that prolonged the siege, but also the business opportunities that the UN-led Sarajevo relief operation created for local black market transactions. The injection of aid, peacekeepers, and other international actors into the besieged city provided an opportunity for a criminalized war economy to flourish. Importantly, international actors on the ground were incorporated and absorbed into the war economy rather than simply kept out or driven out by it (as was the case in Grozny).

International intervention prolonged the siege not only due to the transfer of official aid, but also because it helped to create a lucrative environment for black marketeers, who were empowered to trade across frontlines, slip in and out of closed areas, transform humanitarian supplies into hard currency, and obtain access to weapons and other vital war supplies. Once the siege lines became more settled, informal cross-frontline trading relations developed, greatly benefiting from the stabilizing influence of the UN's presence (and sometimes direct complicity).[7] Thus, official international recognition and relief aid were insufficient causes for the prolongation of the siege; Sarajevo's survival cannot be explained without taking into account cross-frontline smuggling practices and the criminalized defense effort. This is not to suggest that the siege was deliberately prolonged to enrich black marketeers, but rather that such clandestine entrepreneurial activities were essential for Sarajevo's remarkable survival.

The Sarajevo siege was particularly supportive of the black market because it created formally impermeable spaces—front lines—that were closed to most locals, but permeable for many internationals and well-placed Bosnians. The siege lines thus functioned like a heavily policed border—and as elsewhere, borders and border controls generate tremendous incentives and opportunities for smuggling.[8] These incentives were especially powerful in the case of Sarajevo since the city was essentially a large captive market with astronomical price differentials from one side of the siege line to the other. The business of survival in besieged Sarajevo thus involved continually negotiated access across these lines—keeping the siege permeable through formal channels in the form of delivering official aid, and informal channels in the form of smuggling people, goods, and money. Both channels were intimately intertwined, representing the front-stage and backstage action in the prolonged siege drama.

My emphasis on the formal and informal political economy of the siege provides an antidote to the obsessive focus on ethnic identities and animosities in the Bosnia conflict. In the case of Sarajevo, ethnicity certainly mattered, but this does not take us very far in explaining the longevity of the siege. Ethnicity as a master narrative simply does not hold up to close scrutiny when looking at the messy and complex micro-dynamics on the ground.[9] While the mobilization and political manipulation of ethnic nationalist animosities helped to bring about the siege, an ethnicity-driven account would not expect and cannot account for the various forms of clandestine cross-ethnic exchange that helped sustain Sarajevo under siege. Ethnicity cannot explain the considerable variation in local relations across the siege lines, including levels of violence and permeability. These variations were also not always reducible to a simple strategic calculus of maximizing military advantage. The high levels of clandestine cross-frontline trading, the intensity of global attention, the multiple formal and informal roles played by key local and international actors, and the city's stubborn endurance do not fit neatly within a conventional realist understanding of unitary actors pursuing their security interests. At the same time, my focus on the criminalizing effects of the UN-led intervention does not sit comfortably with (and tends to be glossed over by) many liberal advocates of humanitarian responses to conflict.

Lessons from Sarajevo

The Sarajevo siege experience is in many ways distinctive—and indeed this distinctiveness is part of what makes it such a remarkable and significant case. Nevertheless, the Sarajevo story speaks to much broader discussions and debates about contemporary conflict, intervention, and their legacy for postwar reconstruction. My purpose here is not to generate lessons drawn from the Sarajevo experience for sieges per se, but rather to use the siege to help illuminate the nature of contemporary war economies, the relationship between the material and performative dimensions of conflict, and the dilemmas and unintended consequences of international intervention and their aftermath.

At the broadest level, the Sarajevo siege case illustrates the merits of taking topics traditionally considered to be in the realm of criminology and neglected by most security scholars—criminal networks, black marketeering, and underground economies—and making them of more central importance to the analysis of conflict, intervention, and reconstruction. Although this story is grounded largely in the Sarajevo experience, the intersection of violent conflict and clandestine economic activities is very much a global phenomenon.[10] It is also an old phenomenon—the blockade-runners during the American Civil War, for example, were the predecessors to today's UN sanctions evaders and arms embargo violators.[11] War does not simply inhibit trade, as is commonly understood, but rather transforms it, pushing it into the shadows and creating new winners and losers. As Mark

Chingono observes, "While, as Thucydides, Hobbes, and Rimmer speculated, war destroys markets and commerce, it must be stressed that it also *created* others where none existed before, and *more* rewards for those prepared to take the risk."[12] Such a "bottom-up" clandestine political economy approach to the study of conflict provides analytical insights that are not captured by more conventional, "top-down" accounts. Although this does not mean simply reducing war motives to crime motives, it does mean devoting much greater attention to the intersection between the business of war and the business of crime. Rather than perpetuating the tendency to either denounce or ignore the criminalized component of conflict, we need more nuanced approaches to unpack its complexity, ambiguity, and relationship to broader political and economic forces.

In this regard, the Sarajevo siege experience reinforces the conclusion of many scholars that we need to pay much greater attention to economic motives and rewards in conflict.[13] However, the siege dynamics indicate that efforts to neatly and cleanly differentiate between "greed" and "grievance" motives create a false and misleading dichotomy.[14] An analysis of the micro-dynamics of the siege reveals a complex interaction between economic and political objectives, and can involve considerable variation across time and even across place on the siege lines. As the defense of the city illustrates, there can be a fuzzy line between a patriot and profiteer, with some of Sarajevo's leading defenders also robbing those they are supposed to be protecting. Indeed, criminals can be celebrated heroes, and they can also be more heroic or more predatory at different points in time. Similarly, cross-frontline economic collusion can be about private wealth accumulation, but can also serve strategic interests and political objectives. Political and economic ambitions can co-exist and be intertwined. These complex realities of the siege defy easy categorization, and thus do not fit simplified accounts that divorce political and economic agendas.

It should be emphasized that this mixing of patriotism and criminality is an old story. "In the Balkan folklore," writes Aida Hozić, "bandits have often been turned into national heroes."[15] In Indonesia, Jakarta gangsters "blended brigandage with patriotism" in the revolt against Dutch colonialism.[16] Criminals have also long been incorporated into state-making projects, as Karen Barkey demonstrates in her study of the Ottoman empire.[17] George Gavrilis similarly documents how the Ottoman empire and the new Greek state utilized bandits and ex-convicts to secure the Greek-Ottoman border up until the end of the 1870s.[18] More generally, bandits played a key role in the formation of national states in the Central Balkans during the course of the nineteenth century.[19] Today's criminalized paramilitary groups may be more transnationally connected through cross-border crime networks and diaspora communities, but they are in some respects simply the latest versions of Eric Hobsbawm's "social bandits."[20]

Patriotism and political protection have also long provided a convenient cover for plundering and profiteering. During the American Civil War, for instance, Virginia's Confederate rangers "used their recognition by the state as a license to steal and murder."[21] Likewise, James Henderson points out that in Colombia, the *Violencia* "became an umbrella under which every variety of criminality could be found. As the depredations of men under arms grew even more ghastly, it became clear that larger numbers of psychopaths and common bandits had joined those who claimed to be fighting to maintain their political principles."[22] He nevertheless notes that "the political motive was usually present no matter how heinous the crime."[23] Thus, while it is intellectually fashionable to make bold pronouncements regarding the emergence of "new wars" and "postmodern warfare" in which irregular forces increasingly eclipse traditional armies, these historical parallels provoke a strong sense of déjà vu.

The Sarajevo experience not only underscores the need to pay greater attention to the criminalized aspects of conflict but to do so in a manner that recognizes its double-edged nature. This leads to some rather awkward and even unsettling conclusions. Clandestine trading can contribute to the persistence of war but also to its resolution. Smuggling and the use of criminal combatants can contribute to the looting of the country but also to its survival. A shadowy weapons procurement system invites corruption and rewards those with the best connections in the covert world, but it can nevertheless be vital to the defense effort. Smuggling and corruption can stymie and complicate international conflict resolution initiatives, but international interventions can also fuel smuggling and enrich profiteers. Postwar reconstruction is hindered and distorted by black marketeering, but clandestine commerce is also an essential survival strategy for many people in the face of dire economic conditions. These paradoxical and contradictory aspects of the criminalized side of conflict and their aftermath will continue to challenge analysts and present dilemmas for practitioners, given that in some form and to some degree, they are evident not only in Bosnia but in many other war-torn places across the globe.

The Sarajevo story also provides a powerful illustration of why we need to consider the effects that the criminalized aspects of conflict can have on the postwar social order. While the physical scars of war are the most visible, the social repercussions may be more consequential. Understanding of the postwar order should be rooted in an analysis of the wartime dynamics where new political alliances and social relations are forged and cemented. Despite a growing literature on war economies, too rarely is the analysis of the political economy of conflict extended to the post-conflict era.[24] In general, the more criminalized the conflict, the more criminalized will be the state, economy, and society that emerges from conflict. Key players in the criminalized war economy can emerge from the war as part of a new elite. Regardless of whether they are perceived locally as patriots or profiteers (or both), they are among the major beneficiaries of war. At the same time, large numbers of the old elite are violently displaced, often fleeing the fighting as refugees. In other words, war not only involves military confrontation but also a social transformation. As part of this transformation, many who lived on the margins of society experience rapid upward mobility that would have been inconceivable in peacetime. War, in short, can be a highly effective mechanism for criminalized social advancement.

Another crucial lesson of the Sarajevo and wider Bosnian experience is the importance of taking much greater account of the role of various forms of international intervention in the criminalization of local conflicts. Although scholars have increasingly focused on the role of international intervention in resolving intrastate conflict, inadequate attention has been given to the mechanisms through which such intervention can shape and become entangled in the war economy. For instance, while UN sanctions and arms embargoes are politically popular because they provide a convenient substitute for more direct military intervention and signal strong international condemnation (even as some states that formally support these measures may informally tolerate, encourage, and even contribute to circumventing them), they also create an economic opportunity structure for illicit trade that helps to criminalize the political economy of the targeted area. This strengthens the hand of criminal actors, contributes to the proliferation and strengthening of cross-border black market networks, and encourages closer ties between political leaders and the criminal underworld that can become entrenched and persist long after sanctions are lifted and the conflict is over.[25] When international officials subsequently charge that organized crime and corruption are impeding reforms, and apply pressure on local leaders to crack down on criminal networks (as has been the case in Bosnia and Serbia), rarely is there any international acknowledgment of having contributed to creating the problem in the first place.

The Sarajevo siege experience also reinforces and extends the conclusion by some observers that humanitarian action in conflict zones can become deeply enmeshed in the war economy.[26] Aid convoys are "taxed" at checkpoints and partially diverted to the black market, while military and other supplies may be camouflaged as humanitarian supplies (with or without the knowledge of the aid providers). However, what makes the Sarajevo experience particularly striking is that these backstage dimensions of humanitarian action—including being integrated into a criminalized war economy and institutionalizing a symbiotic siege relationship—were entirely compatible with and served the U.S. and Western European policy objectives of containment and avoidance of a major military entanglement. In this sense, rather than Washington's Bosnia policy simply being a failure, it was, in Samantha Powers's words, "ruthlessly effective."[27] Liberal humanitarianism, including its criminalizing consequences and contribution to the war economy, served the realpolitik goal of avoiding more direct and risky military engagement. Western governments ultimately resorted to a more robust international military posture in the form of NATO air strikes around Sarajevo that helped to lift the siege and end the wider war—but only after the military balance on the ground had sufficiently shifted through clandestine weapons procurement channels.

Peacekeeping forces and other international actors on the ground can also become direct and indirect participants in the criminalized side of the war, including through various smuggling schemes—motivated by material gain or political sympathy (or both). In some cases, as shown in the behavior of some of the "Blue Helmet" troops deployed to Bosnia, this backstage behavior may be as important as their front-stage role. As evident in Sarajevo and elsewhere in the country, internationally supported protected enclaves and "safe areas" can also shape the geography of the clandestine political economy of war, since these areas can become commercial centers of black market exchange. The consumer base of such clandestine trading sometimes includes not only the warring parties but also UN personnel, foreign journalists, and aid workers. In Sarajevo and throughout Bosnia, this extended into the postwar period, where the large influx of internationals provided part of the clientele for the clandestine economy, ranging from the purchase of pirated CDs to frequenting the many brothels using trafficked women.

Finally, the Sarajevo siege story provides a powerful illustration of the merits of disaggregating conflict and analytically embracing its messiness.[28] As I have emphasized, the war in Bosnia was not a unitary conflict but rather a series of large and small sieges that varied considerably in their conduct, duration, and outcome—as tragically evident in the dramatically contrasting fates of Sarajevo and Srebrenica. These variations in siege dynamics reflect different levels of internationalization and degrees of permeability. Disaggregating further, the siege of Sarajevo was not a unitary battle but rather was characterized by substantial variation across time and place on the siege lines. Similarly, disaggregating the actors reveals that many of the key local and international players in the extended siege dynamics did not have fixed and unitary roles, but rather played multiple formal and informal roles—with their backstage behavior often at odds with their highly scripted official front-stage performance. This book has attempted to provide a glimpse of these backstage activities and their relationship to the front-stage action.

NOTES

Preface

1. Hereafter, Bosnia.

2. For comparison, the siege of Leningrad, previously the longest siege of the twentieth century, lasted 900 days.

3. David Rieff, *Slaughterhouse: Bosnia and the Failure of the West* (New York: Touchstone, 1996), 216.

4. Interview in the documentary *The Siege: Sarajevo 1992–1996* (Sarajevo: FAMA International, 1998).

5. See, for example, Carolyn Nordstrom and Antonius Robben, eds., *Fieldwork under Fire: Contemporary Studies of Violence and Culture* (Berkeley: University of California Press, 1996).

6. See Michael Burawoy et al., *Global Ethnography* (Berkeley: University of California Press, 2000).

1. The Longest Siege

1. For a general introduction, see Laura Silber and Alan Little, *Yugoslavia: Death of a Nation* (New York: Penguin, 1997). On the conduct of the war, see Branka Magaš and Ivo Žanić, eds., *The War in Croatia and Bosnia-Herzegovina, 1991–1995* (London: Frank Cass, 2001).

2. Estimate by John Fawcett, former director of the International Rescue Committee Bosnia office. Author correspondence.

3. William J. Durch and James A. Schear, "Faultlines: UN Operations in the Former Yugoslavia," in *UN Peacekeeping, American Politics, and the Uncivil Wars of the 1990s*, ed. William J. Durch (New York: St. Martin's, 1996), 193, 238. The authors note that "Bosnia in particular taxed command, control, communications, and tactical intelligence more than any previous UN field operation" (223).

4. See Dietrich Rueschemeyer, "Can One or a Few Cases Yield Theoretical Gains?," in *Comparative Historical Analysis in the Social Sciences*, ed. James

Mahoney and Dietrich Rueschemeyer (Cambridge: Cambridge University Press, 2003). On case study research in general, see Alexander L. George and Andrew Bennett, *Case Studies and Theory Development in the Social Sciences* (Cambridge, Mass.: MIT Press, 2004); and John Gerring, *Case Study Research: Principles and Practices* (Cambridge: Cambridge University Press, 2006).

5. The practice of "trading with the enemy" is an old one, yet is often overlooked by security scholars. See Jack S. Levy and Katherine Barbieri, "Trading with the Enemy during Wartime," *Security Studies* 13, no. 3 (2004): 1–47.

6. The substantial literature on "global cities" rarely examines urban spaces during wartime. See Saskia Sassen, *The Global City*, 2nd ed. (Princeton: Princeton University Press, 2001); and Neil Brenner, ed., *The Global Cities Reader* (London: Routledge, 2006).

7. David Rieff, "Midnight in Sarajevo," *Atlantic Monthly*, April 2000, 104.

8. It is widely estimated that there were over 10,000 war-related deaths in Sarajevo. See the recent calculations provided by the Research and Documentation Center, Sarajevo (available at http://www.idc.org.ba/aboutus.html).

9. See Erving Goffman, *The Presentation of Self in Everyday Life* (New York: Anchor, 1959). On the "dramaturgical" perspective in sociological theory, which Goffman pioneered, see Dennis Brissett and Charles Edgley, eds., *Life as Theater: A Dramaturgical Sourcebook* (New York: Aldine de Gruyter, 1990).

10. More generally, on the importance of access and infrastructure in shaping global reporting of violence, see Howard Ramos, James Ron, and Oscar Thoms, "Shaping the Northern Media's Human Rights Coverage, 1986–2000," *Journal of Peace Research* 44, no. 4 (2007): 385–406; and James Ron, Howard Ramos, and Kathleen Rodgers, "Transnational Information Politics: NGO Human Rights Reporting, 1986–2000," *International Studies Quarterly* 49, no. 2 (2005): 557–587.

11. Nik Gowing, "The One-Eyed King of Real-Time News Coverage," *New Perspectives Quarterly* 11, no. 4 (1994): 45–54.

12. David B. Ottaway, "Mostar's Muslims 'Living Like Rats,'" *Washington Post*, February 21, 1994, A1.

13. Robert Donia, *Sarajevo: A Biography* (London: Hurst, 2006), 287.

14. Stathis N. Kalyvas, *The Logic of Violence in Civil War* (Cambridge: Cambridge University Press, 2006), 39, 41.

15. Ralph Peters, "The Future of Armored Warfare," *Parameters* 27, no. 3 (1997): 5.

16. Stathis Kalyvas, "The Urban Bias in Research on Civil Wars," *Security Studies* 13, no. 3 (2004): 160–190.

17. See in particular Kalyvas, *The Logic of Violence in Civil War*.

18. This common label masks substantial discord, disunity, and diversity. See Beatrice Pouligny, *Peace Operations Seen from Below: UN Missions and Local People* (Bloomfield, Conn.: Kumarian Press, 2006), 128–131.

19. Gil Loescher, *The UNHCR and World Politics: A Perilous Path* (Oxford: Oxford University Press, 2001), 290–296. For a useful evaluation of international organizations more generally, including UN agencies such as the UNHCR, see Michael Barnett and Martha Finnemore, *Rules for the World: International Organizations in Global Politics* (Ithaca: Cornell University Press, 2004).

20. This humanitarian role was articulated in UN Resolution 752 of May 15, 1992—the first of over 150 Bosnia-focused Security Council resolutions and statements.

21. Tim Ripley, *Operation Deliberate Force* (Lancaster, UK: Centre for Defence and International Security Studies, Lancaster University, 1999), 54.

22. The importance of local intermediaries for international actors is evident in conflict zones across the globe. In the case of UN operations, see the discussion in Pouligny, *Peace Operations Seen from Below*, 87–95.

23. "Violent entrepreneurship is a means of increasing private income of wielders of force through ongoing relations of exchange with other groups that own other resources." See Vadim Volkov, *Violent Entrepreneurs: The Use of Force in the Making of Russian Capitalism* (Ithaca: Cornell University Press, 2002), 28.

24. On the role of remittances in conflict and post-conflict zones, see Kevin Savage and Paul Harvey, eds., *Remittances during Crises: Implications for Humanitarian Response* (London: Overseas Development Institute, HPG Report 25, May 2007).

25. Particularly influential was Robert Kaplan, *Balkan Ghosts* (New York: St. Martin's, 1993). For a forceful critique of the ethnic animosity thesis, see V. P. Gagnon Jr., *The Myth of Ethnic War* (Ithaca: Cornell University Press, 2004).

26. Samuel P. Huntington, "The Clash of Civilizations?" *Foreign Affairs* 72, no. 3 (1993): 22–49.

27. The substantial literature on social capital has largely overlooked its various functions in conflict zones. See Nan Lin, *Social Capital: A Theory of Social Structure and Action* (Cambridge: Cambridge University Press, 2001).

28. Ripley, *Operation Deliberate Force*, 32.

29. It should be stressed, as Browning puts it, that "explaining is not excusing; understanding is not forgiving." See Christopher R. Browning, *Ordinary Men: Reserve Police Battalion 101 and the Final Solution in Poland* (New York: HarperCollins, 1998), xx.

30. Kalyvas, *The Logic of Violence in Civil War*, 36. Also see John C. Hammock and Joel R. Charny, "Emergency Response as Morality Play: The Media, the Relief Agencies, and the Need for Capacity Building," in *From Massacres to Genocide: The Media, Public Policy, and Humanitarian Crises*, ed. Robert I. Rotberg and Thomas G. Weiss (Washington, D.C.: Brookings, 1996).

31. The most dramatic events were the mortar shells that exploded in Sarajevo's crowded Markale marketplace in February 1994 and August 1995. Although these bombings "probably killed, between them, fewer people than ethnic cleansing killed on an average day near the start of the war, the visibility of the victims and their familiarity to Western eyes prompted a collective response that the razing of villages and killing peasants (of whatever faith) failed to evoke." See Durch and Schear, "Faultlines," 251.

32. Kalyvas, *The Logic of Violence in Civil War*, 33.

33. David Rieff, "Murder in the Neighborhood," *Dissent* 49, no. 1 (2002): 47.

34. The UNHCR, for example, went to great lengths to define itself as non-political, which was crucial to its public persona and legitimacy even if this did not always match reality. See especially Mark Cutts, "Politics and Humanitarianism," *Refugee Survey Quarterly* 17, no. 1 (1998): 1–15.

35. For a critical review of humanitarianism in general, see Robert Belloni, "The Trouble with Humanitarianism," *Review of International Studies* 33, no. 3 (2007): 451–474.

36. Quoted in Lowell Martin, *Working in a War Zone: A Review of UNHCR's Operations in Former Yugoslavia* (Geneva: UNHCR Evaluation Reports, April 1, 1994).

37. Realists would expect states to use humanitarian aid to achieve strategic objectives. They have difficulty, however, explaining the humanitarian imperative in the first place. On realism, see John Mearsheimer, *The Tragedy of Great Power Politics* (New York: Norton, 2003). On the growing role of humanitarianism in international intervention, see Martha Finnemore, *The Purpose of Intervention* (Ithaca: Cornell University Press, 2003).

38. Vildana Selimbegović, "Abeceda Opsade" (The Siege Alphabet), *Dani* (Sarajevo), April 5, 2002, 20–24.

39. "Nikad Manje Hrane" (Never Less Food), *Oslobođenje* (Sarajevo), May 5, 1993, 5.

40. Information compiled from UNHCR, "Information Notes on former Yugoslavia," November 1993–September 1995 (obtained from the UNHCR library, Geneva).

41. Other food supplies included a modest amount of produce generated from small urban gardens as well as rare and erratic delivery of care packages from friends and relatives abroad via various charity organizations.

42. See, for instance, David Keen, *The Economic Functions of Violence in Civil Wars* (London: International Institute for Strategic Studies, Adelphi Paper 320, 1998); Mats Berdal and David Malone, eds., *Greed and Grievance: Economic Agendas in Civil Wars* (Boulder, Colo.: Lynne Rienner, 2000); Karen Ballentine and Jake Sherman, eds., *The Political Economy of Armed Conflict: Beyond Greed and Grievance* (Boulder, Colo.: Lynne Rienner, 2003); Cynthia Arnson and I. William Zartman, eds., *Rethinking the Economics of War* (Washington, D.C.: Woodrow Wilson Center Press, 2005); Michael Pugh and Neil Cooper, *War Economies in a Regional Context* (Boulder, Colo.: Lynne Rienner, 2004); Dietrich Jung, ed., *Shadow Globalization, Ethnic Conflicts, and New Wars* (London: Routledge, 2002); and Carolyn Nordstrom, *Shadows of War: Violence, Power, and International Profiteering in the Twenty-first Century* (Berkeley: University of California Press, 2004).

43. Recent works include Sarah Kenyon Lischer, *Dangerous Sanctuaries: Refugee Camps, Civil War, and the Dilemmas of Humanitarian Aid* (Ithaca: Cornell University Press, 2005); Alexander Cooley and James Ron, "The NGO Scramble: Organizational Insecurity and the Political Economy of Transnational Action," *International Security* 27, no. 1 (2002): 5–39; Fiona Terry, *Condemned to Repeat? The Paradox of Humanitarian Action* (Ithaca: Cornell University Press, 2002); and S. Neil MacFarlane, *Humanitarian Action: The Conflict Connection* (Providence: Watson Institute for International Studies, 2001).

44. In the case of the Balkans, see especially Paul Hockenos, *Homeland Calling: Exile Patriotism and the Balkan Wars* (Ithaca: Cornell University Press, 2003).

45. See Peter Andreas, "Criminalizing Consequences of Sanctions: Embargo Busting and Its Legacy," *International Studies Quarterly* 49, no. 2 (2005): 335–360;

and R. T. Naylor, *Patriots and Profiteers: On Economic Warfare, Embargo Busting and State-Sponsored Crime* (Toronto: McClelland and Stewart, 1999).

46. Michael Brown, ed., *The International Dimensions of Internal Conflict* (Cambridge, Mass.: MIT Press 1996).

47. Robert Cox, "The Covert World: A Site for Political Analysis," unpublished paper, Toronto, April 1998; and Peter Andreas, "Illicit International Political Economy: The Clandestine Side of Globalization," *Review of International Political Economy* 11, no. 3 (2004): 641–652.

48. This is evident, for instance, by reviewing the table of contents of leading journals in international relations during the past decade, such as *World Politics* and *International Organization*.

49. John Mueller, *The Remnants of War* (Ithaca: Cornell University Press, 2004), 22.

50. This dichotomy is evident in some of the research sponsored by the World Bank on the economics of civil wars: http://www.worldbank.org/research/conflict/index.htm.

51. See U.S. Department of the Army, *Urban Operations*, Field Manual No. 3–06 (Washington D.C., June 1, 2003), 3–17. The United States also has a long history of tolerating and turning a blind eye to drug traffickers considered valuable security assets, such as in Southeast Asia during the Vietnam war, in Afghanistan and Central America during conflicts in the 1980s, and again more recently in its counterinsurgency efforts in Afghanistan. See Alfred McCoy, *The Politics of Heroin: CIA Complicity in the Global Drug Trade*, rev. ed. (Chicago: Lawrence Hill Books, 2003).

52. James Ron, "Territoriality and Plausible Deniability," in *Death Squads in Global Perspective*, ed. Arthur D. Brenner and Bruce B. Campbell (New York: St. Martin's, 2000).

53. John Mueller, "The Banality of Ethnic Conflict," *International Security* 25, no. 1 (2000): 42–70.

54. Janice Thomson, *Mercenaries, Pirates, and Sovereigns* (Princeton: Princeton University Press, 1994).

55. Mary Kaldor, *New and Old Wars: Organized Violence in a Global Era* (Stanford: Stanford University Press, 1999), 31.

56. Charles Tilly, "War Making and State Making as Organized Crime," in *Bringing the State Back In*, ed. Peter Evans, Dietrich Rueschemeyer, and Theda Skocpol (Cambridge: Cambridge University Press, 1985).

2. Imposing the Siege

1. Bosnia was the most ethnically mixed of the former Yugoslav republics. According to the 1991 census, 43.7 percent were Muslim, 31.4 percent were Serb, and 17.3 percent were Croat, with the remainder identifying themselves as Yugoslavs, Jewish, Roma, and so on.

2. Mirko Pejanović, *Through Bosnian Eyes: The Political Memoir of a Bosnian Serb* (Sarajevo: TKD Šahinpašić, 2002), 37.

3. Robert Donia, *Sarajevo: A Biography* (London: Hurst, 2006), 264.

4. Ibid., 289.

5. Ibid., 271, 274.

6. Robert Toscano, "Lessons from the Yugoslav Crisis," *International Spectator* 29, no. 1 (January–March 1994): 6–7.

7. Warren Zimmerman, *Origins of a Catastrophe* (New York: Crown, 1996), 158.

8. Susan Woodward, *Balkan Tragedy* (Washington, D.C.: Brookings, 1995).

9. Carl-Ulrik Schierup, ed., *Scramble for the Balkans* (New York: St. Martin's, 1999).

10. Samuel P. Huntington, "The Clash of Civilizations?" *Foreign Affairs* 72, no. 3 (1993): 22–49; Robert Kaplan, *Balkan Ghosts* (New York: St. Martin's, 1993).

11. Exceptions include Marko Attila Hoare, *How Bosnia Armed* (London: Saqi Books, 2004); and Branka Magaš and Ivo Žanić, eds., *The War in Croatia and Bosnia-Herzegovina, 1991–1995* (London: Frank Cass, 2001).

12. Kalevi J. Holsti, *The State, War, and the State of War* (Cambridge: Cambridge University Press, 1996), 132.

13. Laura Silber and Alan Little, *Yugoslavia: Death of a Nation* (New York: Penguin, 1997), 218.

14. Donia, *Sarajevo*, 276.

15. Norman Cigar, *The Right to Defence: Thoughts on the Bosnian Arms Embargo* (London: Institute for European Defence and Strategic Studies, 1995).

16. E. J. Hogendoorn, "The Impact of the Arms Embargo on the War in Bosnia and Herzegovina," unpublished paper, Princeton University, 2007, 1.

17. See, for example, Adnan Buturović and Filip Švarm, "Ustanak u Kninu i Pokolj u Zvorniku" (The Knin Uprising and the Zvornik Slaughter), *Slobodna Bosna* (Sarajevo), April 20, 1997, and Dejan Anastasijević, "Lik i Delo: Franko Simatović-Frenki" (The Life and Times: Franko Simatović-Frenki), *Vreme* (Belgrade), March 29, 2001, 34.

18. Tim Judah, *The Serbs* (New Haven, Conn.: Yale University Press, 1998), 170.

19. Misha Glenny, *The Fall of Yugoslavia* (New York: Penguin, 1996), 150.

20. James Ron, "Territoriality and Plausible Deniability: Serbian Paramilitaries in the Bosnian War," in *Death Squads in Global Perspective*, ed. Arthur D. Brenner and Bruce B. Campbell (New York: St. Martin's Press, 2000); United Nations Security Council Commission of Experts, *Final Report of the United Nations Commission of Experts Established Pursuant to Security Council Resolution 780 (1992). Annex IV: The Policy of Ethnic Cleansing* (December 28, 1994).

21. Filip Švarm, "Borba do Poslednje Pljačke" (Fight until the Last Robbery), *Vreme* (Belgrade), March 8, 1993, 28–31; and Lana Petošević, "Bio sam Srpski Plaćenik" (I was a Serbian Mercenary), *Vreme* (Belgrade), October 5, 1992, 30–31.

22. Mary Kaldor, *New and Old Wars: Organized Violence in a Global Era* (Stanford: Stanford University Press, 1999), 53.

23. Uroš Komlenović, "State and Mafia in Yugoslavia," *East European Constitutional Review* 6, no. 4 (1997), 70–73.

24. See "Special Dossier: Arkan," *Vreme* (Belgrade), January 22, 2000, 11–21 (Part 1) and January 29, 2000, 8–13 (Part 2); and *UN Commission of Experts Final Report: Annex III.A* (December 28, 1994).

25. *UN Experts: Annex III.A.*

26. Judah, *The Serbs*, 194.

27. John Fawcett and Victor Tanner, *The Political Repercussions of Emergency Programs: A Review of USAIDs Office of Foreign Disaster Assistance in the Former Yugoslavia (1991–1996)* (Washington, D.C.: Checchi Consulting and Co., March 2002), 15.

28. Steven L. Burg and Paul S. Shoup, *The War in Bosnia-Herzegovina* (Armonk, N.Y.: M.E. Sharpe, 1999), 130.

29. Quoted in Fawcett and Tanner, *The Political Repercussions of Emergency Programs,* 15.

30. Jasminka Udovicki and Ejub Stitkovac, "Bosnia and Herzegovina: The Second War," in *Burn This House: The Making and Unmaking of Yugoslavia,* ed. Jasminka Udovicki and James Ridgeway (Chapel Hill: University of North Carolina Press, 2000), 185.

31. Cited in Burg and Shoup, *The War in Bosnia-Herzegovina,* 78.

32. The failure to prepare for the war and lack of weapons and supplies was repeatedly emphasized by former senior Bosnian military leaders in interviews with the author in Sarajevo, July 2002.

33. Author interviews with former police and military personnel, Sarajevo, June 2001, May and June 2006.

34. Cited in David Cortright and George A. Lopez, *The Sanctions Decade* (Boulder, Colo.: Lynne Rienner, 2000), 65.

35. Donia, *Sarajevo,* 277.

36. *Balkan Battlegrounds: A Military History of the Yugoslav Conflict, 1990–1995* (Washington, D.C.: Central Intelligence Agency, Office of Russian and European Analysis, May 2002), 1: 132.

37. Author interview with retired Bosnian army general, Sarajevo, July 2002. Also see Sefer Halilović, *Lukava Strategija* (Cunning Strategy) (Sarajevo: Matica, 1998), 72.

38. Quoted in Norman Cigar, "Serb War Effort and Termination of the War," in *The War in Croatia and Bosnia-Herzegovina,* 209.

39. Donia, *Sarajevo,* 288.

40. Ibid.

41. Quoted in *Balkan Battlegrounds,* 2:345.

42. Donia, *Sarajevo,* 294.

43. *Balkan Battlegrounds,* 2:348.

44. Hogendoorn, "The Impact of the Arms Embargo on the War in Bosnia and Herzegovina," 13.

45. Donia, *Sarajevo,* 298.

46. Judah, *The Serbs,* 212.

47. *Balkan Battlegrounds,* 1:153.

48. Particularly important was a special elite unit within the Ministry of the Interior. A senior member of the special unit described the relations with the criminal defenders as "peaceful coexistence." Author interview, Sarajevo, June 2006.

49. "Juka of Sarajevo," *Vreme News Digest Agency* 120, January 10, 1994.

50. Quoted in *Dani* (Sarajevo), part 2 of series on Juka, June 7, 2002.

51. *UN Experts, Annex III.A Special Forces.*

52. Vehid Gunić, *Shame on You, Europe: Excerpts from a War Diary* (Sarajevo: Plantax, 2001), 71.

53. Ibid., 76–77.

54. On Juka's wartime activities, see the four-part series in the Sarajevo weekly *Dani*, May 31, June 7, June 13, and June 20, 2002.

55. Quoted in Kerim Lučarević, *The Battle for Sarajevo* (Sarajevo: TZU, 2000), 217.

56. Gojko Berić, *Letters to the Celestial Serbs* (London: Saqi Books, 2002), 97.

57. See Mladen Sančanin, "Intervju sa Ismetom Bajramovićem Ćelom" (Interview with Ismet Bajramović Ćelo), *Dani* (Sarajevo), March 10, 1993, 17–19; Vildana Selimbegović, "Ćelo je pod Mojom Komandom bio Pozitivac" (Under My Command, Ćelo Was a Good Guy), *Dani* (Sarajevo), June 9, 2000.

58. Quoted in John Pomfret, "Murderers or War Heroes?" *Washington Post*, May 14, 1993, A34.

59. Author interview with former member of Zulić's unit, Sarajevo, May 2006.

60. Author interview with former Dobrinja military commander, Sarajevo, June, 2006.

61. Author interview with a former senior officer in the Special Unit of the Ministry of the Interior, Sarajevo, June 2006.

62. Author interview with former Bosnian army general, Sarajevo, June 2002; and author interview with former soldier in Zulić's unit, Sarajevo, June 2006.

63. Jovan Divjak, "The First Phase, 1992–1993: Struggle for Survival and Genesis of the Army of Bosnia-Herzegovina," in *The War in Croatia and Bosnia-Herzegovina, 1991–1995*, 164.

64. For a more detailed account see John Fawcett and Victor Tanner, "Birth of the Aid Juggernaut in Former Yugoslavia (1991–1992): Humanitarian Plot or Unintended Consequences?," unpublished paper, Washington, D.C., 1999.

65. Fawcett and Tanner, "Birth of the Aid Juggernaut," 15.

66. Quoted in John Burns, "Mitterrand Flies into Sarajevo: Shells Temper 'Message of Hope,' " *New York Times*, June 28, 1992, 1A.

67. Silber and Little, *Yugoslavia*, 256.

68. Lowell Martin, *Working in a War Zone: A Review of UNHCR's Operations in Former Yugoslavia* (Geneva: UNHCR Evaluation Reports, 1 April, 1994).

69. Silber and Little, *Yugoslavia*, 254.

70. Author interview with senior UN official with extensive experience in wartime Sarajevo, New York, April 2004.

71. Richard Caplan, *Post-Mortem on UNPROFOR* (London: Centre for Defence Studies, University of London, 1996), 2.

72. John Burns, "First Supplies Reach Sarajevo from Airport as Shelling Continues," *New York Times*, July 1, 1992, 8A.

73. Roger Cohen, *Hearts Grown Brutal: Sagas of Sarajevo* (New York: Random House, 1998), 237.

74. Fawcett and Tanner, "Birth of the Aid Juggernaut," 20.

75. Silvia Lauzzana, "Does Relief Aid Prolong Wars? Explaining the Interaction Between Humanitarian Assistance and Conflict During the War in Bosnia-

Herzegovina (1992–1995)" (Ph.D. dissertation, Cambridge University, December 2005), 178.

76. See, for example, T. Brennan, "Final Report on Humanitarian Assistance in Bosnia-Herzegovina," Office of U.S. Foreign Disaster Relief Assistance, December 7, 1992, quoted in Fawcett and Tanner, "Birth of the Aid Juggernaut," 52.

77. Richard Holbrooke, *To End a War* (New York: Random House, 1999), 48.

78. Carol Off, *The Lion, the Fox, and the Eagle* (Toronto: Random House Canada, 2000), 176.

79. Fawcett and Tanner, "Birth of the Aid Juggernaut," 26.

80. Silber and Little, *Yugoslavia,* 254.

81. Quoted in John Burns, "Conflict in the Balkans; UN Takes control of the Airport at Sarajevo as Serbs Pull Back," *New York Times,* June 30, 1992, 1A.

82. Fawcett and Tanner, "Birth of the Aid Juggernaut," 28.

83. Ibid., 15.

84. Mark Cutts, "The Humanitarian Operation in Bosnia, 1992–1995: Dilemmas of Negotiating Humanitarian Access," *New Issues in Refugee Research* (Working Paper No. 8, May 1999), 22.

85. Ibid., 21.

86. Quoted in Fawcett and Tanner, "Birth of the Aid Juggernaut," 29.

87. Quoted, ibid., 44.

88. Cutts, "The Humanitarian Operation in Bosnia," 22.

89. Donia, *Sarajevo,* 300.

90. The siege even became the storyline of a major Hollywood motion picture (*Welcome to Sarajevo*) and an HBO film (*Shot through the Heart*).

91. "Sarajevo Residents Resort to Eating Grass," *CNN,* June 19, 1992, quoted in Fawcett and Tanner, "Birth of the Aid Juggernaut."

92. Quoted in Silber and Little, *Yugoslavia,* 279.

93. Quoted in David Halberstam, *War in a Time of Peace: Bush, Clinton, and the Generals* (New York: Scribner, 2001), 123.

94. Adam Roberts, *Humanitarian Action in War* (International Institute for Strategic Studies, Adelphi Paper No. 305, 1996), 36.

95. Linda Chalker, the British Overseas Aid Minister, argued that "the best way to help people is keeping them on the spot. That is much preferable to a diaspora across Europe." Quoted in Mary Battiata, "Conference on Balkan Refugee Crisis Pledges Aid but not Havens," *Washington Post,* July 30, 1992.

96. Michael Ignatieff, *The Warrior's Honor: Ethnic War and the Modern Conscience* (New York: Henry Holt, 1997), 103.

97. Soros added that the UN was "allowing the Serbs to decide what humanitarian aid should be brought in to enable the concentration camp to survive at the absolutely minimum level. The only justification for the UN's presence here would be if it was lifting the siege. If not, then the UN and especially the European Community must accept responsibility for preserving the concentration camp." Quoted in William Shawcross, *Deliver Us from Evil: Peacekeepers, Warlords and a World of Endless Conflict* (New York: Simon and Schuster, 2000), 23.

98. Gil Loescher, *The UNHCR and World Politics: A Perilous Path* (Oxford: Oxford University Press, 2001), 291.

99. Ibid., 296.

100. Ibid., 296, 290.

101. David Rieff, *A Bed for the Night: Humanitarianism in Crisis* (New York: Simon and Schuster, 2003), 132–133.

102. Cutts, "The Humanitarian Operation in Bosnia," 6.

3. Sustaining the Siege

1. Interview with Amira Sadiković, UNHCR official, *The Siege: Sarajevo, 1992–1996* (Sarajevo: FAMA International, 1998); author interview with former UNHCR officials, June 2006.

2. Bill Carter, *Fools Rush In* (New York: Wenner Books, 2003), 35.

3. Biljana Plavšić, *Svedočim (I Testify)* (adapted as a series for *Nezavisne Novine* [Banja Luka]), part 2, January 14, 2005.

4. Author interviews with former UNHCR and other aid workers, Sarajevo, June 2006.

5. This is commented on in various wartime diaries by Sarajevo residents. See, for example, Nusret Šehić, *Dnevni Zapisi* (Daily Notes), vol. 1 (Sarajevo: RABIĆ, 2003), 243–244, 446, 469, 525; and Valentin Kreševljak, *Sarajeveski Ratni Dani* (Sarajevo War Days) (Sarajevo: Svjetlo Riseci, 1994), 260.

6. Author interviews with former UNHCR and other aid workers, Sarajevo, June 2006.

7. Carter, *Fools Rush In,* 35.

8. Larry Hollingworth, *Merry Christmas, Mr. Larry* (London: Random House, 1997), 65.

9. Author interview with UN official, Sarajevo, June 2006.

10. Chuck Sudetic, *The Nature and Effects of the Flow of Commercial Goods into Sarajevo from May 1992 to October 1995* (unpublished report, 1999), 8. The research and report were undertaken by Chuck Sudetic and commissioned by John Fawcett and Victor Tanner. The information in the report was gathered during interviews conducted with twenty-six persons in Sarajevo, Visoko, Hrasnica, and Pale in December 1998. This included Bosnian government officials, journalists, military officers and soldiers, UN staff members, and local aid workers. I thank Fawcett for providing me with a copy of this report.

11. Ibid., 17.

12. Ibid., 14.

13. Author interview with former UNHCR aid worker, Sarajevo, June 2006.

14. Author interviews with former UNHCR officials, Sarajevo, June and July 2006.

15. Author interview, Sarajevo, June 2006.

16. "Welcome to Hell," *MacLean's,* July 20, 1992, 18.

17. Author interview, Sarajevo, June 2006.

18. Sudetic, *Flow of Commercial Goods into Sarajevo,* 8.

19. Tim Ripley, *Operation Deliberate Force* (Lancaster, UK: Centre for Defence and International Security Studies, Lancaster University, 1999), 37.

20. Vildana Selimbegović, "Abeceda Opsade" (The Siege Alphabet), *Dani*, April 5, 2002, 20–24.

21. Martin Bell, *In Harm's Way* (London: Hamish Hamilton, 1995), 175.

22. Republic of Bosnia and Herzegovina, State Security Service, information memorandum (signed by Mujo Selmanović, Kerim Lučarević, and Vahid Zajko), February 27, 1993 (document originally reproduced in Semir Halilović, *Državna Tajna* (State Secret) (Sarajevo: Matica, 2005).

23. Maggie O'Kane, "UN Soldiers Turning Profit on Tragedy of Sarajevo," *The Gazette* (Montreal), August 26 , 1993, A1.

24. Interviewed in "Romeo and Juliet in Sarajevo," PBS Frontline, May 10, 1994.

25. Peter Maass, *Love Thy Neighbor* (London: Papermac, 1996), 154; *Sarajevo Survival Guide* (Sarajevo: FAMA, 1993), 58; author interviews, Sarajevo, June 2006.

26. Author interview, Sarajevo, June 2006.

27. Maggie O'Kane, "A Piece of the Action," *Ottawa Citizen*, August 28, 1993, B2.

28. Author interview with former UNPROFOR soldier, Sarajevo, June 2006. Also see Sandra Ibrahimović, "Welcome to Marlboro Country," *Dani* (Sarajevo), November 22, 1998, 38–39.

29. *Sarajevo Survival Guide*, 81.

30. Author interview with person smuggled out of Sarajevo in a French APC, Columbus, Ohio, November 2002; and Sudetic, *Flow of Commercial Goods into Sarajevo*, interview with source #1.

31. David Rieff, *Slaughterhouse: Bosnia and the Failure of the West* (New York: Touchstone, 1996), 149.

32. See Milos Stankovic, *Trusted Mole* (London: HarperCollins 2000), 196.

33. Stjepan Šiber, *Prevare, Zablude, Istina: Ratni Dnevnik 1992* (Deceits, Delusions, Truth: War Diary, 1992) (Sarajevo: Rabić, 2000), 119.

34. O'Kane, "A Piece of the Action."

35. Rieff, *Slaughterhouse*, 122.

36. These charges are discussed in Carol Off, *The Lion, the Fox, and the Eagle: A Story of Generals and Justice in Yugoslavia and Rwanda* (Toronto: Random House Canada, 2000), 224–238.

37. Rieff, *Slaughterhouse*, 122.

38. "Akashi Vows to Fight Illegal Activities Within UNPROFOR," Agence France-Presse, January 27, 1994.

39. Ivana Maček, *War Within: Everyday Life in Sarajevo under the Siege* (Uppsala: Uppsala University Press, 2000), 98. This number is even more significant in terms of the city's employable population.

40. Ibid., 87.

41. Interview in the documentary *The Siege: Sarajevo, 1992–1996* (Sarajevo: FAMA International, 1998).

42. Hollingworth, *Merry Christmas, Mr. Larry*, 62.

43. Sudetic, *Flow of Commercial Goods into Sarajevo*, 9. This scheme reportedly involved the collusion of Bosnian Serb officers in Grbavica and Bosnian army or security service members.

44. "Neohumanitarians among the Sarajevans," *AIM*, September 4, 1994.

45. Rasim Delić, *Na Čelu Armije u Ratu i Miru: Lice i Naličje Rata* (Leading the Army in War and Peace: The Front and Back Face of the War) (Sarajevo: Vijeće Kongresa Bošnjačkih Intelektualaca, 2005), 255.

46. Author interview with former UNPROFOR employee, Sarajevo, June 2006.

47. Barbara Demick, *Logavina Street: Life and Death in a Sarajevo Neighborhood* (Kansas City: Andrews and McMeel, 1996), 113.

48. Carol Williams, "A Hell for Have-nots in Sarajevo," *Los Angeles Times*, September 16, 1994, 1.

49. Richard Holbrooke, *To End a War* (New York: Random House, 1999), 47.

50. The agency's headquarters office abroad provided virtually no oversight, with little accounting of aid distribution and use of funds (allegedly including a mysterious slush fund from which the local director of the agency at one point borrowed 70,000 German marks to renovate his house during the war). Author interview with former international aid worker, Sarajevo, July 2006.

51. David Rohde, "Islamic Money Helps Muslims in Bosnia, but Not Enough to Win," *Christian Science Monitor,* January 26, 1995, 1.

52. Mirsada Bosnić, "Neo-Humanitarians among the Sarajevans," *AIM*, September 4, 1994.

53. Vesna Bojičić and Mary Kaldor, "The Abnormal Economy of Bosnia-Herzegovina," in *Scramble for the Balkans*, ed. Carl-Ulrik Schierup (New York: St. Martin's, 1999), 115.

54. Author interview with former UNHCR airlift worker, Sarajevo, June 2006.

55. International Tribunal for the Prosecution of Persons Responsible for Serious Violations of International Humanitarian Law Committed in the Territory of Former Yugoslavia since 1991, Prosecutor v. Stanislav Galić, June 17, 2002, 9931–9932.

56. Sudetic, *Flow of Commercial Goods into Sarajevo*, 6.

57. Ibid., interview with source #2; author interview with former Bosnian soldiers, July 2002.

58. Author interview with former soldier who served as a tarmac crossing guide, Sarajevo, October 2007.

59. Ibid.

60. Unpublished diary, Sarajevo (Dobrinja), 1993–1996, 22 (author has requested anonymity).

61. *Sarajevo Survival Guide*, 81.

62. Muhamed Gafić, *Sarajevski Rulet 2* (Sarajevo Roulette 2) (Ljubljana: Author, printed by Tiskarna Mladinska Knjiga, 1995); author interview with a former soldier who served as a tarmac crossing guide, October 2007; and Saudin Bećirević, *Bore oko Očiju: Dnevnik Bosanskog Vojnika* (Wrinkles around the Eyes: Diary of a Bosnian Soldier) (Sarajevo: Author and Jasminko Halilović, 2007), 259–265.

63. Author interviews with former tarmac runners, Sarajevo, June and July 2006, and with former Bosnian army soldier in Dobrinja who smuggled arms across the tarmac, Sarajevo, October 2007.

64. Rieff, *Slaughterhouse*, 149.

65. Author interview, Sarajevo, June 2006.

66. Author interview, Sarajevo, October 2007.

67. Author interviews, Sarajevo, May, June, and July 2006, October 2007.

68. Gafić, *Sarajevski Roulet 2*, 35.

69. Author interview with former Bosnian army soldier in Dobrinja involved in this event, Sarajevo, October 2007.

70. Sudetic, *Flow of Commercial Goods into Sarajevo*, 8.

71. Author telephone interview with former Bosnian army officer, May 2006.

72. Sudetic, *Flow of Commercial Goods into Sarajevo*, 8.

73. Author interview with former Bosnian army soldier involved in this weapons smuggling operation, Sarajevo, October 2007.

74. Author interview with retired Bosnian army general, Sarajevo, July 2002.

75. Author interview with former soldier who smuggled arms across the tarmac, Sarajevo, October 2007.

76. Author interview with former soldier in Dobrinja involved in smuggling across the tarmac, Sarajevo, October 2007.

77. Sudetic, *Flow of Commercial Goods into Sarajevo*, 8–9, interview with source #4.

78. Ibid., 9.

79. Ibid., 9, interview with source #4.

80. Author interviews with former UNHCR airlift worker, Sarajevo, June 2006.

81. "Discussion: The International Response," in *The War in Croatia and Bosnia-Herzegovina, 1991–1995*, ed. Branka Magaš and Ivo Žanić (London: Frank Cass, 2001), 325.

82. Kerim Lučarević, *The Battle for Sarajevo* (Sarajevo: TZU, 2000).

83. Ibid., 230.

84. Ibid., 231.

85. Author interview with two retired Bosnian army generals, Sarajevo, July 2002.

86. Sudetic, *Flow of Commercial Goods into Sarajevo*, 3.

87. Author interview with former UNHCR airlift official, Sarajevo, June 2006.

88. Quoted in Scott Anderson, *The Man Who Tried to Save the World* (New York: Doubleday, 1999), 142.

89. Author interview with former UNHCR airlift official, Sarajevo, June 2006.

90. Quoted in Anderson, *The Man Who Tried to Save the World*, 144.

91. Sudetic, *Flow of Commercial Goods into Sarajevo*, 13.

92. Author interview with a former international aid worker who helped organize the airport meetings, New York, November 2003; and author interview with former UN Civil and Political Officer for Sarajevo, New York, April 2004.

93. Author interview, Sarajevo, June 2006.

94. John Fawcett (formerly with International Rescue Committee-Bosnia) interview notes, Sarajevo, September 10, 1998.

95. In his memoir, retired Bosnian army general Jovan Divjak claims that the idea of constructing a tunnel under the airport was originally proposed by an Iranian officer in early 1993, who indicated that tunnels had been effectively used during the Iran-Iraq war. Divjak, however, indicates that he was unaware that the tunnel had actually been dug until it was already operational. See Jovan Divjak, *Sarajevo, Mon Amour* (Paris: Buchet/Chastel, 2004), 168.

96. Edis Kolar and Bajro Kolar, *The Sarajevo War Tunnel* (Sarajevo, n.d.), 8–11.

97. Robert Donia, *Sarajevo: A Biography* (London: Hurst, 2006), 326.

98. Author interview with former UN Civil and Political Officer for Sarajevo, New York, April 2004.

99. Author interviews with local journalists, Sarajevo, June–July 2006.

100. For estimates of tunnel traffic, see Nedzad Ajnadžić, *Odbrana Sarajeva* (The Defense of Sarajevo) (Sarajevo: Sedam, 2002).

101. *Sarajevo Survival Guide,* 115.

102. I thank Zvonko Marić for providing me with a copy of this news story.

103. Unpublished diary, Sarajevo (Dobrinja), 1993–1996, 28.

104. Author interview with former member of the military police based in Dobrinja, Sarajevo, October 2007.

105. Unpublished diary, Sarajevo (Dobrinja), 1993–1996, 115.

106. Author interview with a former officer who was a member of this unit, Sarajevo, July 2006.

107. Quoted in Moritz Doebler, "Underground Tunnel a Lifeline for Besieged Sarajevo," *Ottawa Citizen,* December 26, 1994, B2.

108. Sudetic, *Flow of Commercial Goods into Sarajevo,* interview with source #1.

109. See the account of the tunnel by Muhamed Gafić, *Sarajevski Rulet 3* (Sarajevo Roulette 3) (Sarajevo: Vertikale, 1996), 131–142.

110. Interview with Alija Adamović on the Sarajevo television news show *60 Minutes,* October 11, 2004.

111. Author interview with former member of the military police in Dobrinja, Sarajevo, October 2007; author interview with former medic, Sarajevo, June 2006.

112. International Tribunal for the Prosecution of Persons Responsible for Serious Violations of International Humanitarian Law Committed in the Territory of Former Yugoslavia Since 1991, Prosecutor v. Sefer Halilović, April 19, 2005, 32, lines 19–25.

113. Gafić, *Sarajevski Rulet 3,* 131–142.

114. Nidžara Ahmetašević, "Sarajevski Tunel—Kuća Kolarovih" (Sarajevo Tunnel—The Kolar House), *Slobodna Bosna* (Sarajevo), July 10, 1999, 28.

115. John Pomfret, "Steps to Ease Sarajevo Siege Hasten its Partition," *Washington Post,* January 7, 1995, A14.

116. Author interviews, Sarajevo, June and July 2006; Sudetic, *Flow of Commercial Goods into Sarajevo,* 9.

117. Author interview with former member of the military police stationed near the tunnel entrance in Dobrinja, Sarajevo, October 2007.

118. Sudetic, *Flow of Commercial Goods into Sarajevo,* 9.

119. Ibid., interview with source #5.

120. Ibid.

121. Interview in *The Siege: Sarajevo, 1992–1996*.

122. Author interview, Sarajevo, June 2006.

123. Stephen L. Burg and Paul S. Shoup, *The War in Bosnia-Herzegovina*, (Armonk, N.Y.: M. E. Sharpe, 1999), 177.

124. A much larger tunnel under the airport tarmac (big enough to drive a truck through) was reportedly near completion when the war ended. Author correspondence with John Fawcett, International Rescue Committee (Bosnia office).

125. Author interview with former member of the military police stationed near the tarmac, Sarajevo, October 2007. He claims that some of his co-workers would resell confiscated goods on the black market, and that when he complained to his superiors about such behavior he was physically threatened by one of the guards.

126. Plavšić, *Svedočim*, part 15.

127. Ibid.

128. Quoted in Sudetic, *Flow of Commercial Goods into Sarajevo*, interview with source #12.

129. See Republic of Bosnia and Herzegovina, Armed Forces, 1st Corps Sarajevo, Security Sector, Official Memorandum #04/708-1: Jusuf Prazina Juka— Connections and Contacts (signed by Šaćir Arnautović, Deputy Security Commander), April 18, 1993. (Document originally reproduced in Halilović, *Državna Tajna*.)

130. About two-thirds of the siege line did not change from June 1992 to the end of the war in 1995. According to former Bosnian Army general Divjak, "At the beginning of the war the aggressor held Sarajevo in a 46 kilometer ring, but by the end of 1993 we had expanded that to 64 kilometers, and that was how it remained until the end of the war." Jovan Divjak, "The First Phase, 1992–1993: Struggle for Survival and Genesis of the Army of Bosnia-Herzegovina," in *The War in Croatia and Bosnia-Herzegovina, 1991–1995*, 161.

131. The most detailed account of cross-frontline trading routes and relationships is Sudetic, *Flow of Commercial Goods into Sarajevo*.

132. Tim Judah, *The Serbs* (New Haven, Conn.: Yale University Press, 1998), 251.

133. John F. Burns, "Gangs in Sarajevo Worry Diplomats," *New York Times*, October 4, 1993, A3. Sudetic's sources indicate that the trade across these bridges was not as significant as elsewhere on the siege lines. Sudetic, *Flow of Commercial Goods into Sarajevo*, 7.

134. Sudetic, *Flow of Commercial Goods into Sarajevo*, interview with sources #5 and #11.

135. Author interview, Sarajevo, July 2002.

136. *UN Commission of Experts, Annex III*.

137. Burg and Shoup, *War in Bosnia-Herzegovina*, 139.

138. Sudetic, *Flow of Commercial Goods into Sarajevo*, 4.

139. One Bosnian soldier described Stup as "uncertain terrain," where many storehouses were located. Adnan Solaković, interview in *The Siege: Sarajevo, 1992–1996*.

140. Ibid.

141. Šiber, *Prevare, Zablude, Istina: Ratni Dnevnik 1992*, 120–121.

142. Sudetic, *Flow of Commercial Goods into Sarajevo*, 5.

143. Ibid.

144. Ibid.

145. The frequent meetings between Juka and Mandić are discussed in Semir Halilović, *Državna Tajna* (State Secret) (Sarajevo: Matica, 2005), 40–41.

146. Mirsad Ćatić Čuperak, *Sjena nad Igmanom: Ratni Dnevnik 1992–1996* (Shadow over Igman: War Diary 1992–1996) (Sarajevo: Dalsa Bosna, 2000), 164.

147. Šiber, *Prevare, Zablude, Istina: Ratni Dnevnik 1992*, 140.

148. Sudetic, *Flow of Commercial Goods into Sarajevo*, 10.

149. *Dani*, interview, part 1, May 31, 2002.

150. Vehid Gunić, *Shame on You, Europe: Excerpts from a War Diary* (Sarajevo: Plantax, 2001), 73–74. Juka's extensive cross-frontline connections with Bosnian Serbs, especially criminals and police in Grbavica, are detailed in Republic of Bosnia and Herzegovina, Armed Forces, 1st Corps Sarajevo, Security Sector, Official Memorandum #04/708-1: Jusuf Prazina Juka—Connections and Contacts (signed by Šaćir Arnautović, Deputy Security Commander), April 18, 1993. (Document originally reproduced in Halilović, *Državna Tajna*.)

151. Sudetic, *Flow of Commercial Goods into Sarajevo*, 19n43. Also see Suzana Anđelib, "Ratni biznis: Kako je Radovan Karadžić sarađivao sa 'muslimanskim ekstremistima' " (War Business: How Radovan Karadžić Collaborated with the "Muslim Extremists"), *Slobodna Bosna* (Sarajevo), March 25, 2004.

152. Sudetic, *Flow of Commercial Goods into Sarajevo*, 10, 18.

153. Ibid., 10.

154. Ibid., 11

155. Ibid., 6. Sudetic notes that the cemetery director denies these claims.

156. Ibid., 7.

157. Ibid.

158. Author interview with former Bosnian military officer who trained a unit of soldiers from Visoko during the war, Sarajevo, June 2006.

159. Barry Came, "Military Investigates Misconduct," *MacLean's*, July 29, 1996, 10.

160. Judah, *The Serbs*, 247. For more detail on Croats covertly supplying Serbs with fuel, see Ed Vulliamy, "Bosnia: The Secret War: Croats Who Supped with the Devil," *Guardian*, March 18, 1996, 8.

161. "Bosnia: War Profiteering," *Vreme* (Belgrade), March 9, 1996 (summarized and translated by *Balkan Media and Policy Monitor*, available at http://mediafilter.org/mff/Mon.30-31.2.html)

162. Maass, *Love Thy Neighbor*, 118.

163. Robert Fox, "Sex and Drugs—The Price of Peace when Mafia Meets the Military," *Daily Telegraph*, August 27, 1993.

164. Filip Švarm, "Borba do Poslednje Pljačke" (Fight until the Last Robbery), *Vreme* (Belgrade), March 8, 1993, 28–31.

165. Laura Silber and Alan Little, *Yugoslavia: Death of a Nation* (New York: Penguin, 1997), 296.

166. Bell, *In Harm's Way*, 114.

167. Gunić, *Shame on You, Europe*, 269.

168. Donia, *Sarajavo*, 290.

169. Nik Gowing, "The One-Eyed King of Real-Time News Coverage," *New Perspectives Quarterly* 11, no. 4 (Fall 1994): 45–54.

170. Quoted in Gowing, "The One-Eyed King."

171. The fact that the city had hosted the Olympics less than ten years earlier also meant that a larger number of people across the world had heard of Sarajevo and could perhaps even find it on a map. The legacy of the Olympics is emphasized by Aida Hozic, "Making of the Unwanted Colonies: (Un)imagining Desire," in *Cultural Studies and Political Theory*, ed. Jodi Dean (Ithaca: Cornell University Press, 2000), 228–240. Sarajevo's most important earlier claim to international fame, of course, was the June 28, 1914, assassination of Archduke Franz Ferdinand by the Serbian Gavrilo Princip, helping to trigger World War I.

172. Richard Holbrooke, for example, stayed at the hotel during a two-day visit to Sarajevo at the end of 1992. He wrote in his journal: "This Holiday Inn has to be one of the most peculiar hotels ever." Holbrooke, *To End a War*, 48.

173. Donia, *Sarajevo* (London: Hurst, 2006), 315.

174. *Sarajevo Survival Guide*.

175. Hollingworth, *Merry Christmas, Mr. Larry*, 15.

176. Sudetic, *Flow of Commercial Goods into Sarajevo*, 5. Ćorić apparently also made trips to Kiseljak to buy supplies. Sudetic interview with source #7.

177. Ibid., 10.

178. "Welcome to Hell," *MacLean's*, July 20, 1992, 18.

179. Maass, *Love Thy Neighbor*, 122.

180. Anthony Loyd, *My War Gone By, I Miss it So* (New York: Penguin, 1999), 16.

181. Bell, *In Harm's Way*, 50.

182. Maass, *Love Thy Neighbor*, 146.

183. Ibid., 148.

184. Loyd, *My War Gone By, I Miss it So*, 179.

185. Nik Gowing, "Real-Time TV Coverage from War: Does It Make or Break Government Policy?" in *Bosnia by Television*, ed. James Gow, Richard Paterson, and Alison Preston (London: British Film Institute, 1996), 82.

186. Doug Aubrey, "Shell-shocked Art," *Variant* 18 (Autumn 2003) (available at http://www.variant.org.uk).

187. Carter, *Fools Rush In*.

188. Author interview with local translator who worked for a major European television broadcast service during the siege, Sarajevo, June 2006.

189. Gunić, *Shame on You, Europe*, 124.

190. Maček indicates that it cost 50 German marks to take a car battery to be recharged by those with the necessary equipment. See Maček, *War Within*, 80.

191. Demick, *Logavina Street*, 60–61.

192. Unpublished diary, Sarajevo (Dobrinja), 1993–1996, 15.

193. Ed Vulliamy, *Seasons in Hell* (New York: St. Martin's Press, 1994), 190.

194. Kemal Kurspahić, *As Long as Sarajevo Exists* (Stony Creek, Conn.: Pamphleteer's Press, 1997). The numerous awards included the annual Louis M. Lyons award "for conscience and integrity in journalism" from the Nieman

Foundation at Harvard and the International Editor of the Year award by the World Press Review in 1993.

195. Tom Gjelten, *Sarajevo Daily: A City and Its Newspaper under Siege* (New York: HarperCollins, 1995), 121.

196. Kurspahić, *As Long as Sarajevo Exists*, 227.

197. Gjelten, *Sarajevo Daily*, 208.

198. Ibid., 218–219.

199. Ibid., 117.

200. Kurspahić, *As Long as Sarajevo Exists*, 228. Not all UNPROFOR commanders were so helpful. Indeed, after an *Oslobođenje* reporter interviewed Canadian general Lewis MacKenzie and asked for some fuel to get back home, MacKenzie refused. The reporter ran out of gas and was stranded overnight. See Off, *The Lion, The Fox, and the Eagle*, 184.

201. Author interview, Sarajevo, July 2006.

202. Rieff, *Slaughterhouse*, 122.

203. Author interview with former UNHCR airlift worker, Sarajevo, June 2006.

204. Author interview, Sarajevo, June 2006.

205. Ibid.

206. Author interview with journalist working for a leading international news service, Sarajevo, June 2006.

207. Author interview with former local employee of this foreign TV news service, June 2006.

208. Kurspahić, *As Long as Sarajevo Exists*, 211.

209. Author interviews, Sarajevo, May–June 2006.

210. Author interview, Sarajevo, July 2006.

211. Maček, *War Within*, 86.

212. Author interview, Sarajevo, May 2006.

213. Demick, *Logavina Street*, 114.

214. Gunić, *Shame on You, Europe*, 121.

215. Elma Softić, *Sarajevo Days, Sarajevo Nights* (St. Paul, Minn.: Hungry Mind Press, 1995), 89.

216. Demick, *Logavina Street*, 113.

217. Softić, *Sarajevo Days, Sarajevo Nights*, 88–89.

218. O'Kane, "A Piece of the Action."

219. R. A. Bradford, "The Economic Organization of a P.O.W. Camp," *Economica* 12, no. 48 (November 1945): 194.

220. Softić, *Sarajevo Days, Sarajevo Nights*, 88.

221. *Sarajevo Survival Guide*, 45.

222. Maass, *Love Thy Neighbor*, 108.

223. Author interview with former army soldier, Sarajevo, May 2006.

224. Unpublished diary, diary entry for February 19, 1995, Dobrinja (Sarajevo), 86.

225. Gunić, *Shame on You, Europe*, 132.

226. Interview with Šefik Lojo, director of the tobacco factory, in *Siege of Sarajevo, 1992–1996* (Sarajevo: FAMA, 2000), 521.

227. Chuck Sudetic, "Cigarettes a Thriving Industry in Bleak Sarajevo," *New York Times*, September 5, 1993, 3.

228. Divjak, *Sarajevo, Mon Amour*, 100.

229. Stankovic, *Trusted Mole*, 172–173.

230. O'Kane, "A Piece of the Action."

231. *Sarajevo Survival Guide*, 82.

232. Pomfret, "Steps to Ease Sarajevo Siege Hasten its Partition."

233. Williams, "A Hell for Have-nots in Sarajevo."

4. The Siege Within

1. Author interview, Sarajevo, July 2002.

2. David Rieff, "Murder in the Neighborhood," *Dissent* 49, no. 1 (Winter 2002): 47.

3. Semir Halilović attributes this to the "mutual understanding of the warring parties." See Semir Halilović, *Državana Tajna* (State Secret) (Sarajevo: Matica, 2005), 27.

4. See Tom Gjelten, *Sarajevo Daily: A City and Its Newspaper under Siege* (New York: HarperCollins, 1995), 199.

5. See "Thefts and General Misappropriation of Property," Prosecutor v. Sefer Halilović: Judgment, International Tribunal for the Prosecution of Persons Responsible for Serious Violations of International Humanitarian Law Committed in the Territory of Former Yugoslavia since 1991, November 16, 2005.

6. *UN experts, Annex III.A. Special Forces*.

7. Stjepan Šiber, *Prevare, Zablude, Istina: Ratni Dnevnik 1992* (Deceits, Delusions, Truth: War Diary, 1992) (Sarajevo: Rabić, 2000), 140.

8. At the same time, retired Bosnian Army general Šiber noted in his wartime diary that there were allegations that the commander of the French battalion was engaged in smuggling through the Sarajevo airport. See Šiber, *Prevare, Zablude, Istina: Ratni Dnevnik 1992*, 175–177, 203.

9. Author interview with former senior Bosnian government official, July 2002.

10. "Juka of Sarajevo," *Vreme News Digest Agency* (Belgrade), no. 120, January 10, 1994.

11. Stjepan Šiber, *Prevare, Zablude, Istina: Ratni Dnevnik 1993* (Sarajevo: Rabić, 2001), 166.

12. This is evident in the transcript of an intercepted radio communication between Juka, his sister, Ćelo Bajramović, and several others. See Republic of Bosnia and Herzegovina, Ministry of the Interior, State Security Service, Department 6, Official Memorandum number 06-6; February 28, 1993. (Document originally reproduced in Semir Halilović, *Državna Tajna* [State Secret] [Sarajevo: Matica, 2005].)

13. Author interview with former member of Zulić's brigade, Sarajevo, May 2006.

14. Author interview with former Dobrinja platoon commander, Sarajevo, June 2006.

15. Author interview with former soldier in Caco's unit, Sarajevo, June 2006.

16. Rubina Čengić, "Caco Dossier Opened; Crimes Passed Over in Silence," *AIM*, November 18, 1997. The number of Serbs killed within the city during the siege, and the number of bodies disposed of at Kazani, remains a contentious and much debated issue.

17. Halilović, *Državna Tajna*, 163.

18. Author interview with UNHCR official, Sarajevo, June 2006.

19. See Halilović, *Državna Tajna*, 15.

20. Author interview, Sarajevo, July 2002.

21. Interview in the documentary, *The Siege: Sarajevo, 1992–1996* (Sarajevo: FAMA International, 1998).

22. On details of "Action Trebević," see Šiber, *Prevare, Zablude, Istina: Ratni Dnevnik 1993*, and Petar Finci, "Dosije: Borba Protiv Kriminala" (Dossier: The Fight against the Crime), *Dani* (Sarajevo), December 29, 1993, 20–23.

23. Natasha Narayan, "Showdown in Sarajevo," *The Gazette* (Montreal), October 28, 1993, A11.

24. Rubina Čengić, "Caco Dossier Opened; Crime Passed Over in Silence," *AIM*, November 18, 1997.

25. Letter from Jovan Divjak to Alija Izetbegović, November 3, 1996, reprinted in Divjak, *Sarajevo, Mon Amour* (Paris: Buchet/Chastel, 2004).

26. Ibid., 228–230.

27. Ibid., 228.

28. John Pomfret, "Murderers or War Heroes?" *Washington Post*, May 14, 1993, A34.

29. Munir Alibabić, *Bosna u Kandžama KOS-a* (Bosnia in the Claws of KOS) (Sarajevo: NIP Behar, 1996), 98.

30. Vildana Selimbegović and Senad Pećanin, "Porok i Profesija" (Vice and Profession) *Dani* (Sarajevo), September 14, 1998.

31. Republic of Bosnia and Herzegovina, State Security Service, Sarajevo, Information Memorandum (signed by Mujo Selmanović, Kerim Lučarević, and Vahid Zajko), February 27, 1993. (Document originally reproduced in Halilović, *Državna Tajna*.)

32. Halilović, *Državna Tajna* (citing reprinted Alibabić letters). In late October 2007, Alispahić was officially charged with conspiring to illegally import cannabis tea into Bosnia. Mirza Čubro, "Alispahića i Hodžica Osumnjičeni za Uvoz Čaja od Kanabisa" (Alispahić and Hodzić Suspected of Importing Cannabis Tea), *Nezavisne Novine* (Banja luka), October 24, 2007.

33. Alibabić, *Bosna u Kandžma KOS-a*, 88–90. On the treatment of Sarajevo's Serbs, see Mirko Pejanović, *Through Bosnian Eyes: The Political Memoirs of a Bosnian Serb* (Sarajevo: TKD Šahinpašić, 2002).

34. Author interview, Sarajevo, May 2006.

35. Alibabić, *Bosna u Kandžama KOS-a*, 106–108.

36. Sefer Halilović, *Lukava Strategija* (Cunning Strategy) (Sarajevo: Matica, 1998), 118.

37. Author interviews with former senior Bosnian government officials, Sarajevo, July 2002, June 2006. This is also emphasized in Halilović, *Lukava Strategija*.

38. John Fawcett interview notes, Sarajevo, September 14, 1998.

39. Author interview, Sarajevo, July 2006.

40. Pejanović, *Through Bosnian Eyes*, 114.

41. Author interview with former member of the Bosnian presidency, Sarajevo, July 2006.

42. Jovan Divjak, "The First Phase, 1992–1993: Struggle for Survival and the Genesis of the Army of Bosnia-Herzegovina," in *The War in Croatia and Bosnia-Herzegovina*, ed. Branka Magaš and Ivo Žanić (London: Frank Cass, 2001), 162.

43. International Crisis Group, *Bin Laden and the Balkans: The Politics of Anti-Terrorism*, ICG Balkans Report 119, November 9, 2001, 11. The exact number is unknown and remains contentious.

44. The Dayton Peace Agreement required that all foreign fighters depart within thirty days, and the United States pressured the Sarajevo government to enforce this provision by threatening to terminate military aid and other assistance.

45. Such anxieties became especially pronounced after the terrorist attacks on September 11, 2001, as evident in a number of often polemical and sensationalistic books. See, for example, John R. Schindler, *Unholy Terror: Bosnia, Al-Qaida, and the Rise of Global Jihad* (St. Paul, Minn.: Zenith Press, 2007); and Evan F. Kohlman, *Al-Qaeda's Jihad in Europe* (Oxford: Berg, 2005). For an authoritative account by a well-respected Bosnian journalist, see Esad Hecimović, *Garibi-Mudsahedini u BiH 1992–1999* [Garibs: Mijahidin in Bosnia-Herzegovina, 1992–1999] (Sarajevo: Fondacija Sina, 2006). Also see the discussion in Marko Attila Hoare, *How Bosnia Armed* (London: SAQI/Bosnian Institute, 2004), 131–135.

46. Kohlman, *Al-Qaeda's Jihad in Europe*, 59–60.

47. See especially Marko Attila Hoare, "Civilian-Military Relations in Bosnia-Herzegovina, 1992–1995," in *The War in Croatia and Bosnia-Herzegovina*.

48. Ibid., 195. Also see Hoare, *How Bosnia Armed*.

49. Chuck Sudetic, *The Nature and Effects of the Flow of Commercial Goods into Sarajevo from May 1992 to October 1995* (unpublished report, 1999), 11.

50. Ibid., 11 and interview with source #11.

51. Ibid., 12.

52. John Pomfret, "Red Tape and Corruption, Not Serbs, Delayed Drinking Water for Sarajevo," *Washington Post*, August 10, 1994, A13.

53. Quoted in Scott Anderson, *The Man Who Tried to Save the World: The Dangerous Life and Mysterious Disappearance of Fred Cuny* (New York: Doubleday, 1999), 143.

54. John Fawcett and Victor Tanner, "Breaking the Siege by Water: Fred Cuny in Sarajevo," unpublished paper, Washington, D.C., n.d.

55. Quoted in Pomfret, "Red Tape and Corruption."

56. Quoted in Anderson, *The Man Who Tried to Save the World*, 150.

57. Quoted in Pomfret, "Red Tape and Corruption, Not Serbs, Delayed Drinking Water for Sarajevo."

58. Pomfret, "Red Tape and Corruption."

59. Fawcett and Tanner, "Breaking the Siege by Water."

60. Ibid.

61. Anderson, *The Man Who Tried to Save the World*, 151.

5. Lifting the Siege

1. United Nations General Assembly, *Report of the Secretary-General Pursuant to General Assembly Resolution 53/35: The Fall of Srebrenica* (New York: November 14, 1999), 99.

2. See Marko Attila Hoare, *How Bosnia Armed* (London: Saqi Books and the Bosnian Institute, 2004); and *Balkan Battlegrounds: A Military History of the Yugoslav Conflict, 1990–1995*, vol. 1 (Washington, D.C.: Central Intelligence Agency, May 2002). Journalist Tim Ripley writes, "Some journalists and members of UN-PROFOR were convinced the offensive was designed to fail, to show up the impotence of the UN and add pressure for international intervention." Tim Ripley, *Operation Deliberate Force* (Lancaster, UK: Centre for Defence and International Security Studies, Lancaster University, 1999), 141.

3. Ripley, *Operation Deliberate Force*, 245.

4. Quoted in Ripley, *Operation Deliberate Force*, 249.

5. Quoted in Ripley, *Operation Deliberate Force*, 248.

6. Quoted in Ripley, *Operation Deliberate Force*.

7. Ripley, *Operation Deliberate Force*, 318.

8. Adam Roberts, *Humanitarian Action in War: Aid, Protection and Impartiality in a Policy Vacuum* (Oxford: Oxford University Press, 1996), 39.

9. Quoted in Roberts, *Humanitarian Action in War*, 38–39.

10. Robert Donia, *Sarajevo: A Biography* (London: Hurst, 2006), 290.

11. Ripley, *Operation Deliberate Force*, 108.

12. See U.N. General Assembly, *Report of the Secretary-General Pursuant to General Assembly Resolution 53/35: The Fall of Srebrenica*.

13. Martin Špegelj, "The First Phase, 1990–1992: The JNA Prepares for Aggression and Croatia for Defence," in *The War in Croatia and Bosnia-Herzegovina*, ed. Branka Magaš and Ivo Žanić (London: Frank Cass, 2001), 40.

14. Cees Wiebes, *Intelligence and the War in Bosnia, 1992–1995* (New Brunswick, N.J.: Transaction, 2003), 215.

15. The Bosnian Serbs also allegedly received some arms supplies from Russia and Israel. According to one report, Bosnian Serbs made a deal with Israel in which a large part of Sarajevo's Jewish community was allowed to exit the city in exchange for Israeli arms. A late 1994 investigation revealed that the remains of a mortar grenade on Sarajevo's airfield bore Hebrew letters; and in August 1995 an Israeli TV news show claimed that the Bosnian Serbs received supplies from private Israeli arms traffickers. See Wiebes, *Intelligence and the War in Bosnia*, 205.

16. Michael R. Gordon, "Iran Said to Send Arms to Bosnians," *New York Times*, September 10, 1992, A10.

17. Clandestine access to arms supplies through Croatia slowed to a trickle from spring 1993 to spring 1994. Author interviews in Sarajevo with three former Bosnian army generals, July 2002.

18. Richard Holbrooke, *To End a War* (New York: Random House, 1999), 51.

19. Tom Hunter, "The Arms Embargo That Wasn't: Iran's Shipments to Bosnia," *Jane's Intelligence Review*, December 1, 1997.

20. Sefer Halilović, *Lukava Strategija* (Cunning Strategy) (Sarajevo: Matica, 1998), 108–125.

21. Michael Dobbs, "Saudis Funded Weapons to Bosnia, Official Says," *Washington Post*, February 2, 1996, A1. The official also noted that "the covert operation in Bosnia was much easier than in Afghanistan. In Afghanistan, the people who did the dirty work stood out a mile because of their blond hair and blue eyes. We didn't have this problem in Bosnia," referring to the fact that Bosnians and Americans are similar in appearance.

22. Dobbs, "Saudis Funded Weapons to Bosnia, Official Says."

23. In addition to the press reports cited below, see Federal Office of Criminal Investigation (Germany), *Expert Report Concerning the Area 'Financial Investigations' relating to the judicial assistance request, ref. no. INV/10289/T09-PH (245), dated 8/27/2002 of the Office of the Prosecutor of the International Court of Criminal Justice for the former Yugoslavia relating to the 'Third World Relief Agency' (TWRA), Vienna/Austria* (August 28, 2003).

24. See the report on the Third World Relief Agency by Nijaz Džafić in *Dani* (Sarajevo), October 1, 2000, 16–19 (Part 1), and October 8, 2000, 34–36 (Part 2).

25. Not only Islamic countries supported the Bosnian war effort. Slovenia reportedly served both as a transit route for and a supplier of weapons for Bosnia, through deals brokered by Hasan Čengić. See Zoran Odich, "Arms Trade's Last Stop: Sarajevo," *AIM* (Paris), October 9, 1997.

26. John Pomfret, "How Bosnia's Muslims Dodged Arms Embargo; Relief Agency Brokered Aid from Nations, Radical Groups," *Washington Post*, September 22, 1996, A1.

27. Ibid.

28. Ibid.

29. John Pomfret and David B. Ottaway, "U.S. Allies Fed Pipeline of Covert Arms to Bosnia," *Washington Post*, May 12, 1996, A1.

30. Hunter, "The Arms Embargo That Wasn't: Iran's Shipments to Bosnia."

31. Wiebes, *Intelligence and the War in Bosnia*, 176.

32. For a more detailed discussion, see ibid., 177.

33. Ripley, *Operation Deliberate Force*, 62.

34. Wiebes, *Intelligence and the War in Bosnia*, 184.

35. Ripley, *Operation Deliberate Force*, 60.

36. Editorial, "Getting Serious on Bosnian Arms," *New York Times*, November 11, 1994, A30.

37. Phillip Corwin, *Dubious Mandate: A Memoir of the UN in Bosnia, Summer 1995* (Durham, N.C.: Duke University Press, 1999), 85.

38. Wiebes, *Intelligence and the War in Bosnia*, 173.

39. Patrick Bishop, "Bullet Smuggling Case Is Propaganda Gift," *Daily Telegraph*, April 10, 1993; "UN Trucks Used to Smuggle Arms," *Reuters*, May 7, 1993.

40. Wiebes, *Intelligence and the War in Bosnia*, 181.

41. Ibid.

42. Steven L. Burg and Paul S. Shoup, *The War in Bosnia-Herzegovina* (Armonk, N.Y.: M. E. Sharpe, 1999), 307–309, 313.

43. Richard Norton Taylor, "America used Islamists to Arm the Bosnian Muslims: Official Dutch Report Says That Pentagon Broke UN Embargo," *Guardian* (London), April 22, 2002, 13.

44. Quoted in Bruce Hicks, "Lifting the Arms Embargo on the Bosnian Muslims: Secret Diplomacy or Covert Action?" *International Journal of Intelligence and Counterintelligence* 18, no. 2 (2005): 249.

45. Statement of White House Press Secretary Mike McCurry, Washington, D.C., August 1, 1995.

46. Quoted in Anthony Lloyd, "Smuggled Munitions Strengthen Muslim Firepower," *The Times* (London), June 10, 1994.

47. "Arms to Former Yugoslavia," *Jane's Defence Weekly Global Update*, August 1994.

48. This included rifles, ammunition, uniforms, and anti-tank weapons. Doyle McManus and James Risen, "U.S. Had Options to Let Bosnia Get Arms, Avoid Iran," *Los Angeles Times*, July 14, 1996.

49. One Croatian soldier involved in covertly importing howitzers officially listed them as "giraffes" on the paperwork. Author interview, June 2002, Zagreb.

50. Uli Schmetzer, "How West Let Croatia Sneak Arms," *Chicago Tribune*, August 20, 1995.

51. Ibid.

52. Ripley, *Operation Deliberate Force*, 80.

53. Ibid., 85.

54. Ibid., 84, 149.

55. On the importance of the military balance on the ground in Serb decision making, see especially Norman Cigar, "How Wars End: War Termination and Serbian Decisionmaking in the Case of Bosnia," *South East European Monitor* 3, no. 1 (1996): 3–48.

56. Holbrooke, *To End a War*, 73.

57. Mark Danner, "Hypocrisy in Action: What's the Real Iran-Bosnia Scandal?" *New Yorker*, May 13, 1996, 7–8.

58. Quoted in Walter Pincus, "Feds Hid Fact that Iran was Sending Arms to Bosnia," *Washington Post*, May 22, 1996.

59. Holbrooke, *To End a War*, 51.

60. Holbrooke recommended that the new administration consider allowing covert evasion of the arms embargo, possibly through third parties (similar to Afghanistan), in a manner that would reduce Bosnia's exclusive dependence on Islamic nations. Ibid., 50–52.

6. Aftermath

1. For a region-wide overview, see Marko Hajdinjak, *Smuggling in Southeast Europe: The Yugoslav Wars and the Development of Regional Criminal Networks in the Balkans* (Sofia: Center for the Study of Democracy, 2002); and the special issue of *Problems of Post-Communism* (May/June 2004).

2. Paula M. Pickering, "Generating Social Capital for Bridging Ethnic Divisions in the Balkans: Case Studies of Two Bosniak Cities," *Ethnic and Racial Stud-*

ies 29, no. 1 (January 2006): 79–103. Pickering applies social network theory to interethnic relations in postwar Bosnia, but does not consider the role of criminalized social capital.

3. Quoted in Government Accounting Office, *Bosnia Peace Operation: Crime and Corruption Threaten Successful Implementation of the Dayton Peace Agreement* (Washington, D.C., 2000), 13.

4. Author interview, Office of the High Representative, June 2001 author interview, International Crisis Group, Sarajevo, June 2001.

5. See Michael Pugh, "Transformation in the Political Economy of Bosnia Since Dayton," *International Peacekeeping* 12, no. 3 (Autumn 2005): 453.

6. Author interview, World Bank (Sarajevo office), July 2002.

7. This is emphasized in Michael Pugh and Neil Cooper, *War Economies in a Regional Context* (Boulder, Colo.: Lynne Rienner, 2004).

8. Author interview, Customs and Fiscal Assistance Office to Bosnia and Herzegovina—Sarajevo, June 12, 2001.

9. See Vera Devine and Harald Mathisen, "Corruption in Bosnia and Herzegovina—2005," CMI Report (Norway: Michelsen Institute, 2005), 19; Timothy Donais, "The Political Economy of Stalemate: Organized Crime, Corruption and Economic Deformation in Post-Dayton Bosnia," *Conflict, Security, and Development* 3, no. 3 (December 2003): 359–382.

10. Phil Williams, "Organized Crime, Corruption, and Illegal Markets in Bosnia," unpublished paper, University of Pittsburgh, December 2000, 1.

11. See Amra Festić and Adrian Rausche, "War by Other Means: How Bosnia's Clandestine Political Economies Obstruct Peace and State Building," *Problems of Post-Communism* 51, no. 3, (May–June 2004): 27–34.

12. Williams, "Organized Crime, Corruption, and Illegal Markets in Bosnia," 6.

13. See Timothy Donais, *The Political Economy of Peacebuilding in Post-Dayton Bosnia* (New York: Routledge, 2005).

14. See, for example, Gerald Knaus and Felix Martin, "Travails of the European Raj," *Journal of Democracy* 14, no. 3 (July 2003): 60–74.

15. This was part of a global pattern in Western-sponsored reconstruction efforts. For a detailed critique, see Roland Paris, *At War's End: Building Peace after Civil Conflict* (Cambridge: Cambridge University Press, 2004).

16. Gojko Berić, *Letters to the Celestial Serbs* (London: Saqi Books, 2002), 98.

17. Interview with Emin Švrakić, *Start* (Sarajevo), November 18, 2003.

18. David Stark and Laszlo Bruszt, *Postsocialist Pathways: Transforming Politics and Property in East Central Europe* (New York: Cambridge University Press, 1998).

19. I thank Richard Snyder for pointing out this contrast.

20. Quoted in Munir Alibabić, *Bosna u Kandžama KOS-a* (Bosnia in the Claws of KOS) (Sarajevo: NIP Behar, 1996), 73.

21. Author interview, Sarajevo, July 2002.

22. Robert Donia, *Sarajevo: A Biography* (London: Hurst, 2006), 346.

23. Senad Pećanin and Vildana Selimbegović, "Abecada Korupcije" (The Corruption Alphabet), *Dani* (Sarajevo), August 27, 1999, 16–21.

24. Chuck Sudetic, *The Nature and Effects of the Flow of Commercial Goods into Sarajevo from May 1992 to October 1995* (unpublished report, 1999), 14.

25. Michael Pugh, "Post-war Political Economy in Bosnia and Herzegovina: The Spoils of Peace," *Global Governance* 8, no. 4 (2002): 467–482.

26. Timothy Donais, "The Politics of Privatization in Post-Dayton Bosnia," *Southeast European Politics* 3, no. 1 (June 2002): 1. Donais notes that the privatization deal was eventually blocked due to pressure from international officials and police investigations.

27. Chris Hedges, "Leaders in Bosnia Are Said to Steal Up to US $1 Billion," *New York Times*, August 17, 1999, A1.

28. Author interview with a senior official in the Bosnian Intelligence Agency, Sarajevo, July 2002. See also Emir Hodžić and Adnan Buturović, "Kako su SDA i HDZ Zaštitili (prije)Ratni Kriminal" (How SDA and HDZ Protected [Pre-]War Crimes), *Slobodna Bosna* (Sarajevo), June 20, 2002, 5–8.

29. Author interview, Office of High Representative, Sarajevo, July 2002.

30. Berić, *Letters to the Celestial Serbs*, 98.

31. Emir Imamović and Vildana Selimbegović, "10 Najmoćnijih Sarajlija" (Ten Most Powerful Sarajevans), *Dani*, March 5, 2004.

32. Author interview, International Crisis Group, Sarajevo, July 2002; and author interview, Office of the High Representative, Sarajevo, July 2002.

33. Stjepan Šiber, *Prevare, Zablude, Istina: Ratni Dnevnik 1992* (Deceits, Delusions, Truth: War Diary, 1992) (Sarjevo: Rabić, 2000), 147.

34. "Operation Balkan Vice: Crippling the Support Network of Radovan Karadžić, Balkan War Criminal," U.S. Department of the Treasury, Office of Public Affairs, March 7, 2003. Available at: http://usinfo.state.gov/ei/Archive/2004/Jan/07-195546.html.

35. Tamara Skrozza, "Ko je Ko" (Who Is Who), *Vreme* (Belgrade), February 7, 2002, 26–27; and Vildana Selimbegović, "Žetva Posijanog Straha" (Reaping of the Sown Fears), *Dani* (Sarajevo), May 26, 2000.

36. Author interviews with investigators and lawyers, state court of Bosnia, Sarajevo, June 2006.

37. Ibid.

38. Ibid.

39. Petar Kolaković, Jonathan Martens, and Lynellyn Long, *Irregular Transit Migration through Bosnia and Herzegovina* (Geneva: International Organization for Migration, April 2000), 1.

40. Ibid., 10, 28.

41. Author interview with UN officials, Sarajevo, June 2001.

42. Alix Kroeger, "Bosnia Crackdown on Illegal Migrants," *BBC News*, December 8, 2000.

43. Author interview, International Organization for Migration, Sarajevo, June 2001.

44. Paul Henley, "Sarajevo's Refugee 'Business,' " *BBC News*, April 24, 2001.

45. Quoted in Andrew Bomford, "Sarajevo: Gateway to Europe," *BBC News*, February 9, 2001.

46. Drazen Simic, "Human Trafficking: Italy in the Midst of Bosnia," *AIM*, February 7, 2001.

47. Antonio Prienda, "Bosnian Smuggling Ring Smashed," *Balkan Crisis Report*, September 7, 2001.

48. Quoted in Colin Barraclough, "Bosnia Major Hub for Smuggling People," *Globe and Mail*, September 12, 2000, A13.

49. For a region-wide overview, see H. Richard Friman and Simon Reich, eds., *Human Trafficking, Human Security, and the Balkans* (Pittsburgh: University of Pittsburgh Press, 2007).

50. Martina E. Vandenberg, "Peacekeeping and Rule-Breaking: United Nations Anti-Trafficking Policy in Bosnia and Herzegovina," in *Human Trafficking, Human Security, and the Balkans*, 84; Human Rights Watch, *Hopes Betrayed: Trafficking of Women and Girls to Post-Conflict Bosnia and Herzegovina for Forced Prostitution*, Human Rights Watch Report 14, no. 9(November 2002); Sarah Mendelson, *Barracks and Brothels: Peacekeepers and Human Trafficking in the Balkans* (Washington, D.C.: Center for Strategic and International Studies, 2005).

51. Author interview, United Nations High Commission for Human Rights (Sarajevo office), July 2002.

52. Mendelson, *Barracks and Brothels*, 11.

53. One NGO official estimated that there were as many as 2,000 women and girls from the former Soviet Union and Eastern Europe forcibly working in Bosnian brothels. A 2002 UN background paper on anti-trafficking efforts in Bosnia estimated that some 1,000 women and girls had been trafficked into the country. See Human Rights Watch, *Hopes Betrayed*, 4, 11.

54. Mendelson, *Barracks and Brothels*, 12.

55. Human Rights Watch, *Hopes Betrayed*, 4–5.

56. Ibid., 51.

57. Quoted in Mendelson, *Barracks and Brothels*, 65.

58. Human Rights Watch, *Hopes Betrayed*, 53.

59. Ibid., 54.

60. Ibid., 62.

61. Ben Johnston testimony, "The UN and the Sex Slave Trade in Bosnia: Isolated Case or Larger Problem in the UN System?" Hearing before the Subcommittee on International Operations and Human Rights, April 24, 2002, quoted in Mendelson, *Barracks and Brothels*, 36.

62. Human Rights Watch, *Hopes Betrayed*, 66.

63. See especially Richard Caplan, "Who Guards the Guardians? International Accountability in Bosnia," *International Peacekeeping* 12, no. 3 (Autumn 2005): 463–476.

64. Quoted in Human Rights Watch, *Hopes Betrayed*, 64.

65. Vandenberg, "Peacekeeping and Rule-Breaking," 81.

66. Ibid., 91.

67. Mendelson, *Barracks and Brothels*, 65.

68. Ibid.

69. Quoted in Mendelson, *Barracks and Brothels*.

70. Human Rights Watch, *Hopes Betrayed*, 59.

71. Ibid., 28.

72. Ibid., 49.

73. Ibid., 5, 59.

74. Ibid., 59.

75. Mendelson, *Barracks and Brothels*, 62–63.

76. Quoted in "Showdown at Arizona" (available at http://www.netnovinar. org/netnovinar/dsp_page.cfm?articleid=731&specialsection=ART_FULL& pageid=493&PSID=4394).

77. Ibid.

78. Jeffrey Smith, "Bosnian Mart Becomes Den of Criminal Enterprise," *Washington Post*, December 26, 1999, A33.

79. Philip Sherwell, "Guns, Girls, Drugs, Fake Track Suits: It's All Here in the Wildest Market in the World," *Sunday Telegraph* (London), November 19, 2000, 35.

80. Ibid.

81. Smith, "Bosnian Mart Becomes Den of Criminal Enterprise."

82. Quoted in "The Lessons Learned in Bosnia—and How They Apply to Iraq," Army Times.com (accessed June 2007 at http://www.armytimes.com/ print.php?f=1-292925-543796.php).

83. Quoted in Bruce R. Scott and Edward N. Murphy, *Brčko and the Arizona Market* (Harvard Business School case, August 14, 2006), 15.

84. Ibid.

85. Ibid., 17.

86. Quoted in "Showdown at Arizona."

87. Fait and Mortif, "A Neutral Space," USAID, quoted in Scott and Murphy, *Brčko and the Arizona Market*, 16.

88. Scott and Murphy, *Brčko and the Arizona Market*.

89. Sherwell, "Guns, Girls, Drugs, Fake Track Suits."

90. Smith, "Bosnian Mart Becomes Den of Criminal Enterprise."

91. Scott and Murphy, *Brčko and the Arizona Market*, 18.

92. Quoted in Scott and Murphy, *Brčko and the Arizona Market*, 17.

93. "Bosnia: Market Shimmer," *Economist*, September 7, 1996, 48.

94. Quoted in Doug Schwartz, "Real Deals for Peace," *Christian Science Monitor*, December 11, 1997, 7.

95. Quoted in Chris Hedges, "At Last, a Unifying Force in Bosnia: Making Money," *New York Times*, October 17, 1996, A4.

96. "Organizovani Kriminal—Država uzvraća udarac" (Organized Crime: The State Strikes Back), *Slobodna Bosna* (Sarajevo), December 12, 2003.

97. Festić and Rausche, "War by Other Means," 29.

98. Beth Kampschror, "Bosnia's Arizona Market Moving from 'Wild West' to Legitimacy," *Balkan Times*, January 31, 2002.

99. In 2001, there were more than four hundred illegal border crossings in the country and only fifty legal crossings (of which only thirty-five were policed by the State Border Service). Anes Alić and Jen Tracy, "Sanctioned Smuggling in the Balkans," *Transitions Online*, September 14, 2001.

100. Quoted in Scott and Murphy, *Brčko and the Arizona Market*, 19.

101. This is part of a much broader global trend. See Peter Andreas and Ethan Nadelmann, *Policing the Globe: Criminalization and Crime Control in International Relations* (New York: Oxford University Press, 2006).

7. Extensions

1. Official aid delivery levels rarely matched required food levels, and the gap between the two was often enormous. For a useful summary, see Mark Prutsalis, "Too Little, Too Late: Humanitarian Aid," in *With No Peace to Keep: United Nations Peacekeeping and the War in the Former Yugoslavia*, ed. Ben Cohen and George Stamkoski (London: Grainpress, 1995), 84.

2. One UN report notes that in the enclaves, "UNHCR was rarely able to meet the needs of the population," yet also observes that "starvation was almost unknown." The report does not go further in explaining the puzzling survival of these besieged populations. See United Nations General Assembly, *Report of the Secretary-General Pursuant to General Assembly Resolution 53/35: The Fall of Srebrenica* (New York: November 1999), 10.

3. As Danner writes about Srebrenica's defenders: "Militarily the Bosnians had grown weaker during their years languishing in the safe area. They lacked fuel and shells for their two old tanks, they were low on ammunition, and many of their fighters had no working weapons. Some carried only a pistol or a single grenade, others knives or clubs." Mark Danner, "Bosnia: The Great Betrayal," *New York Review of Books*, March 26, 1998.

4. G. Duijzings, *Srebrenica—A Safe Area: Reconstruction, Background, Consequences and Analysis of the Fall of the Safe Area*, part 2, Dutchbat in the Enclave, chap. 4 (available at http://193.173.80.81/srebrenica/).

5. Chuck Sudetic, *Blood and Vengeance: One Family's Story of the War in Bosnia* (New York: Penguin, 1998), 157–160.

6. The relatively few foreign reporters that came to Srebrenica, mostly from the print media, tended to arrive and depart with the convoys, which were erratic and infrequent.

7. Sudetic, *Blood and Vengeance*, 223.

8. Testimony of Thomas Karremans, *Prosecutor v. Radovan Karadžić and Ratko Mladić*, Case No. IT-95-5/18, July 3, 1996, 623–624.

9. Statement of Naser Orić, read in *Prosecutor v. Radislav Krstić*, Case No. IT-98-33, April 6, 2001, 9586.

10. Tim Ripley, *Operation Deliberate Force* (Lancaster, UK: Centre for Defence and International Security Studies, Lancaster University, 1999), 53.

11. Chuck Sudetic, "Desperation Drives Escape of Muslim Refugees," *New York Times*, September 4, 1994, A3.

12. Duijzings, *Srebrenica—A Safe Area*, chap. 7 (available at http://193.173.80.81/srebrenica/).

13. Ibid., chap. 4.

14. Ibid., chap. 7.

15. T. Frankfort, *Srebrenica—A Safe Area: Reconstruction, Background, Consequences and Analysis of the Fall of the Safe Area,* part 2, chap. 8 (available at http://193.173.80.81/srebrenica/).

16. Duijzings, *Srebrenica—A Safe Area,* chap. 7.

17. Ibid.

18. In March 1993, one kilo of tobacco reportedly cost 1,000 German marks, and a package of cigarettes 60 marks. Duijzings, *Srebrenica—A Safe Area,* chap. 4.

19. Ibid.

20. Duijzings, *Srebrenica—A Safe Area,* chap. 7.

21. John Pomfret, "U.N. Offers Bosnians Life, But No Hope," *Washington Post,* January 30, 1994, A1.

22. Letter from Brigadier General Jašarević to General Delić in *Prosecutor v. Vujadin Popović et al.,* Case No. IT-05–88, September 22, 2006, 2035.

23. Testimony of Pieter Boering, *Prosecutor v. Vujadin Popović et al.,* Case No. IT-05–88, September 22, 2006, 2032–2033.

24. William Shawcross, *Deliver Us from Evil: Peacekeepers, Warlords and a World of Endless Conflict* (New York: Simon and Schuster, 2001), 156.

25. Quoted in Duijzings, *Srebrenica—A Safe Area,* chap. 7.

26. Duijzings, *Srebrenica—A Safe Area,* chap. 4.

27. Ibid.

28. Indeed, during the war, one of Orić's commanders, Ejub Golić, attacked the local police station to free two associates. See Duijzings, *Srebrenica—A Safe Area,* chap. 7.

29. Cited in ibid.

30. Quoted in United Nations General Assembly, *Report of the Secretary-General Pursuant to General Assembly Resolution 53/35: The Fall of Srebrenica* (New York: November 1999), 54.

31. See, especially, Esad Hećimović, "Kako Su Prodali Srebenicu i Saćuvali Vlast" (How They Sold Out Srebrenica and Kept Power), Special Issue, *Dani* (Sarajevo), September 1998. Orić claims that the enclave was deliberately sacrificed by higher-ups in the Bosnian government. See David Rohde, *End Game: The Betrayal and Fall of Srebrenica* (Boulder, Colo.: Westview, 1997), 356.

32. For a critical assessment, see Rohde, *End Game,* 353–376. Rhode concludes that the most likely possibility is that Srebrenica was "tacitly sacrificed" because it served the interests of various key local and international actors. Also see Danner, "Bosnia: The Great Betrayal."

33. See United Nations General Assembly, *Report of the Secretary-General Pursuant to General Assembly Resolution 53/35: The Fall of Srebrenica* (New York: November 1999), 53, 106.

34. Shawcross, *Deliver Us from Evil,* 171.

35. Sudetic, *Blood and Vengeance,* 339.

36. Hugh Griffiths, "Striking Fear," *Transitions Online,* April 22, 2003.

37. Ibid.

38. Author observations, Sarajevo, July 2006.

39. Harrison E. Salisbury, *The 900 Days: The Siege of Leningrad* (New York: De Capo Press, 1969), 474.

40. Ibid., 511.

41. See especially Boris Belozerov, "Crime During the Siege," in *Life and Death in Besieged Leningrad, 1941–44*, ed. John Barber (New York: Palgrave, 2005).

42. Ibid.

43. See John Barber, "Introduction: Leningrad's Place in the History of Famine," in *Life and Death in Besieged Leningrad*.

44. Salisbury, *The 900 Days*, 479.

45. Belozerov, "Crime during the Siege," 223.

46. Salisbury, *The 900 Days*, 477.

47. Ibid., 474.

48. David M. Glantz, *The Siege of Leningrad, 1941–1944: 900 Days of Terror* (Osceola, Wisc.: Zenith Press, 2001), 75–76.

49. Barber, "Introduction," 1.

50. Salisbury, *The 900 Days*, 474.

51. Ibid., 478.

52. Glantz, *The Siege of Leningrad, 1941–1944*, 178.

53. Ibid., 63–64.

54. Ibid., 67.

55. Anatol Lieven, *Chechnya: Tombstone of Russian Power* (New Haven, Conn.: Yale University Press, 1998), and Carlotta Gall and Thomas de Waal, *Chechnya: Calamity in the Caucus* (New York: New York University Press, 1998).

56. Anatol Lieven, "Lessons of the War in Chechnya, 1994–1996," in *Soldiers in Cities: Military Operations on Urban Terrain*, ed. Michael C. Desch (Carlisle, Penn.: U.S. Army War College, October 2001), 63.

57. Quoted in "Filling a Vacuum in the Market?" *Jane's Intelligence Review*, March 1, 2000.

58. Lieven, "Lessons of the War in Chechnya, 1994–1996," 72.

59. Ibid.

60. See Olga Oliker, *Russia's Chechen Wars, 1994–2000: Lessons from Urban Combat* (Santa Monica, Calif.: RAND, 2001).

61. Anthony Loyd, *My War Gone By, I Miss It So* (London: Penguin, 1999), 243–244.

62. Minh T. Vo, "Why World Won't Aid Chechens," *Christian Science Monitor*, October 12, 1999.

63. See especially Valery Tishkov, *Chechnya: Life in a War-Torn Society* (Berkeley: University of California Press, 2004).

64. Vo, "Why World Won't Aid Chechens."

65. Shawcross, *Deliver Us from Evil*, 26.

66. See Steven Sampson, " 'Trouble Spots:' Projects, Bandits, and State Fragmentation," in *Globalization, the State, and Violence*, ed. Jonathan Friedman (Lanham, Md.: Altamira Press, 2003).

67. Olga Oliker, *Russia's Chechen Wars, 1994–2000: Lessons from Urban Combat* (Santa Monica, Calif.: RAND, 2001), 63.

68. Patrick Cockburn, "A Lost Victory in Chechnya," *The Independent* (London), October 24, 1999, 25. On the kidnapping of journalists, also see Tishkov, *Chechnya: Life in a War-Torn Society* (especially chap. 8).

69. Author interview with a retired Bosnian army general, Sarajevo, July 2002.

70. Author interview with a former humanitarian organization director, New York, November 2003.

71. See Anna Politkovskaya, *A Small Corner of Hell: Dispatches from Chechnya* (Chicago: University of Chicago Press, 2003), 62, 67, 86–87.

72. "Scars Remain Amid Chechen Revival," *BBC News,* March 3, 2007.

73. As one press report put it, "Among Iraqis, Fallujah is best known for two things: the best-tasting Kebab in the country and enthusiasm for smuggling." Daniel Williams, "Fueling Pacification with Propane," *Washington Post,* June 4, 2003, A14. Also see Christopher Parker and Pete W. Moore, "The War Economy of Iraq," *Middle East Report* 243 (available at http://www.merip.org/mer/mer243/parker_moore.html).

74. Quoted in Mark Thompson and Darrin Mortenson, "How to Squeeze a City," *Time,* April 19, 2004, 43–44.

75. See Bing West, *No True Glory: A Frontline Account of the Battle for Fallujah* (New York: Bantam, 2005), 91, 177.

76. Jeffrey Gettlemen, "The Re-Baathification of Falluja," *New York Times,* June 20, 2004.

77. Dahr Jamail, "Sarajevo on the Euphrates," *The Nation,* April 12, 2004 (available at http://www.thenation.com/doc/20040426/jamail).

78. Pamela Constable, "Hatred Rises with Fallujah Death Toll," *Washington Post,* April 13, 2004.

79. James Hider, "Explosions, Grenades, Gunfire, and Snipers—Fallujah Suffers in 'Peace,' " *The Times* (London), April 14, 2004.

80. "Iraq Sunni/Shiite Marchers Breach U.S. Roadblocks to Bring Aid to Fallujah," *AFX News,* April 8, 2004.

81. Ned Parker, "Fallujah Marines in Strange World—Half War, Half Humanitarian Mission," Agence France-Presse, April 13, 2004.

82. West, *No True Glory,* 190.

83. See Carter Malkasian, "Signaling Resolve, Democratization, and the First Battle of Fallujah," *Journal of Strategic Studies* 29, no. 3 (June 2006): 423–452.

84. "U.S. Won't Let Men Flee Fallujah," Associated Press, November 13, 2004.

85. Aqeel Hussein and Toby Harnden, "Iraqi Rebels Slip Away to Fight Another Day," *Sunday Telegraph* (London), November 14, 2004, 26.

86. Edward Wong, "Provincial Capital Near Falluja Is Rapidly Slipping into Chaos," *New York Times,* October 28, 2004, A1.

87. Sebastian Usher, "Arab Media 'Muted' on Falluja," *BBC News,* November 10, 2004.

88. West, *No True Glory,* 315–316.

89. Ann Scott Tyson, "Increased Security in Fallujah Slows Efforts to Rebuild," *Washington Post,* April 19, 2005, A15. Herring and Rangwala describe Falluja after the U.S.-led siege as "flattened" and "almost totally destroyed." See Eric Herring and Glen Rangwala, *Iraq in Fragments: The Occupation and Its Legacy* (Ithaca: Cornell University Press, 2006), 35, 181.

90. Quoted in Michael Schwartz, "Falluja: City without a Future?" *Mother Jones*, January 15, 2005.

91. "Fearful in Fallujah," *The Guardian*, November 9, 2004.

Conclusions

1. The study of sieges is therefore typically the domain of military historians, who tend to focus on developments in weapons, fortifications, and technologies in past eras. There is also a specialized literature on urban operations and urban warfare, largely aimed at military strategists and practitioners. See, for example, *Urban Operations: An Historical Casebook* (Fort Leavenworth, Kan.: Combat Studies Institute, Command and General Staff College, October 2, 2002).

2. Stephen Graham, "Introduction: Cities, Warfare, and States of Emergency," in *Cities, War, and Terrorism*, ed. Stephen Graham (Oxford: Blackwell, 2004), 2.

3. Ralph Peters, "Our Soldiers, Their Cities," *Parameters* 26, no. 1 (Spring 1996): 43–50.

4. Graham, "Introduction," 4. Graham points out that the effort to annihilate cities nevertheless remains "terra incognita" in urban social science: "Certainly, the attempted annihilation of Verdun, Ypres, Guernica, Nanking, and Rotterdam; of Coventry, London, Leningrad, Stalingrad, Warsaw, Hamburg, and Dresden; of Tengchong, Tokyo, Hiroshima, Nagasaki, Seoul, Phnom Penh, My Lai, Algiers, Beirut, Sarajevo, Jenin, or Grozny, are only very rarely discussed in urban course books and textbooks designed for urban planners, geographers, sociologists, or architects." See Stephen Graham, "Cities as Strategic Sites: Place, Annihilation and Urban Geopolitics," in *Cities, War, and Terrorism*, 32.

5. *Human Security for an Urban Century: Local Challenges, Global Perspectives* (Ottawa: Canadian Department of Foreign Affairs and Trade, 2007), 5.

6. For a general discussion, see Michael Barnett, "Humanitarianism Transformed," *Perspectives on Politics* 3, no. 4 (December 2005): 723–744.

7. Bosnian Serbs sometimes even asked the UN to serve as a broker in making cross-frontline deals, and on at least one occasion the UN agreed. Author interview with former senior UN official in Sarajevo, New York, April 2004.

8. See, for example, Peter Andreas, *Border Games: Policing the U.S.-Mexico Divide* (Ithaca: Cornell University Press, 2000).

9. On the importance of scrutinizing "local messiness" in violent conflicts and its traditional neglect in social science research, see Stathis N. Kalyvas, *The Logic of Violence in Civil War* (Cambridge: Cambridge University Press, 2006), 392.

10. See, for example, Carolyn Nordstrom, *Shadows of War: Violence, Power, and International Profiteering in the Twenty-first Century* (Berkeley: University of California Press, 2004); Dietrich Jung, ed., *Shadow Globalization, Ethnic Conflicts, and New Wars* (London: Routledge, 2003); William Reno, *Warlord Politics and African States* (Boulder, Colo.: Lynne Rienner, 1999); and Mark Duffield, *Global Governance and the New Wars: The Merging of Development and Security* (London: Zed, 2001).

11. R. T. Naylor, *Patriots and Profiteers: On Economic Warfare, Embargo Busting, and State-Sponsored Crime* (Toronto: McClelland and Stewart, 1999), 15–16.

12. Mark F. Chingono, *The State, Violence, and Development* (Aldershot, UK: Avebury, 1996), 110.

13. See, especially, David Keen, *The Economic Functions of Violence in Civil Wars* (London: International Institute for Strategic Studies, Adelphi Paper 320, 1998); and Mats Berdal and David M. Malone, eds., *Greed and Grievance: Economic Agendas in Civil Wars* (Boulder, Colo.: Lynne Rienner, 2000).

14. Recent critiques of this dichotomy include Stathis N. Kalyvas, "The Ontology of 'Political Violence': Action and Identity in Civil Wars," *Perspectives on Politics* 1, no. 3 (September 2003): 475–494; and Karen Ballentine and Jake Sherman, eds., *The Political Economy of Armed Conflict: Beyond Greed and Grievance* (Boulder, Colo.: Lynne Rienner, 2003).

15. Aida Hozić, "Crime and Sovereignty in the Balkans," in *Art of the State*, ed. Douglas Howland and Luise White (Bloomington: Indiana University Press, 2008).

16. Robert Cribb, *Gangsters and Revolutionaries: The Jakarta People's Militia and the Indonesian Revolution, 1945–1949* (Honolulu: University of Hawai'i Press, 1991), 52.

17. Karen Barkey, *Bandits and Bureaucrats: The Ottoman Route to State Centralization* (Ithaca: Cornell University Press, 1994).

18. Cited in Hozić, "Crime and Sovereignty in the Balkans."

19. Alexander Petrović, "The Role of Banditry in the Creation of National States in the Central Balkans During the 19th Century: A Case Study—Serbia" (master's thesis, Department of History, Simon Fraser University, 2003).

20. Eric Hobsbawm, *Bandits* (New York: New Press, 2000). This point is made by Hislope in his discussion of paramilitaries in Macedonia. See Robert Hislope, "Crime and Honor in a Weak State: Paramilitary Forces and Violence in Macedonia," *Problems of Post-Communism* (May/June 2004).

21. Philip Shaw Paludan, *Victims: A True Story of the Civil War* (Knoxville: University of Tennessee Press, 1981), 52.

22. James D. Henderson, *When Colombia Bled: A History of the Violence in Tolima* (Tuscaloosa: University of Alabama Press, 1985), 149.

23. Ibid., 150.

24. Notable exceptions include Michael Pugh and Neil Cooper, *War Economies in a Regional Context: Challenges of Transformation* (Boulder, Colo.: Lynne Rienner, 2004); and Heiko Nitzschke and Kaysie Studdard, "The Legacies of War Economies: Challenges and Options for Peacemaking and Peacebuilding," *International Peacekeeping* 12, no. 2 (Summer 2005): 222–239.

25. For a more detailed account, see Peter Andreas, "The Criminalizing Consequences of Sanctions: Embargo Busting and its Legacy," *International Studies Quarterly* 49, no. 2 (June 2005): 335–360.

26. See, for example, Fiona Terry, *Condemned to Repeat? The Paradox of Humanitarian Action* (Ithaca: Cornell University Press, 2002).

27. Samantha Powers, *A Problem from Hell: America and the Age of Genocide* (New York: Basic Books, 2002), xxi.

28. This is most forcefully argued in Kalyvas, *The Logic of Violence in Civil War*.

Index

Page numbers in *italics* indicate illustrations.